Finding THE PERFECT GIFT

The Ultimate Guide

100's and 100's of Creative, Unique Gift Ideas... and Where to Find Them!

LISA HULLANA
KARL PRESTON

Dog Gone Books
Malibu, California

Finding THE PERFECT GIFT

The Ultimate Guide

By   LISA HULLANA
KARL PRESTON

Published by:

Dog Gone Books
P.O. Box 4054
Malibu, California 90264

Printed in the United States of America

Library of Congress Cataloging in Publication Data
Hullana, Lisa   /   Preston, Karl
Finding the Perfect Gift: The Ultimate Guide

      Includes index.
      1. Shopping.   2. Gifts.   3. Holiday.   4. How to.   I. Title

Library of Congress Catalog Card Number
      94 - 94350

ISBN 0-9641513-8-3 $12.95 softcover

In Memory of...

Bernard, Mary

&

Pops

Who gave us life...& love

CONTENTS

CONTENTS

About The Authors

Lisa Hullana, a Filipino-American born and raised in the San Francisco bay area of Vallejo, California, has effortlessly modeled her life around giving to others. Her kind-hearted nature is a breath of fresh air and a break from the struggles of daily life...a reminder of how life should always be...and feel. She immerses herself into one gift-giving project after another from extravagant surprise parties and gift baskets to a simple note of kindness. No one ever questions her motivations, because they know she derives as much or more pleasure than her recipient. Her only intention is to bring joy and light into the lives of others, which in turn, reflects in her own life. Lucky for her large family and many friends who are touched by this tireless energy and genuine kindness. What better way to expand on her giving spirit than to share with others the rewards of giving. It would be her goal through this book to bring you and the rest of the world a little bit closer to peace...and happiness.

By the way, when Lisa's not pursuing her hectic gift giving schedule, she's busy doing her real job, being an actress, which has brought her to such exotic destinations as a jungle with Beau Bridges, a tropical island with Tom Selleck and a deep ocean abyss with Roy Scheider.

Karl Preston, Lisa's partner in life and on the page, boasts of being one of the few remaining souls born and raised in the Los Angeles area without being...too affected. Karl's ability to edit and organize, along with his talent for art direction has combined beautifully with Lisa's more heart-felt creative side on this project. Between book writing projects, Karl enjoys working on screenplays and writing "freelance" editorials for several newspapers.

They live in beautiful Malibu, California, but opt for a half & half residence split between Marin, California and the island of Maui...some day. For now they're not complaining as their black lab "Betty" takes them out for hearty walks along California's beautiful coastline.

Acknowledgements

A note of thanks and appreciation to all of our friends and family who have supported, helped and have served as our gift-giving inspiration...

Marge & Ken Rumburg, Evelyn & Gary Harris, Dana & Chuck Walker, Bernard & Jesse Hullana, E.J. & Mary Louise Hullana, Jenna Hunt & Hayden, Kellie Harris, Mark Rogerson, Jeff & Kal Rumburg, Karen & James Hooper, Michelle & Justin, Tamara & Roneil, Scott Harris, Helen McDaniel, Janine Bakker, Tracy Mays, Brocky, Joe Gattuso, Mark "Sparky" Trepanier, Kevin Bradley, Tina Bow, Blendi Reynolds, David Pires, Jean Cooper, Jamie & Julie, Dave & Linda Glenn, Nancy Bleier, and of course Betty...and all the 'idea people' who have helped in supplying sources and information vital to the quality of this guide.

...a special thanks to the many people who make it their lives to give....who use their innovative efforts, their God-given talent, and hard work to bring happiness to another being. Here's to the people who are in the service of bringing smiles to mankind.

COVER: An original oil on canvas by world-renound artist Danielle Born in Argentina, raised in Isreal, the artist's latest work can be seen at the Los Angeles County Museum of Art.

Warning - Disclaimer

All matters dealing with companies listed in this guide are to be handled yourselves, aside and separate from this guide. We, the authors and publisher of this guide, are not bound by any agreement, verbal, written or otherwise, with the sources, companies or organizations listed in this guide (except for special permissions needed for copyright purposes). The sources listed here within are simply an unbiased compilation chosen specifically for their creative, unique or otherwise helpful services and products they are able to offer you.

The authors and Dog Gone Books shall have neither liability nor responsibility to any person or entity with respect to any loss or damage caused, or alleged to be caused, directly or indirectly by the information contained in this book. Furthermore, any risk taken by an individual through a gift idea or the process of gift giving with its origin found or taken from this guide will be solely and completely responsible and liable for their own actions. We should go on to say that some gifts are not meant for everyone and could be harmful or dangerous in some instances. Please use intelligent discretion with gifts of this nature. Pay particularly close attention to gifts for children & babies and the outdoor / adventure gift ideas.

Every effort has been made to make this guide as accurate as possible, however, there may be mistakes both typographical and in content, therefore this text should be used only as a general guide, and not as the definitive source on the subject matter contained here within. Furthermore, this guide contains information only up the printing date.

If you do not wish to be bound by the above, you may return this book to the publisher for a full refund.

A GIFT FROM THE HEART & IMAGINATION

The Perfect Gift

The constant struggle of always trying to think of new, exciting, unique gift ideas was our strongest motivation for creating this guide, and it is used continuously by ourselves to stimulate our own gift giving needs. The main emphasis is to not only give you great new, creative gift ideas, but to allow these ideas to stimulate your own imagination and creativity, so that you may customize and personalize a gift for your own particular needs.

Keep in mind that a gift doesn't necessarily have to be a materialistic possession, traditionally wrapped in box. A gift can take any form or shape and be given in as many different ways. In fact, a good portion of our creative gift ideas have to do with events, things to do, and places to go, and you can't very well wrap up in a box something so intangible as a good time...or can you?

Whether it's a store bought gift, dinner at a nice restaurant, personal service, a trip, a gift certificate, tickets to an event or something to do, or simply an evening on the town, use your imagination and creativity to present the gift in a way that makes the process of gift giving rich and fulfilling for all. It has been said that presentation is everything. Presentation expresses the thought put into a gift, which enhances the emotions shared, and the closeness felt. It's the happiness given...and received, that makes the process of gift giving successful. The things that make life simply wonderful.

No matter what form a gift is given in, regardless of its monetary value, if you have truly given from the heart and it has given a person the feeling of being special in any way, you have truly given a perfect gift...and a priceless one. This is a gift that encompasses all gifts, given from anybody to anybody. The only consideration is that the thought behind the gift must be any or all of those good feelings that come directly from the heart. You'll never go wrong when giving to another if you always give from the heart...unconditionally with no expectations in return. One of the best, most creative gifts you could ever give is a gift thought of, planned out, and given souly from the heart...and imagination.

Author's note

This guide is designed to assist you as much as possible in your pursuit of finding the perfect gift...again...and again...and again. It is to be used to stimulate your own ides so that each gift you decide to give can be tailored and personalized to suit your desires.

CATALOGS: About 99.9% of the sources listed in this guide will have catalogs, brochures or other printed matter, all yours for the asking. Most are free, while some companies will charge from 50 cents to a few bucks for their information.

PRICES: Most prices have the potential to range dramatically depending on the source you purchase from and the quality of the item. Our intention is to give you enough accurate information and choices to plan your budget accordingly.

The greatest effort was made just prior to publication to check for accuracy with all sources, companies and information listed in this guide. If you find a toll-free number (1-800...) out of service, check with your toll-free operator (1-800-555-1212) for a new number listed under the same company name. Companies change quickly and move around quite a bit. With each new edition of this guide we will do our best to completely revise all information contained within. If you do have further questions, comments, corrected information or need specific help on something, feel free to drop us a line or send a note and we'll do our best to help you find that perfect gift.

HELP: If you or your company feel that you have a creative gift idea or two that belongs in this guide, please let us know. If it qualifies, we'd be more than happy to include it in our next revised edition and we will be sure to give you proper written credit as well as a free copy of our next edition of *"FINDING THE PERFECT GIFT."* Thanks for your help and continued support. May we fill all your gift giving needs.

Planning Ahead

To get in return the absolute satisfaction and enjoyment from the experience of giving to another, one must **PLAN AHEAD**. This is especially true during popular gift giving holidays such as Christmas and Valentine's Day. There's nothing worse then rushing around last minute, unable to find any parking spaces, then fighting the hostile crowds only to find all the stores out of that special gift, only you could have thought of, or worse...settling for something you don't really want. The amount of stress this creates fights against the very purpose of giving.

Planning ahead will help make the process of gift-giving, shopping for and thinking of a special gift, a thoroughly positive and enjoyable experience. You'll be surprised how one idea will lead to another and this will lead to that when you're free of any time constraints. Soon your original idea has evolved into something quite spectacular, showing the true effort and thought put forth toward someone you care about. Planning ahead, and taking ample time, will make all the difference in the world. Keep in mind that it is the special moments in life that we work so hard to attain. When you reach that moment, recognize it...slow down...and savor it. Day to day life is mostly a facade, created by our culture, technology, and society in general. It is the small moments that stimulate real emotion...that makes life real. Then and only then do we really live.

"Carpe diem" - **SEIZE THE DAY !**

TOP 10 PERFECT GIFT IDEAS

 # 1 THE GREATEST GIFT OF ALL - the most noble gesture - a gift, monetary or otherwise, given anonymously to a needy person, charity or cause **24**

 # 2 VIDEO MEMORIES - the making of your own movie starring your family and/or friends - transferring old films, videos and stills to video, edited with music **223**

 # 3 FANTASY GIFT PACKAGE - the ultimate romantic / erotic adventure & gift package to be shared with the one you love **52**

 # 4 THE MOST NATURAL GIFT - The donation of money, time and/or energy to a noble cause that fights for the protection and preservation of animals and the environment **26**

 # 5 PRIVATE RESERVE - personalized wine or champagne bottles of your favorite vintage - perfect for weddings, anniversaries, birthdays, family and friends **36**

 # 6 FAMILY COOKBOOK - the collection of family recipes to the creation and distribution of your family cookbook **206**

 # 7 THE ULTIMATE ADULT TOY - the Argo Conquest - 6 or 8-wheel-drive off-road amphibious vehicles, climb a mountain or cross the sea...without getting out **41**

 # 8 LIVE TREE - the noble gift of a tree is a miracle of nature, and a symbol of life, beauty & growth in a friendship or relationship **216**

 # 9 MOTIVATIONAL / INSPIRATIONAL / SELF HELP... books & tapes has the potential to create a powerful life-changing impact in one's life **282**

#10 OLYMPIC TICKETS - it's the Olympics, what more is there to say? **132**

SPECIAL KINDS of CREATIVE GIFTS

TOP 10 PERFECT GIFT IDEA SOURCES

 # 1 FINDING THE PERFECT GIFT: THE ULTIMATE GUIDE - it's been said, "It's quite simply the greatest creative gift source and gift reminder in the world" **178**

 # 2 DREAMS COME TRUE - from building sand castles on the beach to flying a fighter jet, this company will arrange anything to "Make your dreams come true." **22**

 # 3 SUCCESSORIES - power through inspirational beauty. Motivational & inspirational visuals, writings and more geared toward personal success and achievement **282**

 # 4 PERSONAL CREATIONS - the greatest collection of personalized products out there. Engraved & monogrammed gifts for everyone...even your dog **183**

 # 5 JOHNSON SMITH COMPANY - the greatest kids catalog in the world. Only the most creative fun stuff found for kids...and inexpensive too ! **248**

 # 6 THE HOME WINEMAKING SHOP - self proclaimed as the greatest store on earth...well, we think it's pretty close - wine, beer, cheese making kits and more **42**

 # 7 THE PLEASURE CHEST - the adult toy store supermarket - an uninhibiting place to shop for all your adult toys and accessories...and more ! **47**

 # 8 AMERICAN FORESTS - the most majestic and patriotic gift in our whole collection - tree saplings originating from famous historical places around the country...and the world **216**

 # 9 AIR COURIER ASSOCIATION - international travel for next to nothing - only for the spontaneous...no reservations accepted **111**

#10 SHIP'S HATCH - only the most beautiful nautical pieces and decorative items found, from ship's wheels, plaques, clocks and much more **31**

The Unique,

The **Unusual**,

The *Original*

The **Unique**, The **Unusual**, The *Original*...
encompass the handmade, the homemade, arts & crafts,
environmental / nature, new age, the different, the bizarre and all of
those other gift ideas that don't easily fall into one of the other
categories. This section may best exemplify our goal to help you
search out, find or even think of all of those great gifts and gift ideas.
This section helps create the backbone for "Finding The Perfect Gift"
and it is our hope that it gives to you more great ideas than you
know what to do with. Allow your creativity and imagination to first
walk...then run. Follow your first instincts. Don't stop yourself from
giving something because you think it's too wild, just not appropriate,
too this, too that. There's nothing worse that saying to yourself, "I
should've..." after the fact. Don't hesitate. Go for it. It's better to be
remembered as being unique, unusual or original than to not be
remembered at all.

*"Give what you have. To someone, it may be better than you
dare to think."*

LONGFELLOW

Unique, Unusual, *Original*

QUICK REFERENCE LIST

ADOPT-A-STAR

Give an absolutely stellar gift of a star through the International Star Registry. Name a star after the one you love and present him or her with a beautiful certificate that denotes the star's coordinates and its new name. Includes certificate, sky charts and gift card.

INTERNATIONAL STAR REGISTRY   **$40 800-282-3333**
THE MINISTRY OF FEDERAL STAR REGISTRATION   **$56 800-544-8841**

ADOPT-A-TREE

With a small donation you can have a tree planted and dedicated in your name, or the name of someone special. "Tree People" will send a beautiful card stating that a tree will be planted, grow, and live in their name.   **minimum donation $15**
TREE PEOPLE   **818-753-4631**
See also ***ADOPT-AN-ACRE, ADOPT-A-WOLF*** *and* ***ADOPT-A-WHALE***

BEADED JEWELRY KIT

Beaded necklaces, bracelets, anklets, earrings...With beads coming back into fashion, many bead stores are cropping up offering beads of all kinds, from wood, plastic, bone, shells, coral, glass, cut stone and more. Most bead suppliers carry all the elements to create your own designs...tasteful or not.   **$15 - $100'S**
BOURGET BROTHERS   **800-828-3024**
     jewelry making supplies: beads, chains, stones, pearls and more
ENTERPRISE ART   **800-366-2687**
     arts, crafts, jewelry supplies: beads, rhinestones and more
ABEADA - beads, bead-stringing kits   **800-521-6326**
BANASCH - beads, pearls and more   **800-543-0355**
BEADS GALORE INTL. - beads and bead-stringing supplies   **800-424-9577**
BUCKS COUNTY CLASSIC - beads, semi-precious stones   **800-942-GEMS**
INDIAN JEWELRY SUPPLY CO.   **505-722-4451**
     precious metals, semi-precious stones, shells, coral & equipment
VICTOR LEVY   **800-421-8021**
     seed, shell, bone and fancy beads, jewelry making supplies, gemstone, stone, metal beads, pearls and supplies
HHH ENTERPRISES   **800-444-0449**
     jewelry components: beads, stones and more
JEWELRY MAKER'S SOURCEBOOK - jewelry making supplies **800-366-2218**

BLIMP RIDE

Be one of the rare few who have taken a ride in a blimp. Isn't it always who you know? Unfortunately you can't buy your way into this gift idea. In fact, blimp rides on any one of the three Goodyear Blimps are always complimentary. To get a ride on one of these airships, one must either know or be a representative that deals with the Goodyear Company, and through them a ride can be arranged. Goodyear has three blimps located throughout the country; one in Los Angeles, Ohio and Florida. Fuji, Budweiser and MetLife also have blimps. If you know a higher up in one of these companies you might try your luck there. **FREE**

GOODYEAR BLIMP
Los Angeles: 213-770-0456
Akron, Ohio: 216-796-3127
Pompano Beach, Florida: 305-946-8300

COLLECTOR'S CORNER

Unique, creative collectibles. Everybody either knows someone or are themselves an avid collector of...something. From expensive, cheap to beautiful and down right ugly...elephants, coins, cars and dolls to weapons, hats, belt-buckles and magazines, there's got to be something for everyone. Where does one start when trying to encompass this endless category. There are about as many different things to collect as there are people collecting them. Many of our creative gift ideas throughout this guide can fall under this category, although we have limited it to just a few sources, some of which are listed nowhere else in this guide. This category has been edited down considerably to only the sources we had found interesting, creative and of good quality.

AMERICAN HISTORICAL GUILD   800-544-1947
original letters / documents from famous people

THE HUNTINGTON COLLECTION   800-777-8126
U.S. made bronze sculptures

THE DINOSAUR STORE   310-589-5988
real dinosaur skulls, skeletons, teeth, claws, eggs and more

MUSEUM REPLICAS LTD. -   **PO Box 840, Conyers, GA 30207**
authentic weapons, battle gear and period clothing

MODEL EXPO INC. - historic ship model kits   800-742-7171

PACIFIC AIRCRAFT - hand carved mahogany warbirds   800-950-9944

REMINGTON COLLECTION - bronze sculptures   **800-521-3179**
AMERICANA CAROUSEL COLLECTION   **800-852-0494**
   full size carousel horses
ELEGANZA LTD. - museum statuary reproductions   **206-283-0609**
DUTCHGUARD   **800-821-5157**
   canes with wood, silver, brass & gold heads, gadget and flask canes,
secrecy sticks in exotic hardwoods
TONY STEFFEN - cans, mugs, steins for collectors   **800-443-8712**
D & A INVESTMENTS - steins and brewery collectibles   **800-336-2055**
KELEY HANEY ART GALLERY   **405-382-3915**
   original Indian, paintings, sculpture, jewelry, baskets, pottery
THE FRONT PARLOR - David Winter cottages   **217-346-3533**
THE NOBLE COLLECTION   **800-8-NOBLE-8**
   replicas of the arms and armor from the medieval times and the samurai
   to antique guns and cannons
WILDLIFE ART NEWS - intl. magazine for wildlife art   **800-626-0934**
WORLDWIDE COLLECTIBLES AND GIFTS   **800-222-1613**
WORLDWIDE CURIO HOUSE   **Box 17095, Minneapolis, MN 55417**
   unusual gifts jewelry and more from around the world
NATURE'S GALLERY   **800-400-0090**
   collectable fine art prints and lithos of wildlife, nature and more
HOUSE OF TYROL   **800-443-1299**
   gifts & collectibles from around the world, beer steins to cuckoo clocks
PLAYBOY CATALOG   **800-423-9494**
   back issues of Playboy Magazine from 1960's to 1990's
THE MYSTIC TRADER   **800-637-9057**
   old world and new age gifts from exotic places around the world
THE CONDE' NAST COLLECTION - antique maps   **800-678-5681**
See also *MOVIE MEMORABILIA, FRAMED AUTOGRAPH, RARE COIN,*
FRAMED MOVIE POSTER, SPORTS MEMORABILIA

THE COUNTRY STORE

From windmills and wood stoves to country clothing, home decor
and hard to find collectible antiques. Give to somebody a gift from
the rich cultural era of 50 years ago, that has been all but forgotten.
The recipient will be sure to appreciate the style and quality not
found these days...not to mention the memories it will bring back of
"the good ol' days."

CUMBERLAND GENERAL STORE   **800-334-4640**
built to last home and farming tools, windmills, woodstoves, Victorian baths and more

COUNTRY STORE   **800-924-1014**
country clothing, home decor, hard to find collectibles

CRATE AND BARREL   **800-323-5461**
country-style indoor and outdoor housewares & furniture

THE POTTERY BARN   **800-922-5507**
indoor & outdoor, country-style furniture, housewares & accessories

CUSTOM AQUARIUM

Have an impressive salt or freshwater aquarium built into a wall, coffee table or other piece of furniture. It may be a little costly, but it's sure to be the center of attention. A saltwater aquarium can be more exotic, although the upkeep may take a little more time and energy.   **$150 - $1,000's (Installed)**

CAPTIVE SEA   **310-657-3232**
AQUALIFE   **213-293-2200**
See also *FISH TANK*

DAVID WINTER COTTAGES

All the way from England, David Winter has put together a one-of-a-kind collection of miniature cottages, ranging in size from about 3 inches to the size of a bread box. These English inspired cottages are available in a variety of different styles, from his charming country homes of England and Ireland, to chapels, castles, and mansions from the same area. These fine pieces of art truly have to be seen to be appreciated. You're sure to fall in love with the "Pudding" or "Snow Cottage," or perhaps the "Robert Burns Reading Room." Certainly a most suitable gift around the holidays...or any occasion. Beware cheap imitations. If you're familiar with his collection, you may order through the following sources, otherwise you can try to find them at a specialty, gift or collectors shops.   **$30 - $700**

THE PICADILLY SHOP   **818-842-2324**
COLLECTORS HAVEN   **213-931-8894**
THE FRONT PARLOR   **217-346-3533**

DREAMS COME TRUE

Drive a race car, fly a 747, blow up a building, or be a chef for a day at Spago. This company will help you to live out your wildest fantasy with pre-arranged or custom-made packages. You can also arrange to fly fighter jets, have a helicopter picnic, a yacht cruise, horseback ride on the beach, or simply build sand castles... or...whatever. Ranks high on our **Top 10 Creative Gift Sources** list. Just let your imagination soar and they'll make your "Dreams Come True."   **$245 - $10,000**
DREAMS COME TRUE - John Alexander   **213-661-1300**

A GIFT THAT GIVES TWICE

The following sources listed below offer creative gifts for the general public to purchase, and, in turn, a portion of their profits will go towards a helpful, needy, good cause, individual or charity. Do something truly gratifying today and give a gift that gives twice.

COST: Priceless

GLOBAL CRAFTS - Christian Children's Fund   **800-366-5896**
THE CHILDREN'S GIFT CATALOG   **800-817-KIDS**
      give the gift that gives twice, Children's Home Society
BEREA COLLEGE CRAFTS   **800-347-3892**
      master craftspeople - college students mostly from Appalachia create quality gifts from the loom, lathe, forge, and potters wheel
FRIENDS OF THE VIET NAM VETERAN'S MEMORIAL   **703-525-1107**
      t-shirts, prints, cards, books and memorabilia, proceeds to support the memorial
UNIVERSITY OF TEXAS MD ANDERSON CANCER CENTER   **800-231-1580**
      children's Christmas cards made by cancer patients
See also MOTHER EARTH, GREATEST GIFT OF ALL

HOMEMADE / PERSONALIZED CHRISTMAS ORNAMENTS

If you feel the need to give something to your fellow co-workers or every single family member around Christmas time, but don't have the budget to get them all a new car, have a personalized Christmas ornament or ornaments made especially for them. If you look hard enough around the holiday season there are creative services that can personalize a variety of different ornaments, stockings, and other

decorative pieces. Add family names to ornaments of similar likeness and gender. You may even find one that looks like the family dog...and his or her dog house. Check your local mall or shopping center for these seasonal businesses. Get ultra-creative and personalize some ornaments yourself. Check arts & crafts supply stores, art stores, specialty stores, and even large discount stores for all the little pieces, paints & fixin's.　　　　**$1 - $11 / ornament**
BORSE　　　　　　　　　　　　　　　　　**800-227-3515**
　　　Old world Christmas ornaments and gifts from Germany
THE CRACKER BOX - Christmas ornament kits　　　　**215-862-2100**

LEATHER-CRAFTING KIT

Give to some creative, artistically inclined person the means to make their own belts and other leather accessories. The possibilities are endless if you supply them with a good leather working guide. You might also include in the kit the essential leather working tools, die stamps, stains and other finishing products, and of course some leather to work with.　　　　　　　　　　**$40 - $200**
LEATHER FACTORY - leather-crafting kits　　　　**615-756-4484**
LEATHER UNLIMITED - leather-crafting kits & supplies　　**414-999-9464**
PYRAMID OF URBANA　　　　　　　　　　　**217-328-3099**
　　　leather-crafting kits, how-to books and more
TANDY LEATHER CO.　　　**P.O. Box 791, Fort Worth, TX 76101**
　　　leather-crafting kits & supplies, books, patterns and videos
VETERAN LEATHER CO. - leather-crafting supplies, kits　**800-221-7565**
See also *WOOD CARVING, SCULPTING, PAINTING, and POTTERY KITS*

LIPO SCULPTURE

One obviously cannot surprise their mate with such a gift. Lipposuction is growing in popularity and acceptability. It is basically the surgical removal of unwanted fat, purely for aesthetic enhancement. We will not go into the details of the process and we certainly don't advocate it. We are simply listing it as an odd yet creative gift idea...for the right person.　　　　**$100's - $1,000's**

The Greatest Gift

*A*n anonymous gift given to a needy individual, a cause you believe in, or your favorite charity is truly a rewarding experience. Whether you give something of direct need, such as food, clothing, etc., or a monetary contribution, this act of giving unselfishly, solely to give help and happiness to others without any acknowledgement in return...is giving in its most pure form.

SELECTED CHARITIES, CAUSES AND NON-PROFIT ORGANIZATIONS

HUMAN AID & ILLNESS

CHRISTIAN CHILDREN'S FUND   804-644-4654
    provides care & education for disadvantaged youths
MADD - Mothers Against Drunk Driving   817-268-6233
    anti-drunk driving organization
SPECIAL OLYMPICS   202-628-3630
    encourages self-esteem of the mentally retarded through sports
ALZHEIMER'S DISEASE AND RELATED DISORDERS ASSOCIATION
    to support research into diagnosis, therapies, causes &   cures
    for Alzheimer's Disease   312-853-3060

. . . Of All

AMERICAN HUMAN ORGANIZATION   303-695-0811
   to prevent neglect, abuse and cruelty to children & animals
NATIONAL COMMITTEE FOR THE PREVENTION OF CHILD ABUSE
   to prevent child abuse in all its forms   **312-663-3520**
THE PEARL S. BUCK FOUNDATION   215-249-0100
   to educate the public to the needs of Amerasian children, to
   educate these forgotten children in their foreign countries and
   to protect them against the prejudices that harm them
SAVE THE CHILDREN FEDERATION   203-226-7272
   to provide direct services for children
VIET NAM VETERANS OF AMERICA
   to promote the improvement and condition of the Viet Nam
   Veteran and to help them adapt better in society
THE NATIONAL VETERANS FOUNDATION   310-642-0255
CHILDREN'S MIRACLE NETWORK   801-942-2200
   all kinds of medical treatments for some 5 million children
   from cancers, AIDS and heart disease to birth defects and
   accidental injuries
MAKE A WISH FOUNDATION   800-722-9474
   grants wishes to children who are terminally ill or have a life-
   threatening condition. Will not turn down any child who
   qualifies, from meeting celebrities, traveling or something as
   simple as making a fish pond
BOYS & GIRLS CLUB OF AMERICA   212-351-5900
   promotes good health, education and social character-
   development of youths
CAMPFIRE BOYS & GIRLS   816-756-1950
   club emphasizing self development & social development
NON-PROFIT TIMES   P.O. Box 408, Hopewell, N.J. 08525
   the non-profit trade publication, for further information
**See also *NON-PROFIT: ANIMALS, WILDLIFE & THE
ENVIRONMENT***

NON-PROFIT NATURE:

ANIMALS, WILDLIFE & THE ENVIRONMENT

NATIONAL PARKS AND CONSERVATION ASSOC.   **800-NAT-PARK**
nature products to help preserve national parks
GREENPEACE   (gift catalog) **800-456-4029**
$30 minimum contribution for membership
THE NATURE CONSERVANCY   **800-628-6860**
adopt and preserve an acre of rain forest, includes personalized
land deed (memberships also available)   **$30 / acre**
THE NATIONAL WILDLIFE FEDERATION   **800-432-6564**
for the education and conservation of wildlife
RAINFOREST ACTION NETWORK (RAN)   **415-398-4404**
supports economic alternatives to rain forest destruction
EARTH ISLAND INSTITUTE   **800-DOLPHIN**
intl. organization to protect dolphins, whales, marine mammals
CHILDREN'S ALLIANCE for PROTECTION of the ENVIRONMENT
(CAPE) - to educate our future generations   **512-476-CAPE**
THE ALASKA WILDLIFE ALLIANCE   **907-277-0897**
merchandise catalog, proceeds go to fight illegal wolf killings
WOLF HAVEN INTL. - wolf tracks catalog   **800-448-9653**
wolf conservation, adopt-a-wolf program   **$20**
includes certificate, photo & biography
INTL. SOCIETY FOR ENDANGERED CATS   **614-451-4460**
gift catalog, proceeds for preservation of endangered wild cats
WHALE ADOPTION PROJECT   **70 E Falmouth Hwy,**
catalog of whale gifts   **E Falmouth, MA 02536**
the protection of humpback whales & other marine mammals
whale adoption: includes certificate, photo and more   **$17**
HUMANE SOCIETY OF UNITED STATES   **2100 L St, N W,**
catalog, proceeds to help animals   **Washington, DC 20037**
AMERICAN HUMAN ORGANIZATION   **303-695-0811**
to prevent neglect, abuse and cruelty to children & animals

...the most natural gift !

SIERRA CLUB	**P.O. Box 7959 San Francisco, CA 94120**
	membership - $35 and up

NATIONAL GEOGRAPHIC SOCIETY MEMBERSHIP   **800-638-4077**
$21 / year + magazine

WORLD GAME INSTITUTE   **215-387-0220**
products for global education

FUND FOR ANIMALS   **212-246-2096**
to prevent the cruel and inhumane treatment of animals

NON-PROFIT TIMES   **P.O. Box 408, Hopewell, New Jersey 08525**
the non-profit trade publication - monthly

AMERICAN SOCIETY FOR THE PREVENTION OF CRUELTY TO ANIMALS   **212-876-7700**

THE WILDERNESS SOCIETY   **202-842-3400**
conservation organization

LCA - LAST CHANCE FOR ANIMALS   **310-271-1409 Office**
(aggressive animal rights group)   **310-271-1409 Hotline**

IDA - IN DEFENSE OF ANIMALS   **415-453-9984**

PETA - PEOPLE FOR THE ETHICAL TREATMENT OF ANIMALS
301-770-PETA

SEA SHEPHERD CONSERVATION SOCIETY - very aggressive
environmentalists to save the great sea mammals
P.O. Box 7000-S, Redondo Beach, CA 90277

WORLD WILDLIFE FUND   **800-CALL-WWF**
For the sake of our endangered wildlife & The Rain Forest Campaign Fund

NAA - NATIONAL ALLIANCE FOR ANIMALS   **703-837-1203**

THE WARM STORE   **800-889-WARM**
non-profit, cruelty-free nature and environmental products

GLOBAL RELIEF   **800-937-3326**
Natural Instinct catalog. products to preserve, conserve and recycle. Donates 5% of profits to environment nonprofit groups.

MAPLE TREE / SAP BUCKET LEASE

Rent mother nature for someone sweet. Lease for them a sugar maple tree or a sap bucket for a year. They'll receive a copy of an authentic 1890 Treasury Department Lease, hand-personalized and suitable for framing. At harvesting season the tree tenant will get at least 50 ounces of 100% pure, wood-fired maple syrup in decorative jugs. Bucket borrowers will receive at least 25 ounces.

RENT MOTHER NATURE -   **617-354-5430**

    Sugar maple tree lease: $40 (at least 50ozs. of pure maple syrup)
    Sap bucket lease: $30 (at least 25ozs. of pure maple syrup)

MIND GEAR

A brainwave synchronizer for relieving stress or reaching a meditative state-of-mind. Specially designed eyewear, headphones and a theta & alpha wave sound system helps achieve specific mind states that promote enhanced creativity, accelerated learning, memory recall, deep relaxation, etc. Works also with your own selection of music, personal improvement or self-hypnosis cassettes. Some of the top executives throughout the country are known to use this futuristic mechanism...and swear by it. Manufacturers claim that a meditative state can be reached in a few minutes equal to that of a Buddhist Monk after 30 years of practice. Haven't tried it personally, but it's in the mail.   **$300 and up**

MIND GEAR   **800-525-6463**
ZYGON - The Supermind, mindware   **800-865-7575   800-925-3263**
MIND LAB   **800-388-6345**
    light / sound technology sync with audio tape, also downloads software

THE MOST MORBID GIFT

The Los Angeles County Coroner has dared to sell gift items relating to their...service. They sell about 12 different items from toe-tag key-chains, baseball hats, wall clocks, watches, mugs t-shirts, towels, tote bags and more, many with a chalk line body outline accompanied with the word "coroner"...heaven forbid.   **$5 - $26**

L.A. COUNTY CORONER - brochure available   **213-343-0760**
PERSONAL CREATIONS   **800-326-6626**
    slate-rock memorial etched with pet's name for when they travel to a better place...that big backyard in the sky

MOTHER EARTH: ANIMALS, NATURE & THE ENVIRONMENT

What else can we say about these gift ideas that you haven't already heard. Nature and the environment is something you are either truly concerned about or something you really don't give much thought to. If the latter case is true because you feel somewhat powerless as an individual, take heed. Most of these sources listed protect, help or give back to nature and the environment...and the results are astonishing. If you remember, ten years ago not much was said about recycling, the rain forests, poaching and endangered species. Our system starts to work when the people truly care about something, which creates public awareness...which ultimately and hopefully creates policy. Help create public awareness through environmental and nature gifts. Give the gift that gives twice.

EARTH CARE PAPER   **800-347-0070**
 Environmental cards, stationery, gift wrap and more
THE NATURE COMPANY   **800-227-1114**
THE WOODLAND CATALOG   **800-610-8800**
 Smokey the bear items and collectibles
NORTHSTYLE - Nature gift catalog   **800-336-5666**
NOAH'S ANIMALS - Animal art & collectibles   **800-368-6624**
NATURE'S JEWELRY   **800-333-3235**
 jewelry & gifts depicting nature's animals & scenics. Some items made
 from nature's naturally beautiful semi-precious stones, minerals & shells
SOUNDINGS OF THE PLANET   **800-93-PEACE**
 tapes & CD's of peaceful, natural earthly sounds, rain forests, etc.
WILDLIFE ART NEWS - intl. magazine for wildlife art   **800-626-0934**
SIGNAL'S FALLING RAIN NATURE CHIMES   **800-669-9696**
RENT MOTHER NATURE   **617-354-5430**
 includes personalized lease and maple syrup
  Sugar maple tree lease: $40 (at least 50ozs. of pure maple syrup)
   Sap bucket lease: $30 (at least 25ozs. of pure maple syrup)
COVESIDE CONSERVATION PRODUCTS   **800-326-2807**
 Bat house, bat condos for the yard. Create a home for these and other
 endangered species and rid your surroundings of unwanted flying insects
 Give a gift for nature and let nature take its course   **$25**
THE GREAT ALASKA CATALOG   **800-326-2197**
 native Alaskan arts, crafts, foods, books, jewelry
NATURE'S GALLERY   **800-400-0090**
 collectable fine art prints of wildlife, nature and Americana **$60 - $450**
SERENGETI - wildlife apparel, jewelry and other gifts   **800-426-2852**

WINTERTHUR MUSEUM COLLECTION   800-767-0500
   rare plants, home decor, garden sculpture, ceramics, jewelry & more
THE DOG MUSEUM - art and history of the dog, catalog   314-821-3647
   tail waggin' gifts for you and your dog
WORLD GAME INSTITUTE   215-387-0220
   global educational and research products
ASTRONOMICAL SOCIETY OF PACIFIC   415-337-1100
   for everyone with an interest in astronomy, videos, software, posters,
   books, observing aids and other unique gifts
NATIONAL AUDUBON SOCIETY - gift membership   800-2-WILDLIFE
   travel programs from $2,760 - $4,770   212-546-9140
   expedition institute for environmental education degrees 207-293-2985
THE TROTTING HORSE MUSEUM   914-294-6330
   horse related items - for horse lovers
RAINFOREST ACTION NETWORK (RAN)   415-398-4404
   supports economic alternatives to rain forest destruction
SIERRA CLUB   **P.O. Box 7959 San Francisco, CA 94120**
                                 membership - $35 and up
NATIONAL GEOGRAPHIC SOCIETY MEMBERSHIP   800-638-4077
                                    $21 / year + magazine
EARTH ISLAND INSTITUTE   800-DOLPHIN
   intl. organization to protect dolphins, whales, and marine mammals
See also *THE GREATEST GIFT OF ALL - NON-PROFIT ANIMALS, WILDLIFE
& THE ENVIRONMENT, LIVE TREE, EXOTIC PLANT*

NATIVE AMERICAN-INDIAN: HANDMADE GOODS & JEWELRY

Native American-Indian goods from the southwest and other parts of
the country can make for a rich, cultural gift idea. As Ralph Lauren
and other fashion designers around the world are influenced by their
colors and designs, Native American-Indian culture is becoming more
popular then ever. These hand-crafted works of art truly have to be
seen to be appreciated. If you travel through the southwest,
particularly, Arizona, Utah, Colorado, and New Mexico, you're likely
to find a good trading post in just about any town. You might also
find a few good sources for these authentic goods in major cities
across the country, but you may have to ask around a bit and prices
will be higher.   **$5 - $1,000 +**

AMERICAN-INDIAN GOODS & JEWELRY

SILVER JEWELRY	BELT BUCKLES	EARRINGS	BRACELETS
TURQUOISE JEWELRY	RINGS	POTTERY	RUGS
LEATHER GOODS	PAINTINGS	...and lots more	

SUNDANCE   800-882-8827
Founded by Robert Redford, offering unique southwestern gifts

CHEYANNE OUTFITTERS   800-234-0432
Various Southwestern inspired fashions and gifts

SIMPLY SOUTHWEST - everything southwest   800-447-6177

SHEPLERS - Western wear and accessories   800-833-7667

PRAIRIE EDGE - Plains Indian arts, crafts, jewelry   800-541-2388

KELEY HANEY ART GALLERY   405-382-3915
original indian, paintings, sculpture, jewelry, baskets, pottery

OXFAM AMERICA TRADING CATALOG   800-426-3282
a non-profit hunger relief agency offering hand-crafted gifts from Asia, Africa and the Americas

See also *NATIVE AMERICAN-INDIAN JEWELRY, GIFT EXOTICA*

NAUTICAL FLAGS, DECORATIVE ITEMS & COLLECTIBLES

Take a look around a good marine supply retailer. There are lots of unique things that might spark your interest and imagination, from authentic brass and wood marine decorator items to nautical flags, portholes, wood-encased barometers and ship's wheels. For the boat or den, nautical flags provide beautiful colors for whatever creative purpose you have in mind. Pick up a sailing manual, ask a boat captain or marine supply dealer what letter each flag signifies and use the symbolic flags to spell out something of meaning. Who knows what you'll find in Neptune's treasure chest. It beats the mall for creative gift shopping.   **$5 - $50 / nautical flag**
$10 on up for decorative pieces & collectibles

PRESTON'S   67-T, Main St. Wharf, Greenport, NY 11944
ships and the sea, nautical ideas for the home

NAUTICAL FLAGS - nautical / U.S. / custom flags   800-536-4002

MOBY DICK MARINE SPECIALTIES   800-343-8044
nautical gifts and decorative accessories

SHIP'S HATCH   703-691-1670
ships clocks, hatch cover tables, jewelry, lanterns, ship's wheels, plaques and other nautical gifts

Unique, **Unusual,** *Original*

HAND CARVED - yacht and estate nameboards and more   203-642-6008
NAUTICAL FLAGS - nautical / U.S. / custom flags   800-536-4002
AMERICAN FLAGPOLES & FLAGS   800-777-1706
    flag poles, American, state, Intl., nautical, historical flags
HOUSE OF FLAGS   800-45-FLAGS
    American, historical, state, foreign, holiday, seasonal, nautical
ACE FLAG & PENNANT FACTORY - boating flags & gifts   516-295-2358
CROWDMASTER FLAGS   800-352-4776
    nautical, patriotic, sports teams, company and custom flags & banners
a couple of bucks - $2000 (30' x 60')

NEW AGE GIFTS

Broaden the scope to new horizons. Enable someone special to discover a passage to the higher self and to tap into that spiritual happiness, best defined as the inner peace that has no monetary value. This quest for the ultimate gift can be an enlightening experience. These gift ideas may be what one would call "New Age", metaphysical, holistic, futuristic, or simply "a different approach." A gift that reaches the spirit and soul of one's being is the ultimate in gift-giving. Having an open mind for the new and the unexplained is the beginning of the journey to spiritual transformation...a journey into the next dimension, known as the "New Age."

THE MYSTIC TRADER   800-637-9057
    old world and new age gifts from exotic places around the world
WINNERS VALLEY OF THE SUN   800-421-6603
    New Age/Holistic /Psychic gifts
PYRAMID BOOKS AND THE NEW AGE COLLECTION
    new age & mystical stuff   800-247-1889
U.S. GAMES - Tarot & fortune telling cards   800-448-4263
FORTUNE'S ALMANAC   800-331-2300
MIND GEAR - new age, meditative sight/sound synchronizer   800-525-6463
ZYGON - The Supermind, mindware   800-925-3263

METAPHYSICAL / NEW AGE / SELF-HELP BOOKS
(found at your local or new age bookstore)

DISCOVERING THE SPIRIT	THE PATH
YOU CAN HEAL YOUR LIFE	THE CELESTINE PROPHESY
THE STAR ROVER	REINVENTING YOURSELF
THE AWAKENING	A COURSE IN MIRACLES

METAPHYSICAL / NEW AGE / SELF-HELP BOOKS Cont.

THE PATH OF TRANSFORMATION   THE LIFE YOU WERE BORN TO LIVE
OUT OF BODY ADVENTURES - Astral Travel

GIFT SUBSCRIPTIONS TO MAGAZINES OF THE NEW AGE

BODY MIND SPIRIT	$16 / year	800 338-5216
VALLEY OF THE SUN WINNERS - magazine & catalog		800 421-6603
NEW AGE JOURNAL	$24 / year	800 234-4556
OF MIND & SPIRIT		800 THE-MOON
SPIRIT SPEAKS		800 356-9104

NEW AGE / METAPHYSICAL BOOKSTORES & RESOURCE OUTLETS

MARLAR PUBLISHING CO.	**Box 17038, Minneapolis, MN 55417**
MALIBU SHAMAN - Malibu, CA.	310 456-5617
BODHI TREE BOOKSTORE - W. Hollywood, CA.	310-659-1733
THE QUARTERLY BOOKSTORE BY MAIL	800 825-9798
FIELD'S BOOKS - San Francisco, CA.	415 673-2027
SHAMBHALA BOOKSELLERS - Berkeley, CA.	510 848-8443
GUIDING STAR - Mill Valley, CA.	415 389-8432
SAMUEL WEISER, INC. - New York, NY	212 777-6363
NEW ALEXANDRIAN BOOKSTORE - Ithaca, NY	607 272-1663
BEYOND WORDS BOOKSHOP - Northampton, MA	413 586-6304
BROTHERHOOD OF LIFE - Albuquerque, NM	505 255-8980
HIGHER SELF - Traverse City, MI	616 941-5805

See also *PSYCHIC READING, PAST LIVES HYPNOSIS, MIND GEAR*

PAINTING KIT

No, not for the house. What kind of gift would that be? An artist's painting kit, complete with canvases, paints, brushes, easel and any other necessities to start that young genius (no matter what the age) on their way to becoming the next Rembrandt. A stress reducing, therapeutic hobby no matter how the critics regard your work.

$40 - $400

CO-OP ARTIST'S MATERIALS	800-877-3242 800-284-3388
paints, brushes, canvases and more	
DICK BLICK ARTIST MATERIALS	800-522-5786
THE JERRY'S CATALOG! - art supplies	800-U-ARTIST
PEARL - art and graphic supplies (discount center)	800-451-PEARL

FLAX - art / drafting supplies from portfolios to pencils   **800-640-5641**
WILLIAM ALEXANDER - painting supplies, kits, books   **800-547-8747**
See also *SCULPTING KIT, LEATHER MAKING KIT, WOOD CARVING KIT, POTTERY KIT*

PAST LIVES HYPNOSIS / REGRESSION

This experience is quickly growing in popularity. It's the "in" thing with many celebrities to make these discoveries of their past lives. Have an experienced therapist or hypno-therapist put the recipient of this unique gift under hypnosis to be brought back in time to another life they may have lived previously. For some people they'll discover they were persecuted in a medieval era, or perhaps picked cotton in the south during the slavery days, or maybe they were even a historical figure. For others, the experience may not be as successful. On the other hand they may be fascinated with the thought that there is more to their make-up than their logical present being. There are also books, tapes and videos available on the subject. Try to get a good referral to a good source by someone who has had a successful experience. You might also try finding one through a reputable psychic, new age store or similar related source. **$40 - $120 / session**
See also *PSYCHIC READING, NEW AGE GIFTS*

PERSONAL JIGSAW PUZZLE

Send in a picture of the friend, family member, the one you love, the two of you, your pet or any other photograph for that matter and they'll make a puzzle out of it...really.   **$25 - $2,000**
CUSTOM MADE JIGSAW PUZZLE   **800-JIG-SAWS**
JIGSAW   **800-854-8208**
STAVE JIGSAW PUZZLES   **802-295-5200**
    hand cut, personalized, wooden puzzles from   **$95 - $2,000**
J. C. AYER & CO.   **508-741-1522**
    computer-designed puzzles made from photographs
BITS & PIECES - puzzles for adults & children   **800-544-7297**
ELMS PUZZLES   **410-583-7535**
    wooden, personalized puzzles with shapes & silhouettes
PACIFIC PUZZLE CO. - educational puzzles for children   **206-293-7034**
THE PUZZLE PEOPLE - children's educational puzzles   **916-637-4823**

PERSONALIZED LICENSE PLATE

A nice accessory by itself, but wouldn't it be nice if it came with a new car? For the license plate, contact your local Department of Motor Vehicles. **Personalized Plate: $41 initial fee, 25 / year** (based on California prices, other states will vary)

PLASTER / STONE SCULPTING KIT

Sculpt your own work of art out of plaster, clay or stone or simply give them a starter kit to do it themselves. A fascinating hobby to involve somebody in, which could lead to hours upon hours of enjoyment. A hobby such as this could very well have a therapeutic effect on someone. Individuals who had been buried under a depression or other psychological ailment have unknowingly climbed out and recovered through such creative endeavors...and gone on to live rich, fulfilling, revitalizing lives. All you really need to start with is the plaster mix, clay or stone...and a pair of willing hands.

$10 - $75

AMERICAN ART CLAY CO.   **800-374-1600**
   modeling and self-hardening clays, molds, paper mache products, casting
   compounds
CHASELLE - ceramic molds, sculpture equipment, more   **800-242-7355**
THE CLAY FACTORY - modeling materials   **800-243-3466**
MONTOYA / MAS INTL. - carving stone and sculpting tools **407-832-4401**
STEATITE OF SOUTHERN OREGON   **503-479-3646**
   soapstone for sculpturing and carving
See also *WOOD CARVING KIT, PAINTING KIT, LEATHER MAKING KIT, POTTERY KIT*

POTTERY-MAKING / CLAY-SCULPTING KIT

There are few things in life more therapeutic or enjoyable than to work with and create something with your own two hands. Working with clay for sculpting or making pottery is one of those hobbies most of us wish we had the time to pursue. The truth is, we just haven't made it a priority or important enough to find out where to get supplies and instruction...and then actually do it. Either that or we're just plain lazy. If it were neatly packaged and placed in front of us...ready to go, we might just be inclined to get involved. Most

likely, this Saturday afternoon hobby will turn into a full or part time
obsession.   **clay: $13 - $25 / 50 pound box (shipping not included)**
   potter's wheel: $100 - $900 and up (for pro quality equip.)
   optional equipment, supplies & accessories: another $100 +
AMERICAN ART CLAY CO.   **800-374-1600**
    modeling and self-hardening clays, molds, paper mache products, casting
    compounds
CHASELLE - ceramic molds, sculpture equipment, more   **800-242-7355**
THE CLAY FACTORY - modeling materials   **800-243-3466**
LAGUNA CLAY CO. - clays, tools, and other supplies   **800-4-LAGUNA**
POURETTE CANDLE MAKING SUPPLIES   **800-888-9425**
    soap making supplies also

PRIVATE RESERVE

For the many friends, family members and co-workers that appreciate
a fine bottle or case of wine, this may be the start of a perfect gift.
To make this idea truly special and creative, have the bottle or bottles
personalized by having names, dates or messages inscribed right onto
the label as if you were the owner of the winery. Many of the better
wineries will provide this personalizing service for an additional fee.
You may also be able to find a custom wine bottle labeler at your
favorite wine outlet or distributer. Many of the wineries will also
package and ship in attractive country-oak wood boxes. Box sizes
vary from one, three, four or more bottles of wine...and if you really
love a particular wine or winery they also carry a line of merchandise
from cork screws and wine glasses to t-shirts and sweatshirts.

FAMILY RESERVE - Give to your parents, grandparents, uncles,
aunts...the whole family, one or several bottles, or even a case of
family reserve. Choose from your, or their favorite winery an
appropriate vintage wine, then have the bottles personalized with the
family name, or perhaps the family crest or coat of arms, dates and
any profound message that sums up the occasion. A guaranteed blue
ribbon gift and topic of conversation on Christmas or any family get-
together. Keep in mind that "family reserve" doesn't necessarily mean
your family. It is the family to whom you are giving to.

COMPANY RESERVE - A great gift for co-workers or the whole
company in general...a prized possession to leave a company
Christmas party with one of these bottles under your arm.

COMMEMORATIVE RESERVE - ANNIVERSARIES, WEDDINGS, BIRTHDAYS

Give to a loving couple on their anniversary or wedding a fine vintage from the year they were married, or first met, then personalize it marking the occasion again with names, dates and any message. The gift will be so well received and become such a prized possession...the wine will undoubtedly go un-drunk. Also a great gift for new-borns...their parents that is. **$10 - $20 + / bottle**
See also ***WINE CONNOISSEURS DELIGHT, WINERY LISTINGS, PERSONALIZING SERVICES***

PROSPECTING, GOLD MINING / TREASURE HUNTING KIT

For those heading to the Gold Country way out west, why not give to them a prospecting, gold mining or rock-hounding starter kit. You might want to include a pan for panning, metal detector, maps, surveys, all the."how to, what to look for and where" instructions... and a nod of good luck. The last taxi driver who gave me a ride in Las Vegas had his heart set on retiring in the near future and heading out on the open road with his wife in their motorhome toward the Gold Country...to stake his claim. The gold rush is back!

$45 - $100's +

D & K PROSPECTING HEADQUARTERS   **800-542-4653**
    metal detectors, prospecting equipment and supplies
HOUSE OF TREASURE HUNTERS   **619-286-2600**
    metal detectors and gold prospecting equipment
D & K PROSPECTING HEADQUARTERS   **800-542-4653**
    prospecting equipment & supplies, metal detectors
FORTYNINER MINING SUPPLY   **310-925-2271**
    treasure hunting supplies, metal detectors, books & magazines
GRAVES CO. - rock-hounding equipment   **800-327-9103**
See also ***METAL DETECTOR, ROCK POLISHING***

PSYCHIC READING

Whether for fun or to be taken very seriously, who can refuse to hear positive, motivating words about future events, relationships, love, life and success to look forward to in their lives. There are also interesting books, tapes and videos relating to the subject. Your best bet would be to find a friend with a strong reference. Try to avoid "showy" gypsy-style crystal ball readers or palm readers who advertise. If you want a serious reading, a good psychic doesn't have to advertise...but they'll know you're coming. Many good psychics will also tape record the session for you, so you can refer back and track their success...and your's. **$35 - $200 and up**

See also *PAST LIVES REGRESSION, NEW AGE GIFTS*

PUBLIC PHONE BOOTH

This may take a little working on your part. As things of recent old come back into fashion, small companies are scrambling to get their hands on whatever artifacts or memorabilia from the past for resale at a considerable profit. Call your phone company to see what they do with all those old phone booths. They've most likely been stored in an outdoor city graveyard by a local agency. Whoever installs them, probably removes them. They're likely to give you a reasonable price...if they're authorized to release it. Public phone companies may be less likely to release their old booths. Your best bet might be to contact any number of privately operated phone companies. Check your local directory under *telephone* or *telecommunications*, and simply ask if they have any old phone booths you can purchase. Do a little restoring. Repaint it fire engine red or raincoat yellow and replace any broken windows. Get one with or without a phone, or have one installed. It can make a fascinating conversation piece or add nicely to your entry way or decor. **booth: $20 - $250**

phone: $75 - $250

CHICAGO OLD TELEPHONE CO. **800-843-1320**
    working, restored old telephones
MAHANTANGO MANNOR **800-642-3966**
    working replicas of telephones from 1900's
TURTLE LAKE TELEPHONE CO. - antique hand-crank tel's **715-986-2233**

SAFE-T-MAN

How would you like to have a traveling partner on the road in your car that always listens and never talks back? No, it's not a dog...It's Safe-T-Man. A life-size, life-like "dummy," so to speak, for your safety and security in your car or at home. Statistics show that crime is reduced dramatically when individuals are in the company of

others. This means that you are less likely to be targeted as a victim if someone is with you. A great gift for that female relative or friend that spends much of their time alone. Decrease the odds of being carjacked, robbed at your ATM, store or gas station, or even followed home. Safe-T-Man also loves to read all night, or while you're on vacation...visible from the front window. Give him a name, this way you'll feel like you know him better. Just don't get too attached. People will start to think you are <u>really</u> weird.   **SAFE-T-MAN: $120**
THE SAFETY ZONE   **800-999-3030**
    helpful products for safety & security, for children, home, car and self
See also ***SAFETY & SECURITY***

SHOOTING STAR

Falling stars or meteorites have landed on earth, been found, then turned into unique jewelry and unusual gifts. Own a real piece of the vast mysterious cosmos. Also available are other exceptional environmental, cultural, and science related gifts. If you ever find yourself in Massachusetts, check out STRATA!   **$5 - $100's**
STRATA - John Barbierie & Will McGrath   **800-466-2992**
JOHNSON SMITH CO.   **813-747-2356, Fax: 813-746-7896**
    things you never knew existed catalog, pieces of meteorites and moon
    rocks and many other things   **actual moon rock: $8**

SKY WRITING

With one to five planes, have written across the sky a special message to be seen over a twenty mile radius. Propose marriage, congratulate someone on a promotion or graduation. Wish someone a "happy birthday" or anniversary...or simply tell the one you love, "I love you." Check your local directory under sky writing or ask a local aviation company to refer you to a source.
                                          Prices start in the $100's

STATUE / SCULPTURE

Sculpt your own work of art out of plaster, clay or stone, give them a starter kit to do it themselves or check your local directory under statuaries. If somebody needs something for the home or yard this might be the ticket. Although you should know the person's taste implicitly if picking out this gift idea yourself. Better yet, casually bring them by the statuary one day as if it were unplanned and you needed something for yourself. See what they love, if anything. If you're unsure keep it small or think of something else. It could get embarrassing to see it at their next garage sale...for two bucks. Some of the more modern, hip statuaries have moved away from the more traditional pieces and are producing some things that are quite extraordinary and for reasonable prices. If you really want to get creative have something custom made...or better yet sculpt it yourself.   **$15 - $100's**

SELF-SCULPTURE - Three-D Sculptures   **213-664-5233**
     Robert Ray will sculpt a foot tall humorous clay caricature from photos and facts given by you.   **Price: $200**
DESIGN TOSCANO   **800-525-1733**
     Deco objects and other sculptured pieces
See also *PLASTER / STONE SCULPTING KIT, POTTERY MAKING / CLAY SCULPTING KIT*

A SUBMARINE

The ultimate toy to explore the other two-thirds of the earth with...your own personal submarine. A costly gift, but well worth it for the serious marine enthusiast or hobbyist. A word of caution though, have thorough confidence and knowledge of the machinery and keep safety a priority, so that you can have total enjoyment in "the deep.".   **build it yourself: $6000 - $8000**
INTERNATIONAL VENTURE CORP. - 2-3 man submarine   **604-436-5657**

SUNKEN TREASURE

Own a piece of sunken treasure. Get your hands on some real "Pieces of Eight" recovered recently from a 1622 spanish Galleon that sunk off the coast of Florida. The coins by themselves make a great gift for any kid...as long as a good story comes with it. Don't forget about your distant French relative, Pierre "the pirate" and how he left your family with part of the treasure he battled Blackbeard over. A "pieces of eight" pendant or other piece of pirate jewelry also makes for an interesting and beautiful gift.
RESORT GRAPHICS   **800-621-2440**
     pieces-of-eight made into pendants and other jewelry   **$35 - $85**

SEVEN SEAS TRADING CO - Mike Dunigan   **800-433-3715**
   pieces-of-eight, spanish treasure cobbs in jewelry and other rare coins
   from ship wrecks around the world
JOHNSON SMITH CO.   **813-747-2356, Fax: 813-746-7896**
   things you never knew existed catalog, replica ship wreck coins,
                            pieces -of-eight: silver $28, gold $40
                            200 yr old ship wreck coin: $15

TIME CAPSULE

Enclose in a water, weather & time-proof container, memorabilia
shared between your life mate, friends, or family. Bury it in a secret
location or just tuck it away somewhere safe, then detail in a note,
card, or letter a future reunion to relive old memories. You might
want to include photographs, a video tape of what was on TV that
day, the news, a movie, a weekly show, or a home video, a cassette
tape of music taped off the radio, notes, cards, letters, a trinket, piece
of jewelry, a family heirloom, a page out of your daily schedule or
diary, etc. If you use your imagination, you'll probably need a bigger
capsule. Make one yourself, or for the more serious check out the
following source.   **Store bought: $50 - $1,000's**
                            Homemade: FREE - $75
TIME CAPSULES   **800-527-7853**

THE ULTIMATE TOY (for grown-ups)

The name says it all...The Argo Conquest...An 8 or 6-wheel drive
off-road amphibious vehicle. It sounds like something used in a
James Bond film...and probably was. The ultimate big toy. "One not
need worry about anything else in life with 'Argo Conquest'."
Imagine having total freedom to drive anywhere...land and sea. Roll
over the rugged terrain like a tank, across the sand and into the
ocean. Why haven't these things been mass-produced? Wouldn't it be
nice to drive to work in the morning, then do some big game fishing
in the afternoon...all from the driver's seat of the same vehicle. Go
where no vehicle has gone before...with the Argo Conquest.
The ARGO CONQUEST   **800-561-9508**
   8-wheel or 6-wheel drive off-road amphibious vehicles

WILD WEST LAND DEED

You can still purchase a piece of the wild west. Millions and millions of undeveloped acres throughout the west and Alaska can still be purchased for as little as a few bucks an acre. This is not the same thing as homesteading where you have to occupy and work the land for a number of years before you can call it your own. As of this publication date we had not received complete details on this gift idea. A word of advice would be to inspect the land personally or have a professional look into it...no matter what the cost. The wild west has been there forever, I think it can wait a little longer.

PUBLIC LANDS TITLE   **P.O. Box 2945, Port Angeles, WA 98362**
     20-acre claim program   **$1 an acre (not homesteading)**
GOVERNMENT LAND FOR CLAIM   **707-448-1887**
FEDERAL LAND CO.   **Box 21598, Washington DC 20009**
     govmnt. land at $2.50 / acre
THE NATURE CONSERVANCY   **800-628-6860**
     adopt and preserve an acre of rain forest (includes personalized land deed / memberships also available   **$30 / acre**
P. BROWN AND COMPANY   **4803 Duval Rd. West, Austin, TX 78727**
     Own a real piece of the old west, North of the Pecos, just this side of the Rio Grande.
     You'll own one square foot of historic Texas land for just $12.

WINEMAKING KIT / HOME BREWERY

Try your best to reproduce your favorite wine, beer, or even cheese...at home. For the beer or wine connoisseur, this original, creative gift can enhance their appreciation and even elevate their expertise on the subject. It may even turn into a serious hobby filled with hours and hours of tasty enjoyment. You'll reap the rewards years later as the recipient of this gift feels compelled, out of gratitude, to send you cases and cases of award winning wine from their thriving new winery.   **$15 on up**
THE HOME WINEMAKING SHOP   **818-884-8586**
     Woodland Hills, CA - beer, wine & cheese making kits available
NEW BOOTLEGGERS OF AMERICA   **818-701-0557**
     beer making supplies   **$20 - $130**
THE BREWERY - home brewing supplies   **800-762-2560**
SEBASTIAN BREWERS SUPPLY   **800-780-SUDS**
S.P.I. WINE & BEER - beer & winemaking supplies   **800-852-9545**

JAMES PAGE BREWING CO. - beer making supplies   **800-892-8606**
JOHNSON SMITH CO.   **813-747-2356, Fax: 813-746-7896**
    things you never knew existed catalog   **WINE MAKING KIT: $25**
                             BEER MAKING KIT: $30
THE WINE ENTHUSIAST - wine cellars and unique gifts   **800-356-8466**

...WITH MY OWN TWO HANDS

We mustn't forget the truly original, creative gift idea of arts & crafts, made from scratch, with your own two hands. Many of the gifts in this section, and others, also fall into this group of gifts created by yourself. In fact, it is recommended by us that any and all of these gifts listed in this guide, and thought of by yourself, should always have your personal touch added to it. Whether you put it into the gift itself, the wrapping, the way you give it or what you give it with, a gift that shows caring thought is always appreciated above and beyond any assembly line factory gift...no matter what the cost. This gift idea is so vast it would be impossible to do justice to it in this guide. We will list only a few of the most creative ideas and sources.   **COST: supplies, enjoyable time & creative energy**

HANDMADE IDEAS

KNITTED GOODS	POTTERY	SCULPTURE
CERAMICS	WOOD CARVING	WOOD WORKING
FURNITURE	PAINTING	SKETCH
DRAWING	JEWELRY MAKING	LEATHER WORKING
ORNAMENT MAKING	STAINED GLASS	WEAVING
CALLIGRAPHY	PHOTOGRAPHY	RUG MAKING
BASKET MAKING	CLOCK MAKING	MODEL MAKING
STONE CARVING	BEAD MAKING	CLOTHES MAKING

NASCO   **800-558-9595**
    arts & crafts supplies, calligraphy, leather crafting, metal enameling, needle crafts, ceramics and photography
EARTH GUILD   **800-327-8448**
    basket-making, weaving, spinning, dyeing, pottery, rug-making, knitting, woodcarving supplies and more
CHASELLE   **800-242-7355**
    ceramic, sculpting, stained glass, weaving, leather crafting, etching supplies and more

CRAFT RESOURCES   800-243-2874
  needlework kits, string art supplies, basket making, metal & wood craft,
  stained glass supplies and more
CLASSICS   800-227-7418
  ship model kits, clocks, weather instruments, music boxes and more
CRAFT CATALOG   800-777-1442
  supplies & accessories for arts & crafts
WARSCOKINS - arts & crafts supplies   800-225-6356
See also

LEATHER CRAFTING	*POTTERY MAKING / CLAY SCULPTING*
PAINTING KIT	*WOOD CARVING / WOOD WORKING*
CHRISTMAS ORNAMENTS	*PLASTER / STONE SCULPTING*
JEWELRY MAKING	*BEADED JEWELRY MAKING*
THE HOBBY STORE	*PHOTOGRAPHY BAG*

WOOD CARVING & WOOD WORKING KIT

Carve your own piece of art out of an exotic piece of hardwood and
give something handmade and homemade to someone you care about.
There's nothing more special or holds more value than something
made with your own two hands that took a considerable amount of
time, effort, thought...and love. If you don't feel too artistically
inclined, but know somebody who is, simply give them a starter
package to do it themselves. Include the wood, all the starter tools
and any finishing products. If you need to be pointed in the right
direction, ask at your local lumber yard for a good hardwood dealer.
Some will even have pieces specifically for carving and whittling.

                                                      $35 - $100
WOODWORKER'S SUPPLY   800-645-9292
THE WOODWORKER'S STORE   800-279-4441
  domestic and exotic hardwoods, tools, books and plans
GILMER WOOD CO.   503-274-1271
  rare & exotic woods in logs, planks & squares
WARREN TOOL CO   914-876-7817
  whittling & woodcarving tools, books, woods & supplies
WOODWORKER'S SOURCE   800-423-2450
  exotic & domestic lumber, turning squares and blanks
ADAMS WOOD PRODUCTS   615-587-2942
  kiln-dried woods, pine-turning squares, carving blanks
See also *LEATHER MAKING KIT, POTTERY KIT, SCULPTING KIT,*
PAINTING KIT

Romance

Erotica

G ifts of Romance & Erotica...

is quite possibly our favorite, and most popular section. Of course there are the big gift giving occasions of Valentine's Day, Anniversaries, and birthdays for the romantic and wild at heart, but the following creative gifts can be even more successful for no occasion at all. Whether you use one of these gift ideas as a surprise, or as a well thought of and planned out event by the two of you, romantic and erotic gifts can put a spark in your life, a lilt in your step, and a glint in your eye. It could turn a bad day into a great one and a rocky road into smooth sailing. Ask yourself the question, "Does our relationship lack any romance or erotica?" If it even remotely lacks a little of one or both of these vital elements to a happy successful relationship, give to your partner something no marriage counselor, psychologist, psychiatrist, psycho-analyst, or psycho could ever give...a creative gift of romance or erotica. And if that doesn't work...you won't find it here.

> *"All the beautiful sentiments in the world weigh less than a single lovely action."*
> **JAMES RUSSELL LOWELL**

QUICK REFERENCE LIST

ADULT TOY BOX

Vibrators, edible undies, sexual enhancing creams & oils, leather, rubber, sex games, an assortment of condoms, and other sexual aids and stimulants can be the most interesting or exciting gift, whether given seriously or as a gag. In major cities across the country, more respectable "Adult" stores offering a less intimidating atmosphere are opening up in greater numbers. In Los Angeles, for instance, there is the adult toy store "The Pleasure Chest," which many of your favorite stars are known to frequent...but we won't name any names. A difficult source to track down if you are not already familiar with one. Your best bet would be to ask at your favorite lingerie or adult book store. Good Luck...and enjoy! **$1 - $100's**

THE PLEASURE CHEST - Adult Toys　　　　　　**800-75-DILDO**
IT'S A SECRET LINGERIE - lingerie, lotions, oils, games, etc. **800-390-3528**
THE STAMFORD COLLECTION P.O. Box 1160 Long Island City, NY 11101
　　videos, books, condoms, sex toys, lotions, lingerie and more
THE XANDRIA COLLECTION　　P.O. Box 31039 San Francisco, CA 94131
　　adult toys and gifts
INTIMATE TREASURES - lingerie and much more　　**415-896-0944**
THE NAUGHTY BASKET CO.　　　　　　　　**800-321-4-FUN**
　　outrageous, risque' gift baskets for naughty guys & gals, choose from the "Stud Bucket," "Passion Pail," "Tonight's the Night" & more
　　　　　　　　　　　　　　　　　　　　$25 - $100
SINCLAIR INSTITUTE - sexual positions for lovers video　**800-955-0888**
See also FANTASY & EROTIC GIFT PACKAGE, SENSUAL MASSAGE　$30

BOUDOIR PORTRAIT

For the woman wanting to give something truly special to her mate, a sexy, sensual, erotic, yet tasteful photograph is hard to beat. Don't be put off or intimidated by this gift idea. Make the experience as relaxed and comfortable as possible by selecting a female photographer who specializes in photographing women. Just be sure to mention that a woman photographed it. We wouldn't want anyone to get jealous...would we? A sure fire hit for any occasion.

Hair & Make-Up: $15 - $45
Photographer: $50 - $250
Prints: $10 - $50 each
Total: $75 - $345

BREAKFAST IN BED...DELIVERED

What a great way to start someone's day. One can always wake up early, prepare a wonderful breakfast and surprise the one they love, their parents, a friend or roommate...but to have something prearranged and delivered like room service to your own house, now that's special. In most cities throughout the country you'd be sure to find a local high-end restaurant, a diner or a dive (depending on your budget) that will deliver breakfast. Most eating establishments have done it all at least once. It doesn't hurt to ask. For a couple of extra bucks, they'll do just about anything. Try the recipient's favorite breakfast house first...and don't forget the fresh squeezed and a rose. Many of the larger cities, you may find, have companies that do this sort of thing as a business. Look in the yellow pages under "WAITER" or even ask that restaurant who can provide that delivering service. If worst comes to worst, you can always slip out of bed early to pick it up yourself. Have a good breakfast !

$10 - $40 / person

See also **CATERED DINNER WITH PERSONAL WAITER**

BUBBLE BATH CHAMPAGNE EVENING

Simply buy the one you love a champagne bottle of bubble bath to be enjoyed alone, by themselves, or together. Add a nice note or card with some heart-felt words, or any other accessories that may enhance the start of a beautiful evening. Also makes a great part of any gift basket. **$3 - $15**

See also **ROMANTIC / EROTIC GIFT PACKAGES, BATHROOM IN A BASKET**

CAPE COD CLAMBAKE

The Clambake Company of Cape Cod will send you a lobster feast, expressed overnight, anywhere, ready to cook in its own steamer pot. The traditional New England Dinner-for-two includes lobsters, clams, mussels, Codfish, corn, potatoes and sausage. Plan a whole evening around it with just as much taste and creativity.

CLAMBAKE CELEBRATIONS **800-423-4038**
From 1 to 10 servings: $80 - $464

CATERED DINNER WITH PERSONAL WAITER

There are several sources in most major cities that offer this service. Look in your local directory under "Waiter," or simply call your favorite restaurant to have it arranged. If you find prices too steep, ask a friend to help you out for the night. They might look good in a tux pouring wine. A terrific gift on Valentine's Day, anniversaries, or birthdays. Go the whole nine yards and hire some live music to go along with this dinner extravaganza. This may also be a fine romantic time to...pop the question.   **Catered Dinner + Waiter: $65 - $200 +**
Breakfast in bed, delivered: $10 - $75

THE CHOCOLATE CLUB

Anything chocolate...from long-stem chocolate roses, custom chocolate bars with your name stamped in gold, to chocolate covered foods, sculptures, brownies, logo cookies and lots more for the chocoholic. If you have a chocolate friend (not made of chocolate, just likes it), arrange with one of the following companies to have a different kind or type of chocolate delivered every month. The following sources will provide you with enough chocolate diversity to last...at least a week.

THE CHOCOLATE GALLERY - chocolate kits   800-426-4796
                                                            $10 - $60
THE CHOCOLATE COLLECTION   800-654-0095
       chocolate cakes from around the world
CHOCOLATE PHOTOS - custom molded choc. novelties   212-714-1880
GHIRARDELLI CHOCOLATE CO.   415-474-1413
       chocolates from world famous Ghirardelli Square in San Francisco
HERSHEY'S CHOCOLATE WORLD - chocolates & novelties   800-544-1347
PRIVATE PARTS ADULT CHOCOLATES   215-627-0512
MIRAMAR - custom made chocolate bars   800-222-1624
WITTAMER   **Place Du Grand Sablon 12-13, 100 Brussels, Belgium**
       The best chocolates in the world
TEUSCHER CHOCOLATES OF SWITZERLAND   212-246-4416
CHOCOLATE LONG STEM ROSES   800-527-6566
                                                          $34/dozen
CUSTOM CHOCOLATE BARS   800-222-1624
                                                          $30 and up
FLICKS - chocolate sculptures, logo cookies, kits   818-398-8808
                                                          $4 - $50 and up

Flowers, Flowers, Flowers

Flowers for a friend, family member, or a loved one, are always appropriate and always priceless...as often as you like.

Flowers for just about any occasion, for just about anyone...especially women...are always appreciated. It's always sure to brighten a room and a spirit.

Don't forget Secretary's Day, Mother's Day...your grandparents, and of course flowers on Valentine's Day are always appreciated whether or not love is in the air.

If you're on a budget or have just been too busy and you're on your way to grandma's house for Easter, there are beautiful, "free" wild flowers to be found virtually all–year–'round if you just take a look around. Wild flowers, picked from the local mountains or a nearby field has a genuine old–fashioned feel. The sweetness, thought and physical effort of this gift makes this more valuable then something prepared, and bought from a store or florist. Do avoid Oleanders, which are poisonous, and your state flower, which are usually illegal to pick...and beware the angry bee.

WHAT ARE THE MEANING OF THESE ROSES ?!

RED - Passion, Undying Love   **PINK -** Friendship
YELLOW - Respect / Friendship   **WHITE -** Purity

ROSE X-PRESS	800-366-6202	**800-FLOWERS**
LONG DISTANCE ROSES	800-LD-ROSES	**800-MY-FLORIST**
BLACK TIE ROSES	800-USA-24HR	
THE FLOWER SOURCE	800-344-9898	

DAN'S GREENHOUSE - direct from Hawaii   **808-661-8412**
    Antheriums - Hawaiian love bouquets & more   **$28 - $32**
ANN PLOWDEN - pressed flowers artist   **617-267-4705**
    preserve bridal bouquets and other special flowers in beautiful gift creations

ENCHANTED EVENING

Love, laughter and romance in a box. A romantic board game created for couples that want to share in the richness and warmth of their relationship. The winner gets his or her wish fulfilled.

GAMES PARTNERSHIP LTD., INC. 800-776-7662

Enchanted Evening: $25

Getting to Know You...Better: $25

You Just Became a Millionaire: $25

STRATTON & COMPANY 408-464-1780

The Loving Game: $15

Romantic Journey: $20

PENTHOUSE THE LOVING GAME - $20 800-466-9435

RENDEZVOUS: A CELEBRATION OF LIGHT 408-464-1780

romantic kit & game, includes invitation, guidebook, floating candles, chocolate, inspirational cards and more **$32.50**

EROTIC GIFT PACKAGE

Use your imagination and put together a daring, creative assortment of adult toys and erotic paraphernalia. Don't forget to include the appropriate lingerie, condoms, and list of fantasies to choose from. Take a little time and put a little thought into shopping for and planning an erotic gift package. Start at your favorite lingerie boutique then continue on to the adult toy store. Plan out an exciting evening at home or an exotic weekend away. If you'd like it to be a surprise, wear some hot sexy lingerie that are sure to be seen at any given moment...and don't forget that men can be just as sexy with his under garments, or lack thereof. Set the mood and prepare the house before your lover arrives, with candles and other creative lighting, music, and all the erotic accessories pre-placed, loaded, and ready for action, including yourself. Take control, fulfill a fantasy and continue on with your plans as long as your partner is willing. If you'd like to plan this time together, wrap up in a box or other appropriate creative means any lingerie, adult toys, condoms, "Penthouse Letters," a card or letter describing your own desires or fantasy to be fulfilled, and anything else you can think of that might add creatively and erotically to this gift. **0 - $100 +**

PLAYBOY - videos, magazine, lingerie and more **800-423-9494**

THE NAUGHTY BASKET CO.   800-321-4-FUN
outrageous, risque' gift baskets for naughty guys & gals, choose from
"Stud Bucket," "Passion Pail," "Tonight's the Night" and more **$25 - $100**
RENDEZVOUS: A CELEBRATION OF LIGHT   408-464-1780
romantic kit & game, includes invitation, guidebook, floating candles,
chocolate, inspirational cards and more   **$32.50**
See also *FANTASY GIFT PACKAGE, LINGERIE, ADULT TOY BOX*

EVENING ON THE TOWN

Have flowers delivered during the day, then surprise your mate as
you step out of a limo to pick them up from work or home and
continue on to a fine restaurant. Spend the late night being
chauffeured around town. Find some after-dinner entertainment or
travel on to an after hours club. Don't forget to make a stop a
Inspiration Point on your way home...to see all the city lights of
course.   **Flowers, Dinner & drinks $50 - $150 +**
Limousine $45 - $65 / hour
Entertainment (Optional) $14 - $150 +
See also *LIMOUSINE RENTALS and ENTERTAINMENT SECTION*

EXOTIC CAR RENTAL

Surprise the one you love, your date, a friend or even your buddies
when you show up in a new Mercedes, Jaguar, Rolls, Ferrari, Range
Rover, Porsche, Maserati, Jeep, or a restored classic. Who needs the
trouble and expense of owning such a beautiful automobile when you
can use and abuse someone else's. Rent for a day or weekend an
exotic automobile. Go for a long drive up the coast or into the
mountains...and enjoy! It can also become a great part of any
Romantic or **Fantasy Gift package,** or even as part of a great
weekend getaway.   **$65 - $300 / day**
See also *ROMANTIC / FANTASY GIFT PACKAGES and WEEKEND
GETAWAYS*

FANTASY GIFT PACKAGE

If you share a special erotic, romantic or sexual relationship with
someone, or would like to, design and write out in detail on an
appropriate card or letter, a specific fantasy you or your special

partner truly desires...or be as mysterious as you like, just giving a date, time, place, and necessary elements to bring. Meet at a local hotel, motel, the beach, or start at a club or restaurant. If you have the means, get ultra-creative and leave instructions and as much or as little of your fantasy on a cassette tape, or better yet...video. Imagine your mate coming home to find a note and video tape. A personal teasing, tantalizing video of yourself is a great way to warm things up...and don't forget the candles, music, lingerie, and any other appropriate paraphernalia. You're sure to find lots of help and good ideas through the following sources.

$0 - $75 + (for various accessories, necessities or paraphernalia)
THE "BETTER SEX" VIDEO SERIES   **800-888-1900**
                                        (3 TAPES) $30 EACH
See also *LINGERIE (store listings), HOTEL STAY, ROMANTIC & EROTIC GIFT PACKAGE, ADULT TOY BOX*

FANTASY LETTER / TAPE / VIDEO

Write to your partner in full detail your favorite romantic or erotic fantasy to be lived out on some future special occasion...or maybe later that night. Try not to edit yourself. Go out on a limb and let your written words speak your mind. You might be surprised how similar your fantasies and secret desires really are.   **Cost: FREE**
See also *FANTASY / EROTIC GIFT PACKAGES*

FESTIVAL OF EROTICA

In Spain every July...erotic films, sculptures, poems, and romantic dramas are all part of this event. You'll want to cruise on over to the "Wild Island" of Ibiza after all that body heat.

$900 - $2,000 + / person (including air fare)
SPANISH TOURIST BUREAU   **213-658-7188**
IBERIA AIRLINES OF SPAIN   **800-772-4642**

HOT AIR BALLOON RIDE

Definitely not for the person who is even just a little bit squeamish of heights, because once you lift off the ground, you can't exactly land immediately. A thrill, and exhilarating for anybody willing to give it a try. The scenery is usually breathtaking and the whole experience leaves you with an indescribable feeling. Most prices include a champagne lunch or brunch. To find some hot air closer to home, call your local Chamber of Commerce or check your local directory under "balloons, manned."

$80 - $200 + / person (including champagne brunch)

BALLOON FEDERATION OF AMERICA	515-961-8809
BALLOON LIFE MAGAZINE - Sacramento, CA	916-922-9648
IN THE AIR - ballooning catalog	800-444-1629
BALLOON AVIATION - Napa Valley	800-367-6272
FANTASY BALLOON FLIGHTS	800-GO-ABOVE
Palm Springs, San Diego, CA	
BALLOONS ABOVE THE VALLEY - Napa Valley, CA	800-464-6824
SUNSET BALLOONING - San Diego, CA	800-350-9122
Palm Springs, CA	800-464-9122
BALLOONING - Seattle, WA	206-881-9699
BALLOONING - Reno, NV	702-323-1443
VISTA BALLOONING - Portland, OR	800-622-2309
TRAVCOA	800-922-2003

balloon over parts of Kenya as part of a 'round-the-world trip

HOTEL STAY

Don't feel that it is absolutely necessary to leave town. Booking yourselves into a local motel or hotel often saves time, and money, while still allowing you to enjoy a comfortable, relaxing "Get away from it all" atmosphere. This idea can also add wonderfully to a fantasy gift package. Imagine receiving a mysterious note from your lover to meet at a nearby hotel. Nothing beats this for excitement and anticipation for both. Also, don't miss out on some of the nicest, most reputable hotels right in your own back yard...so to speak. Go to the max and get a suite, complete with a jacuzzi right in your own room. A great gift also for the folks or a friendly couple needing a much deserved weekend away.   **$40 - $600 + / night**

See also *FANTASY GIFT PACKAGE, SPA WEEK/WEEKEND, BEVERLY HILLS HOTEL STAY, BED & BREAKFAST STAY*

JEWELRY

Pearls, Diamonds, Gold & Silver...
as well as other precious stones and metals always make an ideal gift. For something so personal, it's good advise to have the person with you when shopping for this gift, or to at least know the persons taste implicitly. When shopping for a piece of valuable jewelry, you'll find prices reduced as much as 80% through a good jewelry wholesaler. Just be sure to check for top quality with both precious metals and stones. Here are a few creative as well as classic suggestions:

JEWELRY IDEAS

RING / PENDANT w/ BIRTHSTONE or INITIAL	$35 - $100's
PROMISE / ENGAGEMENT RING	$35 - $1,000's
SIGNET RING (with name initial)	$35 - $100 +
"BROKEN" COIN or HEART PENDANT / CHARM	$25 - $85
ART DECO WATCH	$12 - $300 +
POCKET WATCH	$45 - $300 +
STRAND OF PEARLS	$85 - $300
ANYTHING WITH A DIAMOND IN IT	$55 on up
FRIENDSHIP RING / BRACELET	$2 - $100 +

METROPOLITAN MUSEUM OF ART   800-468-7386
     art, jewelry & other unique collectibles
SERRV - African Handcrafts   800-423-0071
TIFFANY & COMPANY   800-421-4468
NATURE'S JEWELRY   800-333-3235
     jewelry & gifts depicting nature's animals & scenics. Some items made from nature's naturally beautiful semi-precious stones, minerals & shells
CARTOUCHE   800-AT-EGYPT
     handmade pendants with your name in ancient Egyptian hieroglyphics
PRAIRIE EDGE - Plains Indian arts, crafts, jewelry   800-541-2388
SIMPLY SOUTHWEST   800-447-6177
     everything southwest, fashions, jewelry, & decor
ROSS-SIMONS   800-521-7677
     the finest jewelry, watches, diamonds, china and collectibles
JOHNSON SMITH CO.   813-747-2356, Fax: 813-746-7896
     things you never knew existed catalog, pendants, charms, pocket watches and much more $7 - $40

KING / QUEEN FOR A DAY

Start with breakfast in bed. Include a meaningful card, one red rose, and maybe a small gift. Bathe him or her in a warm bath. Take care of all chores around the house, and have lunch prepared and an afternoon planned. In the evening, prepare a special home cooked meal, with champagne or wine, and a fabulous dessert. End the evening by offering your personal services of a massage, playing a game of "ENCHANTED EVENING" or unwrapping a gift of lingerie...although here you may find the evening just beginning. The object is to spoil and pamper the person into relaxation...and ecstasy.

Cost: a few bucks for groceries and some simple pleasures

LIMOUSINE RENTAL

A wonderful part of any gift or gift package, whether for your mate, friend, family member, or other loved ones, for any number of occasions. Always fun!   **$45 - $65 / hour**

See also *EVENING ON THE TOWN*

LINGERIE

Always a winning gift for both him and her no matter who gives to whom. Enjoy shopping together for this gift, or risk it alone. An essential part of any **Romantic, Fantasy,** or **Erotic Gift Package.**

$4 - $100 +

LINGERIE MAIL ORDER CATALOGS

PLAYBOY - videos, magazine, lingerie and more	800-423-9494
VICTORIA'S SECRET - Lingerie	800-888-8200
INTERNATIONAL MALE - men's hot, sexy fashions	800-854-2795
UNDERGEAR - sexy underwear catalog for men	800-854-2795
FREDERICK'S OF HOLLYWOOD - hot lingerie	800-323-9525
KRISTI'S - Hot swimwear and other fashions	800-334-6541
KOALA - Men's hottest swimwear from the world	800-238-2941
IT'S A SECRET LINGERIE - lingerie, lotions, oils...	800-390-3528
STORMY LEATHER - leather & lingerie	415-626-1672
MAITRESSE - Lingerie from small to plus sizes	800-456-8464
INTIMATE TREASURES - lingerie and much more	415-896-0944
PANTY-OF-THE-MONTH CLUB	718-PANTIES
JOCK-OF-THE-MONTH CLUB - men's sexy briefs	800-972-JOCK

LOVE PIZZA

Order a pizza in the shape of a heart for the one you love on Valentine's Day, an anniversary, or birthday. Most pizza joints will do it, but it may take longer than the normal 30 minutes. If they won't, take your business down the road.   **$9 - $20**

MUSIC BOX

Who could resist the romance of a beautiful music box that plays *AS TIME GOES BY* or the theme from *DOCTOR.ZHIVAGO*...especially if it had a diamond engagement ring inside, with the phrase "Will you marry me?" etched into the bottom. A beautiful music box is timeless...a gift that may one day be a valuable family heirloom for generations to come. Definitely not for everyone. Be confident of the person's tastes before contemplating this idea.   **$25 - $100's**

KLOCKIT - music box kits   **800-556-2548**
MUSIC BOX WORLD   **718-626-8153**
RICHTER'S MUSIC BOXES - from around the world   **415-441-2663**
SAN FRANCISCO MUSIC BOX CO.   **510-653-3022**
     reproduction antique music boxes and others

PEARLS

...Are a beautiful, classic, feminine gift that any woman would appreciate and treasure, but is often over looked by men. A string of pearls are not necessarily a new creative gift idea, but they can be if you use a little ingenuity and imagination. Slip the strand into a large clam or oyster shell and present it as such.   **$45 - $250**
See also JEWELRY for other ideas

PERSONAL SERVICE

...For an evening, day, weekend, etc. Offer your complete services for however long you feel the other person deserves...or you can put up with. Cater to their every whim and need: Breakfast in bed, a planned, exquisitely prepared dinner, car wash & wax, personal chauffeur service anywhere they desire, run their errands, a daily massage...you get the idea. Pamper and spoil them with every creative, simple, or indulging need or luxury they may desire but

never ask for. Use your imagination and creativity and state your intentions in a card or in the form of a gift certificate or coupons.
See also GIFT COUPONS and GIFT CERTIFICATES   **FREE...on up**

PERSONALIZED ROMANCE NOVEL

Evelyn Brown will make you and your partner the stars and main characters in a full length Romance Novel. Choose from three titles.

SWAN PUBLISHING   **800-535-SWAN**
   OUR LOVE (a California Romance)   **$60 - $200 each**
   PARADISE DREAM (a Hawaiian Adventure)
   LOTTO LOVE (Romance and winning the lottery)
See also THE WRITTEN WORD

PICNIC BASKET & LUNCH

A Picnic basket, complete with all the trimmings & accessories, is an ideal gift for couples, weddings, showers or anniversaries. Stock it with all their favorite fixin's and they'll have the makin's for a fantastic outdoor feast. An exquisite romantic gift package can be easily revolved around a picnic lunch.

        $18 - $250 + (including basket & accessories)
PICNIC TIME - many different kinds of picnic baskets and accessories
PICNIC WORLD   **805-529-7400**
WILLIAMS SONOMA   **800-541-1262**
   country home accessories & housewares
CRATE AND BARREL   **800-323-5461**
   country-style indoor and outdoor housewares, furniture and more
        picnic baskets: $30 - $90

See also ROMANTIC GIFT PACKAGE

POLO MATCH

Take your date to a different but exciting equestrian polo match, either on the outdoor sunny grounds on a Sunday afternoon or the more sporty event at an equestrian center where you can cheer on your city's least known professional sports team at night. **FREE - $15**

ROMANTIC DESTINATIONS

below is simply a list of recommended romantic destinations and sources to help you get there. It's always nice to look forward to that one or two weeks off a year to make your great escape, but the wife might not appreciate you bringing the fishing gear. Let's not forget about those beautiful long weekends. There's just enough time to hit that mountain hideaway, ocean retreat or country bed & breakfast...and just enough time together. Don't make any excuses...work can wait, it's only work...take the time! **$100 - $1000's**

OLD ROMANTIC FAVORITES

SAN FRANCISCO	**NEW ORLEANS**
THE POCONOS	**THE SOUTH**
VERONA or VENICE, ITALY	**PARIS, FRANCE**

ROMANTIC TRAVELING - travel publication **$15 / year** 415-731-8239
FROMMER'S HONEYMOON DESTINATIONS
HONEYMOONS: A ROMANTIC TRAVEL GUIDE
ROMANTIC WEEKEND GETAWAYS
NATCHEZ PILGRIMAGE TOURS - Natchez, Mississippi 800-647-6742
   experience southern hospitality, plantation dinners & more

ROMANTIC / EROTIC BOOKS, VIDEOS & TAPES

A few creative, quality books and videos for you to choose from. Any of these can make a key part of any romantic, fantasy or erotic gift package...or a simple gift to start an evening off in the right direction. **$5 - $29 each**

VIDEOS
(also found at video stores)

PLAYBOY VIDEOS 800-423-9494
   The Art of Sensual Massage   Secrets of EuroMassage
   Oriental Massage   Secrets of Making Love
   101 Ways to Excite Your Lover   Erotic Fantasies video series
   Intimate Workout for Lovers   and lots more...
THE "BETTER SEX" VIDEO SERIES 800-888-1900
   (3 TAPES) $30 EACH
SINCLAIR INSTITUTE - sexual positions for lovers video 800-955-0888
THE STAMFORD COLLECTION P.O. Box 1160 Long Island City, NY 11101
   videos, books, condoms, sex toys, lotions, lingerie and more

KAMA SUTRA
BRAINSTORMS - MASSAGE YOUR MATE   800-621-7500
RED SHOE DIARIES (cable movie / video series)

BOOKS
(check your local bookstore to order the following)
THE EROTIC MIND
THE WONDERFUL LITTLE SEX BOOK
HOW TO GIVE A WOMAN AN ORGASM EVERY TIME
ULTIMATE SEX GUIDE TO BETTER LOVING & SEX
MEN ARE FROM MARS, WOMEN ARE FROM VENUS
SECRETS: AN INTIMATE JOURNAL FOR TWO
237 INTIMATE QUESTIONS...EVERY WOMAN SHOULD ASK A MAN
A GARLAND OF LOVE: Daily Reflections on the Magic & Meaning of Love
HE SAYS, SHE SAYS: Closing the Communication Gap Between the Sexes

CASABLANCA PRESS   800-444-2524
    1001 WAYS TO BE ROMANTIC, 1001 MORE WAYS TO BE ROMANTIC,
    & ROMANCE 101   **$12 / softcover, $19 / Hardcover**
PLAYBOY BOOKS   800-423-9494
    a wide selection of romantic / erotic "how to" books
YELLOW SILK: JOURNAL OF EROTIC ARTS   **P.O. Box 6374**
    $30 / year (quarterly)   **Albany, CA 94706**
TIMELESS LOVE REFLECTIONS   **714-992-4961**
    Romantic Love Books   **$12 each**
MARRIAGE MAGAZINE   **612-454-6434**
    for promoting the limitless potentials of marriage   **$15 / year**
EROTIC ARTWORK by Stephen Hamilton   **708-291-9023**
    original paintings & drawings. He will also do personal creations given
    the subject...and the money

TAPES (MUSIC)
(recommendations, found through your favorite music source)
AS TIME GOES BY AND OTHER CLASSIC LOVE SONGS by Henri Mancini
THE BODYGUARD SOUNDTRACK by Whitney Houston
THE HOURS BETWEEN NIGHT $ DAY by Ottmar Liebert
PHANTOM OF THE OPERA Soundtrack
PARIS SYMPHONIES by New York Philharmonic & Leonard Bernstein
LOVE'S GARDEN Solo Harp by Cynthia Lynn Douglass
WHEN HARRY MET SALLY by Harry Connick Jr.
UNFORGETTABLE by Natalie Cole   **Anything** by Sade
BOLERO   **SONGBIRD & BREATHLESS** by Kenny G

ROMANTIC TAPES (MUSIC) Cont.

IN MY TIME by Yanni

CHEEK TO CHEEK by Pete Fountain

TIMELESS LOVE REFLECTIONS
Romantic Music

714-992-4961
$8 tape, $15 CD

ROMANTIC / EROTIC PLEASURE HUNT

Leave a trail of notes and clues leading your desired one to the destined pot of gold. Leave several notes around the house, each clue or riddle leading to the next. Make it mandatory that the individual must collect each item the note is attached to. Start with a bag, then a piece of lingerie, an adult toy, a hundred dollar bill, etc. The last note attached to a set of car keys or the car itself will lead the person to a local hotel or motel...where you'll be impatiently waiting for the pleasure hunt to continue. You can take it from here. **FREE - $100 +**

RENDEZVOUS: A CELEBRATION OF LIGHT   408-464-1780
   romantic kit & game, includes invitation, guidebook, floating candles, chocolate, inspirational cards and more   **$32.50**

THE NAUGHTY BASKET CO.   800-321-4-FUN
   outrageous, risque' gift baskets for naughty guys & gals, from the "Stud Bucket," "Passion Pail," "Tonight's the Night" and more   **$25 - $100**

LATTY MARKETING GROUP - romance kits   800-368-7978
   THE FRENCH RABBIT - A romantic treasure hunt, includes treasure hunt cards & envelopes, a rabbit & rabbit accessories, instruction booklet & suggestions   **$30**

ANN FIEDLER CREATIONS   310-838-1857
   custom valentines, romantic gift baskets and more

ROMANTIC GIFT PACKAGE

Hopefully this gift will come naturally. When it comes to romance, it is not cost or impressive extravagance. It is the thought, actions, feelings and time taken to "Celebrate Romance." Whether it's a single rose and a card, a picnic in the countryside, a planned out evening for two or a night of pleasure, you have already succeeded. Create something from your heart, plan some time, then allow romance to flourish. The following sources may be able to help you out a bit.
          FREE - The cost of some simple to extravagant pleasures

TIMELESS LOVE REFLECTIONS   **714-992-4961**
Cupid's Care Packages (bridal or couples)   **$45 - $55**
Wedding Album   **$17**
Romantic Music: **$8 tape, $15 CD**   Romantic Love Books**$12 each**
See also *EROTIC, FANTASY GIFT PACKAGES, SENSUAL MASSAGE* for
sources & more ideas

ROMANTIC WEEKEND

Take your second half away for a weekend of non-stop romance to
an exotic hideaway with all the trimmings: A suite with hot tub &
view, room service, champgne, fine dining, entertainment, flowers,
and gifts.   **$75 - $100'S**
STRATTON & COMPANY - Romantic gifts   **408-464-1780**
FIGI'S VALENTINE GIFTS   **715-384-6101**
See also *TRAVEL SECTION* for ideas, *HOTEL STAY, BEVERLY HILLS HOTEL
    STAY, BED & BREAKFAST*

SENSUAL MASSAGE

This gift is always a winner whether it's planned out or spontaneous.
It can be a vital part to any fantasy, erotic, or romantic gift package.
Oils, costume, music, an adult film, and other such elements can only
enhance the experience. Professional as well as sensual massage
videos and books are available at most video libraries and adult book
& toy stores.   **FREE (aids, enhancers and paraphernalia extra)**
BRAINSTORMS - COMPLETE MUSICAL MASSAGE KIT   800-621-7500
    includes soothing music, massage oils & massage guide, all in a beautiful
    gift box   **$20**
PLAYBOY MASSAGE VIDEOS   800-423-9494
    The Art of Sensual Massage, Secrets of EuroMassage, Oriental Massage
THE "BETTER SEX" VIDEO SERIES   800-888-1900
                                        (3 TAPES) $30 EACH
SINCLAIR INSTITUTE - sexual positions for lovers video   **800-955-0888**
See also *ADULT TOY STORE* listings   **$30**

SUNSET SAIL / CRUISE

Take a boat out yourself if you're qualified, or have it taken out by
your own private crew...or join several other people on a large sailing
yacht who have the same good idea. It can be one of the most

romantic adventures to the wildest rip-roaring parties you've ever experienced.

Your own sailboat - FREE
Rented sailboat - $20 - $65 / hour
Party Boat - $15 - $75 / person
See *SAILING, YACHT CHARTERS, BOOZE CRUISE, BOAT RENTALS and YACHT CLUB MEMBERSHIP*

THE WEDDING GIFT BASKET / HONEYMOON KIT

When you're too creative to do the bridal registry...or too late, put together a wonderful wedding gift basket / honeymoon kit. Create a theme around the romance of a new relationship. You might want to include a personalized photo album / scrap-book with their names & a meaningful date, a personalized bottle of wine of a significant vintage year with their names, dates & a message, a practical relationship guide, romantic music, candles and anything else you run across or create that will add the perfect touch...you get the idea. We can't do everything for you. For the honeymoon kit, give it a spicy, more sexy twist. Add a piece of provocative lingerie for both him and her, some "optional" condoms and perhaps something fun to play with, but do be careful not to offend or embarrass anyone. Keep in mind that these gifts will probably be opened in front of a lot of people. Good luck, plan ahead and enjoy the process. If all else fails...give cash!

$35 - $200 +
TIMELESS LOVE REFLECTIONS   **714-992-4961**
Cupid's Care Packages (bridal or couples)   **$45 - $55**
Wedding Album: **$17**   Romantic Music: **$8 tape, $15 CD**
Romantic Love Books   **$12 each**
See also ***TRAVEL KIT, GREAT EXPLORER GIFT BAG, ROMANTIC GIFT PACKAGE***

WEDDINGS, ENGAGEMENTS, ANNIVERSARIES

Why is it always so difficult to think of just one unique, creative wedding gift. There's usually the bridal registry, which, I suppose, is useful in its traditional housewares sort of way. Then you have cash gifts, which I'm not arguing with. But what if they're not registered anywhere?...or what if you're too late to find something under $250 on their bridal registry?...or what if you don't want to take the easy way out and give them the 20 bucks you budgeted for their wedding?...and what if those garage sale vases just won't come clean or fit into a Macy's box. What if...

THE ENGAGEMENT & PLANNING A WEDDING

CREATIVE, DIFFERENT BRIDAL REGISTRIES
Crate & Barrel

THE COMPLETE WEDDING ORGANIZER   800-7WED-PRO
by Debbie Ludovico - call for free wedding planner

ANN'S WEDDING STATIONERY   800-821-7011
wedding story books, bridal accessories, gifts, invitations & access.

CREATIONS BY ELAINE   800-323-2717
invitations, cake knives, reception accessories & jewelry

DAWN INVITATIONS - invitations and gifts for attendants   800-528-6677

TIMELESS LOVE REFLECTIONS   714-992-4961
Cupid's Care Packages (bridal or couples)   **$45 - $55**
Wedding Album: **$17**   Romantic Music: **$8 tape, $15 CD**
Romantic Love Books: **$12 each**

MEMORIES INC.   800-462-5069
handmade wedding albums & picture frames, garters and other accessories

NOW & FOREVER   800-451-8616
invitations, accessories for reception & ceremony, gifts for attendants

EVANGEL WEDDING SERVICE   800-342-4227
invitations, programs and other accessories with a Christian theme

WEDDINGS FROM THE HEART: CEREMONIES FOR AN UNFORGETTABLE WEDDING - available at bookstores

EVERYBODY'S FAVORITE WEDDING MUSIC   800-262-6604

THE WEDDING ALBUM   800-221-8180

THE BETTER WEDDING GIFT IDEAS & SOURCES

THE WEDDING GIFT BASKET	*HONEYMOON KIT*
PRIVATE RESERVE	*ADOPT-A-STAR*
HOT AIR BALLOON RIDE	*ROMANTIC GIFT PACKAGE*
PERSONALIZED ROMANCE NOVEL	*PICNIC BASKET*
PERSONAL POSSESSION	*FAMILY HEIRLOOM*
BATHROOM IN A BASKET	*CREATIVE GIFT BASKETS*
PERSONALIZED GIFTS	*AMERICAN EXPRESS GIFT CHECK*
PERSONALIZED CHRISTMAS ORNAMENTS	
MOVIE SCRIPT LIBRARY	*...CASH*

THE AMERICAN WEDDING ALBUM   **800-428-0379**
    wedding invitations & gifts
ANN PLOWDEN - pressed flowers artist   **617-267-4705**
    preserve bridal bouquets, and other special flowers in beautiful gift creations
PERSONAL CREATIONS   **800-326-6626**
    personalized wedding creations and more from personalized bottles of wine, frames, champagne flutes, wedding cake knives and celebration accessories
INITIALS - personalized / monogrammed gifts   **800-444-8758**
THINGS REMEMBERED - engraved / personalized gifts   **800-274-7367**

HAPPY ANNIVERSARY !

YEAR 1	PAPER	YEAR 25	SILVER
YEAR 5	WOOD	YEAR 30	PEARL
YEAR 10	TIN	YEAR 40	RUBY
YEAR 15	CRYSTAL	YEAR 50	GOLD
YEAR 20	CHINA	YEAR 60	DIAMOND

THE WRITTEN WORD

...Is always a priceless gift. No, we're not talking about the bible. It's a song, poem, love letter, or card thought of and created only by you. It's a feeling in the form of words, coming directly from the heart, mind, and soul. Here are several different ideas and sources to help you.   **FREE on up**

SWEET SERENADE - Compose a song & serenade him or her.

WRITTEN LOVE SONG - Copy down on paper the lyrics to your favorite song and present it to the person whom the song reminds you of. Use nice paper and your best handwriting so that it may be displayed and referred to again and again.

FANTASY LETTER - Write to your partner in full erotic detail your favorite romantic or erotic fantasy.

CUSTOM LOVE LETTER - Have a custom love letter, Wedding, Holiday, or Get Well letter handwritten in calligraphy on fine paper, tied off with a nice ribbon or rolled up as a scroll, then delivered.

LOVE LETTERS INK - Martine Greber   **800-448-WORD**
     $17 and up

ANN FIEDLER CREATIONS   310-838-1857
   custom valentines, romantic gift baskets and more
CREATIVE CALLIGRAPHY   800-942-7471
   personalized lithographs for all occasions
SECRETS: AN INTIMATE JOURNAL FOR TWO (order from your bookstore)
LOVE LINES - letters & poems for all occasions: $30   310-551-0014
GREAT DAYS PUBLISHING   800-447-7817
                        $10 - $30, frame: $14 -$29 extra
   personalized birthday, wedding, anniversary scrolls
See also *PERSONALIZED ROMANCE NOVEL*

YOURSELF

Tie a big ribbon around yourself. Combine this with the gift idea of
Personal Service of any kind...Or perhaps you can find a large empty
box to wrap up and put yourself in as a homecoming surprise or for
whatever other reason you might want to wrap yourself up in a box
for.   **FREE**
See also *GIFT CERTIFICATES, GIFT COUPONS*

THE GREATEST LOVER IN THE WORLD IS

Nominated and Chosen by a committee of one:

_____

For earning this title, you deserve an evening of pure joy and ecstacy. You are to be pampered and spoiled. You are not to touch, but to be touched. You are to allow me to derive pleasure from giving you pleasure.

This Certificate Acknowledges

_____

has just been Approved For Charter Membership in the

Lingerie of the Month Club

Members in good standing are entitled to one new piece of lingerie each month for a year. To sustain membership the recipient must bare each new piece regularly.

Presented by

_____

On This _____ Day Of _____ , 19 _____

THIS GIFT CERTIFICATE ENTITLES YOU TO A FABULOUS

Weekend GetAway

Planned just for you, _____, is a weekend away to the
destination of your desire. The weekend will include transportation, fine
dining, luxury accommodations and more...for your total enjoyment.

DESTINATION: _____   TRAVEL DATES: _____

PRESENTED BY _____

ON THIS _____ DAY OF _____, 19 _____

ADVENTURE

Add a thrill, some excitement, or life altering experience with a creative gift of adventure. Throw a wrench into the hum-drum life or routine of a friend, responsible family member, or workaholic. It's a dangerous thing to get too caught up in a well planned out, safe, secure lifestyle day after day, year after year. Soon a good part of their life has passed before your eyes. The human spirit is most healthy, productive, and alive when put under extreme or stimulating circumstances. Change is good, and the more often the better. The rush of adrenaline can be a most addictive feeling. A one time gift adventure may just turn into a life-long ambition. At the very least, the experience may reopen a window in one's life and awaken their soul, making it far greater than the monetary value of any gift you could give.

"You give but little when you give of your possessions. It is when you give of yourself that you truly give."

KAHLIL GIBRAN

ADVENTURE

QUICK REFERENCE LIST

GREAT ADVENTURE SOURCES

OUTWARD BOUND   800-547-3312 800-243-8520
For 50 years has been the largest outdoor program in the world. From canoeing, kayaking and rock climbing, to sailing, skiing and more. For self improvement and a new outlook on life...through the outdoors

CLUB ADVENTURE   800-621-4611
Biking, hiking, ballooning, rafting

THE CALIFORNIA NATIVES   310-642-1140
From white water rafting, sea kayaking, soaring, caving, to adventures through New Zealand, Costa Rica, The Yukon, Siberia, Yosemite, Patagonia, Bolivia, and Copper Canyon to start.

BART'S WATERSPORTS   800-552-2336
OLD TOWN CANOE CATALOG   800-848-3673
SEA SAFARIS   800-821-6670
SCIENTIFIC EXPEDITIONS   619-450-3460
join marine biology and archeology projects around the world

BIOLOGICAL EXPEDITIONS   800-548-7555
whales and wildlife journeys

INNER ASIA EXPEDITIONS   800-777-8183
Eastern Europe & Asia

BAJA EXPEDITIONS   800-843-6967
whales and other wildlife adventures in the Sea of Cortez

HOLBROOKS TRAVEL WORLD   800-451-7111
safaris, cruises and exotic adventures

INTERNATIONAL EXPEDITIONS   800-633-4734
travel adventures around the world

CROW CANYON ARCHAEOLOGICAL CENTER   800-422-8975
long-term research projects and excavation

CAMPING WORLD   800-626-5944
THE MOORINGS - 50' - 100' yachts   800-437-7880
rent yourself or sail with a cook and crew to the most exotic destinations in the world...the Caribbean, Spain, Tahiti, Tonga

THE COMPLETE GUIDE TO AMERICA'S NATIONAL PARKS $13
proceeds to non-profit nat. park foundation   800-285-2448

OUTSIDE MAGAZINE   800-678-1131
BACKPACKER MAGAZINE   800-666-3434
TOUR WEST - whitewater adventures   800-453-9107

Auto Racing / Precision Driving Course

For the adventurous man...or woman, a training course with a high-performance vehicle at a raceway is truly a one-of-a-kind experience. Be careful though, if you fall in love with this adrenalin pumping addiction, as most people do who try it, it may wind up being the most expensive hobby you've ever dreamed of. A checkered-flag-hit for the man in charge, or woman for that matter. As many celebrities buy their way into this expensive sport, so do less high-profile individuals. Let's just hope a week or weekend of this natural high does the trick.

THE SKIP BARBER RACING SCHOOL	800-221-1131
Formula Ford's & BMW's - 20 locations in U.S.	$275 and up
JIM HALL II - kart racing schools	805-654-1329
BRIDGESTONE RACING SCHOOL	613-969-0334
ROAD ATLANTA	404-967-6143
KART RACING SCHOOL	800-243-1310
sprint cars, Orlando, Florida	1/2 day - 2 day: $200 - $580
RUSSELL RACING SCHOOL	408-372-7223
CAR GUYS INC.	800-800-4897
several locations: Pocano, Road Atlanta, Virginia, N Carolina and other locations	1-day: $175, 3-day: $395

Bungee Cord Jump

The new thrill! Free fall from hot air balloons, helicopters, bridges, cranes, and anything else they can safely think of. Enjoy watching the recipient of your gift find a new appreciation for life after this free fall of faith. **$35 - $85 / jump**

Camping Survival Pack

Load up a new backpack or two with all the necessary camping equipment. Include a tent, sleeping bag, cookware, flashlight, maps, a compass, and...don't forget the TP. You might want to include in the pack, tickets or a gift certificate to get them started towards their favorite camping destination. Put the tickets or gift certificate in the tent or sleeping bag or a more affordable accessory. Use your creativity...just as long as they can find it. If necessary, cut the gift down some according to your budget. **$75 - $400 + (incl. pack)**

CAMPMOR - camping and clothing catalog	201-445-5000
KELLY'S - camping / backpacking catalog	800-69-KELLY

ALL OUTDOORS MOUNTAIN EQUIPMENT   800-624-1466
L.L. BEAN - tents, backpacks, boats and much more   800-221-4221
CAMPING WORLD   800-626-5944
THE SAFETY ZONE   800-999-3030
　　FIRST AID KITS: **$150**, SURVIVAL KITS: **$40 - $90**, TRAVELER'S
　　HEALTH KIT: **$50**
FLAGHOUSE CAMPING EQUIPMENT   800-221-5185
SIERRA TRADING POST   307-775-8000
　　discount, name brand outdoor clothing & equipment
OUTSIDE MAGAZINE   800-678-1131
BACKPACKER MAGAZINE   800-666-3434
THE COMPLETE GUIDE TO AMERICA'S NATIONAL PARKS   800-285-2448
See also **TENT & CAMPING EQUIP., GREAT EXPLORER SURVIVAL KIT**

DUDE RANCH ADVENTURE / CATTLE DRIVE

In the likes of *CITY SLICKERS* or maybe not so like it, these western adventures are growing in popularity and come highly recommended with a high percentage of repeat business. Spend a few days or even a week or more hanging out on the ranch, roping, riding, and eat'n some good grub. If you want more details call your travel agent or contact the following sources.

GREAT DIVIDE TOURS - horseman's holiday adventures   **800-458-1915**
　　Lander, Wyoming   **$950 / one week**
　　Cattle Roundup/Drive, Pony Express / Oregon Trail Ride, Wagon Train,
　　a Ride with the Wild Bunch, Outlaw Trail Ride
RED'S MEADOW WESTERN HORSE DRIVE   **800-292-7758**
　　Mammoth/Crowley Lake, CA   **3 days: $475**
COLORADO DUDE AND GUEST RANCH ASSOCIATION   303-724-3653
THE HIDEOUT - a working cowboy adventure in Wyoming   **800-831-7433**
　　wild horses, the old pony express route, or visit Little Big Horn
BRUSH CREEK RANCH - Saratoga, Wyoming   **800-RANCH-WY**
　　horseback ride, fly fish, rope, barn dancing and barbecues

EXPEDITIONS, JOURNEYS, TREKS & ONCE-IN-A-LIFETIME ADVENTURES

For the person who's always had an inkling to pursue this kind of adventure, this may be the perfect opportunity. With the world getting smaller and smaller, so to speak, the uncharted territories and undiscovered lands & creatures are becoming fewer and farther between. The whole world is out there. Don't deny yourself or someone you care about an adventure of a lifetime. Don't wait till tomorrow. Tomorrow is upon us today. Go for it ! **$1,000 - $1,000's**

SCIENTIFIC EXPEDITIONS   **619-450-3460**
join marine biology and archeology projects around the world

BIOLOGICAL EXPEDITIONS   **800-548-7555**
whales and wildlife journeys

INNER ASIA EXPEDITIONS - Eastern Europe and Asia   **800-777-8183**

BAJA EXPEDITIONS   **800-843-6967**
whales and other wildlife adventures in the Sea of Cortez

POWER PLACES TOURS   **800-234-TOUR**
conference / trips to study and explore the power places

HOLBROOKS TRAVEL WORLD   **800-451-7111**
safaris, cruises and exotic adventures

INTERNATIONAL EXPEDITIONS   **800-633-4734**
travel adventures around the world

CROW CANYON ARCHAEOLOGICAL CENTER   **800-422-8975**
long-term research projects and excavation

ARCHAEOLOGICAL TOURS   **212-986-3054**
worldwide archaeological tours led by noted scholars

EXPEDITION WORLD - travel publication   **203-967-2900**

Fishing Charter : Ocean

A half day, all day, or several day fishing trip given to the avid fisherman has the makings of an unbeatable gift. Have dad take son or "tomboy" daughter on a charter off the Coast. Getting them out of the house for all or part of the weekend could end up being the greatest gift of all...for you. You'll find several different public and private charters to take you out. They usually start at dawn, or earlier, and take you out to an off shore island, or simply follow the fish up and down the local coastline. There may also be a barge or two anchored off the coast, or try your luck from one of the several piers you can fish from for free. On any given day you can be sure to catch at least a couple of fish, from the more common perch, mackerel, cod, and rock fish, to the larger halibut, bonito, tuna, barracuda, and an occasional ray or shark, among others. What makes fishing in the ocean so popular is that you never know what you may find at the other end of the line...it may just be bigger than you are.

Call your local sporting goods, fishing & tackle store for information and details. **Charter: $35 - $65 half day, $45 - $150 all day**
Barge: $25 - $45
Pier & Shore: FREE
Fishing License: $5 - $25 (varies from state to state)
See also *FISHING TRIP, FISHING ROD & REEL*

FLIGHT SCHOOL

If you can't afford to give the 40 hours of flying instruction needed for a Private Pilot's License at $40 + an hour, maybe just an hour, or introductory flight will be just enough to see whether or not the individual is into and "up to" the challenge. Who knows, this may just be one of those gifts that could change a person's life...for the better, of course. What a great gift for today's angry youth. Believe me, the skies are much safer than the drug-filled streets, and this new adventure may just offer the responsibility, enthusiasm and excitement to turn someone around. It could even lead to a promising career. But let's not exclude dad, who's always wanted to learn how to fly too. Call your local airport. They'll refer you to ground and flight schools nearby. For the more hobby-minded amateurs, the minimum standards require you to pass three vital parts in order to obtain your private pilots license: a written ground school test, an oral ground school test and a flight training program & test. If you're more serious, a full-time six-month training course can get you your professional pilot's license, although this doesn't mean you'll be flying Boeing aircraft for American Airlines.

AMERICAN FLYERS - For a professional flying career
California: (4 locations) **800-282-9595**, Florida: **800-327-0808**
private pilot program: **$5,000 - $6,000**
professional pilot program: **$27,000 and up**
FLIGHT TRAINING INTL. - Private / Commercial   Florida: **407-221-0838**
OCALA FLIGHT CENTER - Private / Commercial   Florida: **800-578-7188**
Private Pilot's License, 40 hours: **$1,800** (includes flight time cost only)
AVTAR - Airline training programs   Florida: **800-AVTAR-55**
Commuter Airline: **$8,500**   Turbo-Prop: **$16,000**
Boeing 727-200: **$19,800**
Includes 100 hours of flight time, ground school and more
See also *HELICOPTER FLIGHT SCHOOL*

GREAT EXPLORER TRAVEL PACK

Put together a gift package for the world traveler venturing off overseas for the first time, or for that person who is finally fulfilling their life-long adventure. Put all the appropriate and creative accessories and necessities into a carry-on piece of luggage or day pack. Every destination has its own particular needs. If they're off to Europe, include maps, an electric converter, and maybe a few Francs or few million Lire. If they're going down the Nile or up the Himalayas, you might want to keep it a little leaner and lighter. Think of practical and useful items. They'll appreciate it and think of you every time they need one of those things you thought to include. You'll find lots of good ideas at your local sporting goods, mountaineering store, book store, travel agency, and general merchandise stores. We'll list just a few possibilities to start you off.

$40 - $100'S

MAPS	COMPASS	GLOVES	PAIR OF SHORTS
SUNGLASSES	SUNSCREEN	SOCKS	SWIM SUIT
DAY PACK	CARRY ON BAG	SNACKS	FOREIGN CURRENCY
TRAIN PASS	FANNY PACK	CAMERA	TRAVELER'S CHECKS
FILM	BOOKS	HAT	AIRLINE TICKETS
BATHROOM KIT	LANGUAGE TRANSLATOR		LETTER WRITING KIT

THE SAFETY ZONE   800-999-3030
  helpful products for safety & security, for children, home, car and self
                                        TRAVELER'S HEALTH KIT: $50
See also *TRAVEL KIT, ROAD TRIP, CAMPING SURVIVAL PACK*

HANG GLIDING

Talk about a leap of faith, how would you like to get a running start off the edge of a 500 foot cliff? It's much safer than it used to be...really. Technology has evolved these kites into something very sophisticated, yet easy to operate. Harness yourself in next to an experienced pilot for a one-time adventure. After an exhilarating flight, feeling the wind in your hair as you gracefully drift over a cliff with your manmade wings, your weekends may be booked up the rest of the year. Our favorite pick would be Hang Glider Point, above Black's Beach in San Diego. Glide back and forth above all the nude sun-bathers. Ask around at a local sporting goods store or even your local airport for a certified and qualified hang glider pilot.

One time ride: $45 - $105
Certification Course: $500 - $1500
LOOKOUT MOUNTAIN FLIGHT PARK - Chattanooga TN   404-398-3541
TRUE FLIGHTS CONCEPTS - hang gliding school, CA   818-367-6050
WINDSPORTS - hang gliding, paragliding school, CA   310-474-3502
U.S. HANG GLIDING ASSOCIATION   719-632-8300
   hang gliding magazine & publications available
See also PARAGLIDING

HELICOPTER FLIGHT SCHOOL

Slightly more expensive then obtaining a private pilot's license, a helicopter pilot's license requires at least 40 hours of flight time plus a written and medical exam. The investment may be worth a profitable career for an individual. A gift that could last a lifetime, if that's where their desires lay. Check your local directory under helicopter or contact your area airport to locate a heliport or heli-service.   **$3,000 - $23,000 for license**
$140 + / hour, flight training rental
ALEXAIR HELICOPTERS - Torrance, California   310-236-3338
HILLSBORO HELICOPTER FLIGHT TRAINING   800-345-0949
   Portland, Oregon
QUANTUM HELICOPTERS - Arizona   602-814-8118
TITAN AVIATION   800-FLY-TITAN
PLANE & PILOT   800-283-4330
U.S. HELICOPTERS   310-497-0390

HELICOPTER RIDE / CHARTER

Weather away at an exotic location or right here at home, a helicopter ride...if never tried...can be a thrilling, one-of-a-kind experience. Check your local directory under helicopter or contact an area airport for information. For their hourly rate, they'll take you literally anywhere you want.   **$40 - $85 + / hour**

HISTORICAL MURDER MYSTERY ADVENTURE

A tour covering Scotland Yard, Dartmoor Prison, and many other destinations in and around England. Included in the package is a formal mystery solving weekend at the seaside resort of Dartmoor, England. All that's missing is Sherlock Holmes...or Angela Lansbury. **17 Nights: $2960**
GROUNDS FOR MURDER **800-946-3864**

JET SKI

There are few things that are more fun than being on the water on a warm, sunny day with a wet bike, Sea Doo or jet ski. Whether you're going to buy as a gift or rent out some time for some lucky individual at a local water resort, this is a gift that almost anyone would truly enjoy and appreciate. The jet ski industry has quickly grown and expanded to give you versatility and many options to choose from. There are high performance "stand-up" jet skis (Yamaha's Wave Blaster) with motorcycle-like power and handling for the wave jumping "hot dog," and the larger, more versatile family oriented "sit-down's" or "boats" as they call them (2-3 passenger SeaDoo's, Yamaha's Wave Runner, Polaris and Kawasaki 750's to name a few). Many of the models are even capable and legal for pulling water skiers. The Sea Doo Explorer can hold up to 5 people and combines jet ski technology with a zodiac-type inflatable boat for skiing, fishing, diving or cruising. The only trouble is, if you are just teasing the recipient with a two-hour rental, they'll want one or two of their own next birthday. **$30 on up / Hour rental**
SEA DOO, JET BOAT, SPEEDSTER
   1 to 2-person water craft **$4400 - $6300**
SEA DOO EXPLORER **800-882-2900**
   5-person water craft, combines jet ski technology with Zodiac-type inflatable boat for versatility
YAMAHA - 750'S, 1-person jet skis   **(Wave Blaster): $5400 - $6200**
   2-person "sit-downs"   **(Wave Raider): $$6400**
KAWASAKI
   1-person jet skis, 2-person "sit-down" **(Wave Runner): $5500 - $6200**
POLARIS - known for their snowmobiles and ATV's   **800-POLARIS**
   650's, 750's (1 - 3 seaters) **$5000 +**
See also *MOTOR BOAT RENTAL, SAILBOAT RENTAL*

Outward Bound

Their motto: "How to recharge your batteries 100 miles from the nearest outlet." Outward Bound has been around for decades creating an avenue for people to gain a new outlook on life. They offer more than 600 outdoor programs in hiking, sailing, skiing, canoeing, rock-climbing and more. No special skills or training required. You'll walk away with a new kind of confidence and a feeling that you can accomplish anything you set your mind on.

From 4-day family adventures starting at $500...
their average one - two week outdoor adventures from $700 - $1500...
to their 28 - 83 day outdoor school semesters from $2650 - $6800
OUTWARD BOUND   **800-243-8520**

Paragliding

You might just want to skip Hang Gliding and sky diving all together for the more innovative and quickly growing relative, paragliding. This sport, hobby, adventure, whatever you want to call it, combines the two. Its a rectangular shaped parachute with the control and loftability of a hang glider. If jumping out of a plane with one, landings become soft and effortless. You can also launch yourself off a cliff or a sloping hillside. Ask around at a local sporting goods store or even your local airport for a certified paraglider.

One time ride: $45 - $105
Certification Course: $500 - $1500
WINDSPORTS - hang gliding, paragliding school, CA   **310-474-3502**
See also ***HANG GLIDING***

Parasailing

...Differs from sky diving and paragliding in that you are towed by a line from the back of a boat over a body of water and the shoreline. Growing in popularity around the country along our water recreation areas, harness yourself in for the breath-taking ride of your life. They'll reel you out, then reel you in from a speed boat, or simply launch you from shore. Landings are usually not as graceful. Be prepared to get wet. No previous experience required.

ADVENTURE ADDICTS   **310-379-3340**
     Surf Camp, Parasailing and other adventures   **$25 - $50 / flight**

OUTRAGEOUS RECREATIONAL VEHICLES & CREATIVE TOYS

Next to tools, what could be closer to heaven on earth for a man than "BIG" recreational toys? If I had only had these sources...and the resources to fill a garage with these as a youngster, although it's never too late. My wife will never forgive me. One should always play as hard as one works. After all, isn't that why we work so hard? Pursue that hobby, sport or interest you've always kept just out of reach. Get that private pilot's license, that SCUBA certification, buy that fishing boat, expensive car, plane or helicopter...and don't look back. Take those who are willing to come with you to the other side, leave those on the side of the road who hold you back...Seize the day!

RECREATIVES INDUSTRIES - ATV's   **800-255-2511**
6 wheel drive, 2 or 4 passenger amphibious ATV's
KART WORLD - Go-Karts / Mini-Bikes   **216-357-5569**
SEA EAGLE   **800-852-0925**
5 passenger inflatable boat with outboard
JET-PACK - Build your own personal jet pack   **900-835-UFLY**
REVOLUTION HELICOPTER   **816-792-1011**
build your own helicopter
HELICRAFT - Build your own helicopter   **410-583-6366**
WOLFF TANNING BEDS - Tan at home   **800-462-9197**
BLASTER - Water Balloon launcher   **800-441-1047**
DEEPROCK   **800-333-7762**
drill your own well for all the free water you want
WESTERN CANOE - Canoes & Kayaks   **604-853-9320**
INTERNATIONAL VENTURE CORP.   **604-436-5657**
2 - 3 man submarine
HR ENTERPRISES   **800-547-9755**
The Spud Scud, potato missile launcher   **$40**
PARASCENDER TECHNOLOGIES   **305-242-1340**
fan propelled aircraft with parachute
KIWI KAYAK COMPANY - Kayaks   **800-K-4-KAYAK**

WAR AIRCRAFT REPLICA   805-525-8212
one & two person low wing monoplanes, Corsair & Mustang
SEA DOO EXPLORER   800-882-2900
combination jet ski and Zodiac type inflatable boat. ski, fish, dive
or just cruise
POLARIS - four-wheel, all-terrain vehicle (ATV)   **800-POLARIS**
THE POKE BOAT - better than a canoe at **$800**   606-986-2336
IN THE AIR - hot air balloon (ballooning catalog)   800-583-8038
PERFECT PLAY COMPUTER - blackjack computer   708-823-2500
technology the casinos fear the most, perfect probability betting
& strategy decisions   **starts at $4000**
ROTEC ENGINEERING - power hang glider kits   214-298-2505
BIKE NASHBAR   **800-NASHBAR**
serious mountain bikes & accessories
REAL GOODS - electric cars   800-762-7325
electric conversions: replica of 1955 Porsche Spyder, 4-wheel
drives, pick-ups, passenger vehicles and more   **9 - 30 K**
HEARTLAND AMERICA   800-229-2901
Blackjack Wizard (odds / probability computer)   **$50**
NORTHERN   800-533-5545
inflatable boat with electric motor **$50,** water balloon launcher
$17, motorized go-carts, **$500 - $900,** non-motorized go-carts
$75 - $130
OVERTON'S DISCOUNT BOATING ACCESSORIES   800-334-6541
NAMCO - pool supplies & recreational toys   800-732-6262
DORAN MOTOR CO   702-359-7356
electric cars, go-carts & scooters
JOHNSON MAYO   **516 N 2nd, Cherokee, Iowa 51012**
patented hydroplane (runs circles around jet skis)
ARGO CONQUEST   800-561-9508
8 & 6-wheel drive off-road amphibious vehicles
SOLAR CAR & TRIKE   **P.O. Box 430491, Big Pine Key, FL 33043**
SNORKEL STOVE CO   **108 Elliot Ave W, Seattle, WA 98119**
wood-fired hot tubs   **starting at $1365**
HELICRAFT - home built helicopter kits   410-583-6366
SNO-BIRD AIRCRAFT - gyroplane kits   206-857-3200
SORRELL AIRCRAFT - biplane kits   206-264-2866
CARLSON AIRCRAFT - monoplane & ultralight kits   216-426-3934

Sailing Instruction / Certification

Come on! This is one of those interests that some special person you're thinking of has always wanted to do, but hasn't taken the initiative or the time to do it. Well, we've just made it easier. Learn how to sail on the tiniest of sail boats up to 40 foot + sailing yachts. Once you're certified, you'll be able to rent these sailboats and yachts for your own sailing pleasure. To reap the benefits of giving this gift, have them take you on a sunset sail or to an off-shore island for the weekend. Take the whole family or group of friends for the day or weekend on one of the 40-footers. For anybody who's ever dreamed of sailing from tropical island to tropical island on their own private sailing yacht, this gift will certainly be a start in the right direction. A sailing certification also opens up a world of adventurous possibilities. Most people can't afford a two hundred thousand dollar sailing yacht, let alone have the time to sail it to all those exotic destinations. With the right certification, depending on how large and what type of boat you wish to sail, you now have worldwide access to renting or leasing a sailing vessel of your choice from virtually any port of call, to your desired destination. Imagine flying to The Virgin Islands, where you then pick up your yacht and proceed to meander from deserted island to deserted island...at your leisure. Many marinas along the coast rent medium size (25 - 40 ft.) sailing yachts and offer certification courses. Within five weeks the recipient of this gift will be tacking back and forth heading out to sea aboard a 40-footer with their friends and family. Check your local marina directory under Boat Rental, Sailing, or Yacht Clubs. Forget the cruise ship. Wouldn't you rather have an island all to yourselves?

$300 -$500 (5 week cert. course)
Yacht Rental depending on size of boat: $70 - $150 / half day
$90 - $300 / day

ANNAPOLIS SAILING SCHOOL   **800-638-9192**
    4 locations: MD, FL (2), US Virgin Islands   **up to $2,700**
CALYPSO YACHT CLUB - Marina Del Rey, Newport, CA   **310-823-4338**
    certification and boats supplied   **$250 initial, $30 / month**
YACHTING MAGAZINE   **800-999-0869**
    for sailing / yacht charters, sales, leases, rentals
MOORINGS   **800-437-7880**
    sailing yachts from 50-100 feet available from Bahamas, Virgin Islands & the Caribbean, Tonga, Tahiti, French Riviera, Corsica & Spain

BOATING WORLD MAGAZINE   **800-827-0818**
SEA - magazine for sailing / yacht charters, sales, leases, rentals
See also BOAT RENTAL

SCUBA DIVING CERTIFICATION COURSE

For the gutsy individual who wishes to explore the other two thirds of our earth. People either love it or hate it. There is no in-between, but one thing is for sure. The individual must have a strong desire to start with...and who knows, they may wind up being one of the fortunate few who discover that indescribable beauty and inner-peace in the mystical depths below the surface of the ocean. Once certified there are a wide variety of scuba adventure vacations to virtually any destination in the world from the Cayman Islands, the Great Barrier Reef and our own Pacific and Atlantic coasts to Tonga, Fiji, The Soloman Islands, the Red Sea, the Seychelles, and Belize just to name a few. Plan a gift vacation package to an exotic seaside location and include in it a certificate for you and your traveling partner to get certified together. Your underwater adventures will be remembered for a lifetime. Check your local sporting goods store, dive shop, or under "Skin Diving or SCUBA" in your local directory. Also a terrific group activity to meet lots of new friends.

Certification Course Costs about $235
DYNAMIC ADVENTURES   **310-434-0079**
   Go shark diving and watch your guide become human shark bait in his stainless steel dive suit.
NAUI - National Association of Underwater Instr.   **800-553-6284**
INTL. COMMERCIAL DIVING INSTITUTE   **800-964-ICDI**
SKIN DIVER MAGAZINE   **213-782-2121**
SCUBA DIVING MAGAZINE   **800-666-0016**

SKY DIVING

Simply free fall towards earth at 90 miles an hour until your chute eases you back to safety. Hold on! First it's necessary to take sky diving lessons before you ever leave the ground. Free fall with an instructor, or jump with a static line, but you won't own bragging rights until you free fall...solo!   **One Jump: $110 (static line)**
Free Fall: $175

SKYDIVE CHAMBERSBURG, Pennsylvania, brochure / video   **800-526-3497**
SKY DIVING ADVENTURES - Hemet, CA   **800-526-9682**
CALIFORNIA CITY SKYDIVE CENTER   **800-2-JUMP-HI**

SOARING: SAILPLANE/GLIDER FLYING

Give somebody a truly exhilarating, unique experience of soaring through the air in a motorless aircraft. For a one time flight, an experienced pilot can take them for the ride of their life. If they get hooked, they can build up enough experience and hours to solo and test for a license. On a good day, you could remain in flight for over three hours.   **One time piloted flight: $40 - $110**

Licensed: $5,000 +

SAILPLANE ENTERPRISES - Hemet, CA   **714-658-6577**
SKY SAILING - CA   **619-782-0404**
CRYSTAL SOARING - CA   **805-944-3341**
SOARING ADVENTURES - Vermont   **802-496-2290**

WHALE WATCHING EXCURSION

Between the months of January and April, the Gray Whale, along with their newly born calves, begin their long journey back up the Pacific coast from Baja California to the arctic waters of Alaska. Whale watching excursions can be fascinating, exciting, and even give you a new perspective on life...that is, if you see any whales. Also, don't forget your Dramamine for those of you who don't have sea legs. More expensive whale watching events take place off the coast of Alaska (Gray Whale), the coast of Maui, Hawaii (Humpback Whale), and Norway (Sperm Whale) just to name a few. A whale "breaching" out of the water should be one's goal to see at least once in their lifetime.   **$10 - $45 / day or half day trip on up**

OCEANSIDE SEA LIFE ADVENTURE   **619-722-2133**
     San Diego, California Whale Watch   **$15**
WHALE WATCHING ADVENTURES - Los Angeles   **800-888-5939**

$10-$12

BIOLOGICAL EXPEDITIONS - whales & wildlife journeys   **800-548-7555**
BAJA EXPEDITIONS   **800-843-6967**
     whales and other wildlife adventures in the Sea of Cortez
ANDENES WHALE CENTER - Norway, Sperm Whales   **011-47-761-42-611**

WHITEWATER / RIVER RAFTING

Hold on...! My Aunt and Uncle, who are in their seventies, recently rafted down an advanced section of the Colorado...and loved it. Make it a day, weekend, or whole week of this one-of-a-kind experience. You'll be sure to come back year after year. Just keep paddling if you hear any banjos playing. Be prepared, this adventure is not for the doubtful or hesitant. Just as with a roller coaster, once you start, you can't get off...unless of course you're involuntarily ejected. Rivers are rated from a 1 to 6 class difficulty. One being easy moving water, three being medium to difficult rapids, and six being too difficult and unrunnable. Popular river rafting waterways include, of course, the Colorado River and its tributaries, Gauley River in West Virginia, the Salmon River in Southern Idaho and the Sacramento & Merced Rivers in California among many others. Cowabunga!!!

EARTH TREK EXPEDITIONS   **800-229-TREK**
Central / Northern California: $59-$390
Colorado River: $319-$1896 for a 12 dayer
A WHITEWATER CONNECTION   **800-336-7238**
ACCESS TO ADVENTURE   **800-441-9463**
ALL-OUTDOORS ADVENTURE TRIPS   **800-942-7238**
EARTHTREK EXPEDITIONS   **800-544-8735**
OARS RAFT TRIPS   **209-736-4677**
RIVER RUNNERS, INC.   **800-525-2081**
Colorado, Royal Gorge: $75-$269
COLORADO RIVER RUNS   **800-826-1081**
$20-$40
A WANDERLUST ADVENTURE   **800-745-7238**
Colorado Whitewater: $27-$295
WHITEWATER VOYAGES   **800-488-7238**
CHUCK RICHARD'S WHITEWATER   **800-624-5950**
WESTERN RIVER EXPEDITIONS   **800-453-7450**
TOUR WEST WHITEWATER ADVENTURES   **800-453-9107**
Grand Canyon, Colorado, Idaho: $555 for 4 nights to
$1975 for a 12 nighter

WILDLIFE SAFARI

See what may very well be the last of the wild African Elephants or the odd prehistoric-looking Rhino. Both these species are in danger of becoming extinct in the wild, as well as many other wild animals found on the African continent due to poaching. Consult a travel agent who specializes in Africa to find the most safe, politically secure countries to travel while offering the most exciting, adventurous look at one of the world's greatest animal kingdoms.

ZOOLIFE TRAVEL	**800-234-2585**
JOURNEYS - Himalaya Trek, 2-35 days	**800-255-8735**
VOYAGERS - African safaris	**800-633-0299**
AFRICATOURS	**800-23-KENYA**
GALAPAGOS TRAVEL	**800-969-9014**
WILDLAND ADVENTURES - Galapagos Islands	**800-345-4453**
HIMALAYAN TRAVEL	**800-225-2380**
BUSHTRACKS - African Safaris	**800-995-8689**
SEA SAFARIS	**800-821-6670**
GREAT DIVIDE TOURS	**800-458-1915**

Kenyan Safari - 13 days: **$2800**

BIOLOGICAL EXPEDITIONS	**800-548-7555**

whales and wildlife journeys

INNER ASIA EXPEDITIONS - Eastern Europe and Asia	**800-777-8183**
HOLBROOK'S TRAVEL WORLD	**800-451-7111**

safaris, cruises and exotic adventures

QUESTERS - worldwide nature tours	**800-468-8668**
AFRICAN SAFARI CLUB	**800-544-0934**

Nile cruise and Kenya -14 days: **$2,000)**

INTERNATIONAL EXPEDITIONS	**800-633-4734**

travel adventures around the world

ADVENTURE COMPANIES	**800-882-9453**

African Safaris **$2200 and up**

GLOBAL TRAVEL PUBLISHERS - Travel Guides: **800-882-9453**
 AFRICA'S TOP WILDLIFE COUNTRIES: **$16**, *TRAVEL JOURNAL AFRICA* - Wildlife & language guide, trip organizer and diary **$13**

FOOTHILL SAFARI CAMP - Texas wildlife safari **800-245-0771**
Be a part of the only North American Safari...in Texas? No it's not an armadillo ranch. It's a 3000 acre wildlife game reserve and home to herds of giraffes, zebras and rhinos and almost a thousand other exotic and endangered species. This adventure is for the traveler who prefers luxury...with air conditioned tents, private baths, filet mignon, and chocolate souffle'.

ENTERTAINMENT

Unless you're a jaded movie star, just about everybody loves a brush with the entertainment industry. Weather you're looking for just plain great entertainment or something a little more personal, getting inside Hollywood and the entertainment industry may be easier than you think.

> *"Each one should give as you have decided in your heart to give. You should not be sad when you give, and you should not give because you feel forced to give. God loves the person who gives happily."*
>
> **PAUL**
> (2 Corinthians 9:7, New Century Version)

ENTERTAINMENT

FILM / TV STUDIOS

DISNEY STUDIOS
500 S Buena Vista St, Burbank
818-560-5151
818-840-5246   **Studio Store**
No Tours
Check local listings for their studio
store at a mall near you
800-237-5751   **Catalog**

MGM STUDIOS
10000 W Washington Bl, Culver City
213-280-6000
310-449-3300   **Studio Store**
No Tours

PARAMOUNT PICTURES
5555 Melrose Ave, Hollywood
213-956-5000
213-956-5575   **Tapings**
Tours   **$10**
213-956-5292   **Studio Store**
Free Show Tapings

20TH CENTURY-FOX STUDIOS
10201 W Pico Bl, Los Angeles
310-277-2211
310-203-3087   **Studio Store**
No Tours

UNIVERSAL STUDIOS
100 Universal Plaza, Universal City
818-777-1000
Tour   **$23 - $29**
818-777-4210 Corner Studio Store
818-777-1600   **Company Studio**
     Store

WARNER BROTHERS
4000 Warner Bl, Burbank
818-954-1951
818-954-1744   **Tours: $25**
800-223-6524 Studio Store Catalog
Check local listings for their studio
store at a mall near you

ABC TV
4151 Prospect Ave, Hollywood
213-557-7777   **Logos-To-Go**
     Studio Store
Free Show Tapings
No Tours

CBS TV
7800 Beverly Bl, Los Angeles
213-852-2345
213-852-2488   **Studio Store**
Free Game Show Tapings
No Tours

NBC TV
3000 W Alameda Av, Burbank
818-840-4444   **818-840-3572**
818-840-3537   **tours: $4-$6**
818-840-3559   **Studio Store**
Free Show Tapings

SUNSET-GOWER STUDIOS
1438 N Gower St, Hollywood
213-467-1001
many TV Show Tapings

FOX TELEVISION CENTER
5746 Sunset Bl, Hollywood
213-462-7111
many TV Show Tapings

AUTOGRAPHED CELEBRITY PHOTO

...Of their favorite movie star. This happens to be one of the easiest...and one of our favorite gifts in the list. A celebrity photograph of an actor, singer, politician, sports legend, news person...anybody in the public eye, can be obtained with little effort. Simply decide whose autographed picture you would like for yourself or to give as a gift, construct a short fan letter of admiration or adoration and request a signed photograph, then send it off to the studio or production company with whom they are working with, or worked with last. The odds are, that within a few short weeks you'll be happy to find a large envelope in your mail box containing a photograph with a personal inscription...and their signature. Remember to write the letter in the person's name or explain how big of a fan your friend so that the picture is signed to the right person. Sometimes the celebrity will have a fan club who will handle it and ask for a small donation. Add a nice frame and the recipient will think you are the celebrity's best friend. If it's a person on TV, be sure to put down the show name as part of the address. Always a huge hit with kids, although you do risk being replaced as their hero.

FREE - $20 (through fan club)
See also **FRAMED CELEBRITY PHOTO, FRAMED MOVIE POSTER, FILM & T.V. STUDIO LISTINGS**

AWARD SHOW TICKETS

Be a part of the "in" crowd. Make the investment and the commitment to attend an awards show at least once in your lifetime and live vicariously through your favorite stars. If you do it once, you'll be sure to be back year after year...it's that good. Nothing beats the feeling of cheering on your favorites in person. Be sure to make arrangements well in advance...they fill up fast. If the award show is televised as most are, the TV gods prohibit the selling of tickets to these live events...some sort of regulations or something. The producers, who are smarter than the TV gods, were able to get around it by selling expensive tickets to the dinner following the show. In most cases, it is still difficult to get tickets unless somehow you are directly involved, know somebody or are a major contributor to someone's charity. If you are not able to come up with that elusive pair of tickets, there is a last resort. You can become one of the infamous seat-fillers. Seat-fillers are needed to sit in the vacated seats when stars and their guests leave to go to the bathroom, accept an award, etc. Production does this to make it appear to the TV viewing audience that the place is jam-packed and everyone is having a great time. Just a little more wool TV likes to pull over our eyes. The odds are, you're likely to get a part-time front row seat next to a big celebrity and probably get your face on television. To become a seat-filler you'll probably have to wait around most of the day and go through a screening process. Call the network or production company for details. **FREE - $1,500 (not including travel)**

AMERICAN MUSIC AWARDS
DATE late January
PLACE the Shrine Auditorium
Los Angeles 213-749-5123
PRODUCER Dick Clark
Productions 818-841-3003

GRAMMY AWARDS
DATE beginning of March
PLACE usually at New York's
Radio City Music Hall

EMMY AWARDS
DATE middle of September
PLACE Pasadena Civic Audit.
Los Angeles 818-793-2121

SOAP OPERA AWARDS
DATE late February
PLACE Beverly Hilton Hotel
Bev. Hills 310-274-7777

ACADEMY OF
COUNTRY MUSIC AWARDS
DATE middle of May
PLACE Universal Amphitheatre
Los Angeles 818-980-9421

CABLE-ACE AWARDS
DATE middle of February
PLACE Pantages Theatre
Hollywood 213-468-1770

OSCARS (ACADEMY AWARDS)
Academy of Motion Pictures Arts & Sciences 310-247-3000
DATE late March
PLACE Dorthy Chandler Pavillion
L.A. 213-972-7211

See also ACADEMY AWARD TICKETS, FILM & TV STUDIO Listings

ENTERTAINMENT GIFT PACKAGE

If you have decided to purchase tickets to a live performance as a gift, try adding a little creativity...dress it up a bit. Plan as part of the gift a full day or evening along with it. If it's more of an up-scale show, put the set of theatre tickets inside of an appropriate card along with a gift certificate to limousine service on that specific date, or to a fine restaurant preceding the show...or for a nice hotel stay after the show. If you like the idea of the person unwrapping a gift you have given them, as opposed to just handing them an envelope, wrap up in a nice box along with the envelope a pair of opera glasses, a playbill or book on the subject, a new article of clothing or fashion accessory for the evening, anything you think might be appropriate as a part of the gift. Use these ideas to stimulate your own. Mix and match any of the above according to your budget, taste and style. It could even be as simple as a good movie and a frozen yogurt...or a good frozen yogurt and a movie, anyway.   **$20 - $100's**
See also *LIVE PERFORMANCE TICKETS, EVENING ON THE TOWN*

ENTERTAINMENT MAGAZINE SUBSCRIPTION

An ideal gift by itself or as part of a gift package for the individual in pursuit of a dream, with stars in their eyes, or simply for an entertainment buff, A magazine subscription to one's favorite entertainment industry insider can provide hours and hours of enjoyment, good gossip and important industry information.

PREMIER   **800-289-2489**
$13 / year (12 issues)
HOLLYWOOD REPORTER   **213-525-2000**
$89 / year (once a week publication), $155 / year (daily publication)
DAILY VARIETY   **213-857-6600 800-552-3632**
$39 / 3 months, $97 / 6 months, $145 / year (daily)
AMERICAN MOVIE CLASSICS (AMC) MAGAZINE   **800-669-1002**
$12 / year (12 issues)

FILM FESTIVAL: THE ULTIMATE GIFT IN ENTERTAINMENT

Invite someone along with you for a couple of days or up to a week of nothin' but film, film and more film...some pretty good, some great, and a lot bad, but that's just my opinion. If you're close to someone who likes to be on the cutting edge of the film industry, this is the gift for them. The beauty of it is that most of the smaller film festivals are hungary for a good audience and thus are very inexpensive. Combines beautifully as a travel / vacation getaway for that "movie buff" couple. The larger, more prestigious festivals are more difficult to be a part of...unless your last name is Spielberg. The final rule is, "If there's a will, there's a way." Now, if you'll just sit down we can get on with the show...Roll 'em!

Free - $100's (not including travel exp.)

CANNES INTL. FILM FEST.	May in France	011-42-66-92-20
SUNDANCE FILM FEST.	Feb. Park City, Utah	801-328-3456
THE WORLD FILM FEST.	Aug - Sept in Montreal	514-848-3883
CHICAGO INTL. FILM FEST.	mid-Oct.	312-644-FILM
HAWAII INTL. FILM FEST.	early Dec. (free)	808-944-7007
NEW YORK FILM FEST.	late Sept.	212-877-1800
AMERICAN FILM INSTITUTE FEST.	Los Angeles	213-856-7707
SEATTLE INTL. FILM FEST.	early June	206-324-9996
TELLURIDE FILM FEST.	late Aug.	603-643-1255
THE WINE VALLEY FILM FEST.	mid-July in Napa, CA	707-935-FILM

FILM / TV STUDIO TOUR

If you and your intended recipient happen to live in or around, or plan to visit the Los Angeles area, give the awe-inspiring gift of a studio tour. The old faithfuls such as 20th Century, Universal, Disney, Paramount, and Warner Brothers still have famous remnants of sets, backdrops and locations from the great films of the 40's up 'till present day. An unforgettable experience of the Hollywood phenomenon. It may move you or your friend so much that you'll close the "exciting" accounting practice to persue you dreams in the entertainment industry...even if it's moving around a bunch of phony boulders. **FREE - $28**

See also *TV and FILM STUDIO listings for details*

FRAMED AUTOGRAPH

There are several different autograph "brokers," "dealers," or galleries from which you can purchase autographs of just about anyone even remotely famous, past or present...for the right price. Whether it's on a piece of paper, a check, document or a photograph, the perfect autograph can be the perfect gift for the perfect person. Through the following sources you'll find autographs and documents from politicians, sports legends, movie stars, scientists & inventors and just about anyone who's done anything that everyone knows about...past or present. **FREE - $100's or even $1000's**

UPPER DECK AUTHENTICATED   800-873-7332
   autographed sports memorabilia
BOOK CITY COLLECTIBLES - star autographs past, present 800-4-CINEMA
EILEEN DELANEY AUTOGRAPHS   800-966-7448
   autograph rarities from stars, presidents, inventors and more
WILLIAM LINEHAN AUTOGRAPHS   800-346-9827
   movie star costumes & autographs
AMERICAN HISTORICAL GUILD   800-544-1947
   original letters / documents from famous people
JOSEPH M. MADDALENA   800-942-8856
   letters, photos, documents, signed books and other memorabilia
See also *AUTOGRAPHED CELEBRITY PHOTO, FRAMED CELEBRITY PHOTO, MOVIE SCRIPT LIBRARY, MOVIE MEMORABILIA*

FRAMED CELEBRITY PHOTO

If you're interested in a celebrity from the past or present, there are a few places that carry a grand selection of movie star headshots, posters, and other movie industry pictures and printed memorabilia for as little as two bucks. A couple of minutes planned out to pick up a photograph or two soon turns into a couple of hours as you thumb through literally thousands of fascinating photographs. If you're a movie buff yourself, you might want to bring a pillow and your PJ's. Be sure to bring a list of names and movies...they got it! Check under theatrical or cinema bookstores in major cities. If they don't have a good selection, they'll know who does. Here are some of the better known sources.   **All Black & White Photos $2.50 - $5**
                    All Color Photos $5
                    Posters $10 - $100's
EXPOSURES - photo accessories, frames, albums, etc   800-222-4947
LARRY EDMUND'S CINEMA BOOK SHOP   213-463-3273
MOVIE WORLD   818-846-0459
BACK LOT BOOKS   213-876-6070
HOLLYWOOD MOVIE POSTERS   213-463-1792

HOLLYWOOD POSTER EXCHANGE   310-657-2461
CINEMA COLLECTORS - movie posters / star photos   213-461-6516
JERRY OHLINGER'S - movie posters / star photos   212-989-0869
See *FILM AND TV STUDIO listings, FRAMED MOVIE POSTER, AUTOGRAPHED CELEBRITY PHOTO*

HOLLYWOOD STUDIO STORE GIFT

Almost all of the major Hollywood Studios have "Studio Stores" on their lot that sell their studio related garb, paraphernalia, and memorabilia, complete with logo for all the world to see. Angelinos may be somewhat jaded to the Hollywood scene and its over-commercialization, but for Aunt Bessy from Ohio, there's a whole slew of TV and movie related stuff they'd give a month's wages to get their hands on. The originality of this gift idea may not last too long as more and more "Studio Stores" crop up in local malls throughout the country. It's worth a stop in to see what they have if you're in Hollywood, otherwise many of the studios do have a catalog available. You'll probably pick up more things for yourself than for other people. Our favorite pick would be the Warner Brothers Store at Caesar's Palace, Las Vegas.   **$6 and up**
MCA/UNIVERSAL PROPERTIES
    TV show and movie merchandise
TIME WARNER'S SOUND EXCHANGE   800-854-1681
    music, videos and collectibles
CHEERS - bar and TV show memorabilia   800-852-9692
See *FILM / TV STUDIOS* for studio store listings and information, and *MOVIE MEMORABILIA*

LIVE PERFORMANCE SEASON TICKETS

...to any venue is a marvelous gift for the sports fanatic, avid Theatre-Goer, music lover, etc. Just be sure the person will appreciate and use this gift. Sticking a person with a couple of tickets is bad enough, but a whole set of 'em...   **$40 - $100's**
ANY ARTISTIC OR CULTURAL SEASON OF EVENTS:
    THEATRE OR PLAYHOUSE
    MUSIC / JAZZ FESTIVAL
    SEASON OF MUSIC PERFORMANCES
    SPORTING EVENT SEASON

LIVE PERFORMANCE TICKETS

Perhaps the largest category of our creative entertainment gift ideas is that of a live performance. Giving a material possession as a gift is always a little difficult in that everyone's tastes are different. Live entertainment generally communicates a universal language. Either a performance is good...or it ain't, but, of course, there are some extremes which do require an acquired taste, such as Opera, Ballet, Shakespearian Theatre, etc. Otherwise, tickets to the following are a pretty safe bet for a cultural experience, or just a plain good-old-fashioned evening of enjoyable entertainment. Just use your common sense and keep in mind who you are giving to. Check your newspaper or local theatre, entertainment guide for the following choices. And try to plan in advance for best selection and prices.

COST: Two-drink minimum to $100's

TYPES OF ENTERTAINMENT	WHERE TO FIND ENTERTAINMENT
THEATRICAL PLAY	LARGE LIVE PERFORMANCE THEATRES
MUSICAL	SMALL LIVE PERFORMANCE THEATRES
OPERA	COMEDY / CABARET CLUBS
BALLET	CONCERT / NIGHT CLUBS
DINNER THEATRE	CONCERT THEATRES
CABARET / VARIETY	STADIUMS
STAND UP COMEDY	TICKET SERVICES
AWARD SHOWS	
TV SHOW TAPINGS	

MUSIC CONCERT - COUNTRY, ROCK, JAZZ, BLUES, METAL, NEW AGE, CLASSICAL, EASY LISTENING, ORCHESTRA

MOVIE MEMORABILIA

How would you like a collection of Edith Head Academy-Award-winning costumes or part of the magnificent set from *BEN HUR*. Wouldn't we all. All it will take is a few million bucks and even then you have to have a name like Ted Turner or Michael Eisner. There are however smaller less expensive collectibles from decades of films. The hard part is first getting your hands on it, and second, getting a deal. Like most things in Hollywood it helps considerably to be on the inside. Unfortunately they just don't have a garage sale on Paramount's back lot every Saturday. Although, if you live in the Los Angeles area, your avenues of pursuit are much greater. There are estate sales you might get lucky with or even auctions, but they usually command high prices. There are also several collector's shops opening up around Hollywood selling things such as movie set photographs, scripts, actor's 8 x 10's and many smaller items. You can also go into Western Costume and buy a costume that was known to be in one of the big films. If you're a real movie buff you may just stumble onto a recognizable prop or piece of furniture at one of the large prop houses outside of the studio lots.

WESTERN COSTUME - outlet, North Hollywood, CA　　**818-508-2123**
　　authentic movie costumes
COLLECTOR'S PARADISE - scripts, movie photos　　**800-436-6236**
CINEMA CITY - movie scripts, posters, photos, autographs　**616-722-7760**
SCRIPT CITY　　　　　　　　　　　　　　　　**213-871-0707**
　　movie & TV scripts, film books, photos, posters
WILLIAM LINEHAN AUTOGRAPHS　　　　　　**800-346-9827**
　　movie star costumes & autographs
PROP HOUSES - props and furniture often used in many movies
LORAINE BURDICK MOVIE MEMORABILIA　　**206-845-0340**
THE MOVIE SCRIPT LIBRARY　　　　　　　**800-766-9998**
　　bound, collector's edition reproductions of some of the most popular screenplays in movie history　　**$15 each (including color movie stills)**
TIME WARNERS VIEWER'S EDGE GIFT COLLECTION　　**800-847-6753**
　　movie & TV related mugs,T's, watches, ties, posters, videos, books
See also FRAMED AUTOGRAPH, FRAMED CELEBRITY PHOTO, MOVIE SCRIPT LIBRARY

THE MOVIE SCRIPT LIBRARY

Add a beautiful addition to your living room, den or library with bound collector's edition reproductions of some of the most popular screenplays in movie history. Choose from such greats as *THE WIZARD OF OZ, STAR WARS, SOME LIKE IT HOT, GONE WITH THE WIND, IT'S A WONDERFUL LIFE*...and more. With a purchase you'll also receive a package of full color movie stills.

THE MOVIE SCRIPT LIBRARY　　　　　　　**800-766-9998**
　　　　　　　$15 each (including movie stills)
COLLECTOR'S PARADISE - scripts, movie photos　　**800-436-6236**
CINEMA CITY - movie scripts, posters, photos, autographs　**616-722-7760**
SCRIPT CITY - movie/TV scripts, film books, photos, posters **213-871-0707**

MURDER MYSTERY DINNER THEATRE

This event makes for an unforgettable experience for the family, co-workers, group of friends, or the love of your life. The spirit and comradery that develops with total strangers over the course of an evening is unsurpassed. If you let yourself play into the experience, you're likely to run a gamut of positive emotions of which you hadn't felt in a long, long time. Fun! Fun! Fun! These productions are usually put on in a closed off section of a restaurant, but they can also be hired out to play at hotels, private residences, a train car, or a yacht. As the actors incognito mingle and dine beside you, try to figure out "Who done it?" Beware the person sitting next to you, there is a murderer amongst us! Look hard through your local theatre or entertainment guide.   **$15 - $75 / person (including dinner)**

A PHONY CELEBRITY

...Of your very own. Do like Kathy Bates in *MISERY* and have your favorite celebrity live with you against their will. Feel free to speak to them, be angry at them or...whatever you want to do to them. Only drawback is that they don't respond back, because they're phony. They're free-standing life-size cardboard cut-outs. Choose a sports legend, a movie star, a cartoon character, a president, and a movie monster among others. Great for parties, keeping you company or even keeping the burglars away at night from your front window.
ADVANCED GRAPHICS   **$20 - $30 510-370-9200**

TV SHOW TAPINGS

A terrific gift of a memorable experience if you're not too exposed to the Hollywood element, or if you, your friends or your relatives are coming to tinsel town (Hollywood). Watching a LIVE taping of your favorite sit-com, game show, or local talk show, can be a fascinating, fun-filled day or evening of entertainment. Often times though, the warm-up comedian hired to entertain the live audience before and between takes is more entertaining then the actual show. The best thing of all is that the tickets are free. You're actually doing them a service by adding your laughter and reactions at the appropriate moments. A blast for kids, but make sure there isn't an age limit before you pack up the car. Many Hollywood shows require you to be at least 18 or older. For tickets to high demand, top rated shows write to the studios several months in advance of your travel plans. You can also pick up tickets the morning of a live taping, but get there early. You can also find your favorite talk shows in Chicago and New York. Just tune in and turn on the show you wish to see and they'll give you their address and number for tickets right on your TV screen.   **FREE**

HOLLYWOOD SIT-COM'S   **TALK SHOWS**
MORNING SHOWS   **GAME SHOWS**
See *FILM & TV STUDIO* listings

THE VIDEO EDITOR

Do you have a friend or family member that desires to be a part of the movies and is somewhat mechanically inclined?...Okay, if they can set the clock on the VCR, they're qualified. I'm predicting that the following may be standard equipment in every home following the camcorder revolution...or they'll most likely be standard equipment on the new wave of VCR's or even computer equipment. I'm talking about the ability to edit your own home movies, or even someone else's for that matter. With a simple set up consisting of an editing and special effects keyboard, two TV's (or monitors), a couple of VCR's and a good sound source (cassette tape or CD player), you're ready to make some pretty high quality amateur films. You can cut and splice together and add special effects to existing tape such as fading, freeze frame and more. It's an addicting hobby. Don't be surprised if this next wave of technology produces our future generation of creative film-makers.

Editing / Special Effects board: $150 - 100's
The whole set-up: several $100 - several $1,000
(Editor, Special Effects, Monitors, VCR's, CD player and other equipment)
A/V DIRECT - video editing equipment   **800-939-8858**

VIDEO GIFT PACKAGE

If you haven't been into a well stocked video store lately, you may discover an abundance of gift-giving ideas. Recently, there's been an explosion of video productions of not only the latest feature film releases, but of a whole plethora of subjects and different genres. Many video distributors have already met you half way by packaging sets or series of tapes together. From exercise and instructional to documentary series, movie classics, music videos, TV series, and on and on, to just about anything you can think of. An appropriate video or video set would also make an excellent part of many creative gift packages...or, simply start here by creating a video gift package all by itself.   **$40 - $100 +**

SERIES AND SUBJECTS

INSTRUCT. SPORTS VIDEOS	**INSTRUCT. BUSINESS VIDEOS**
DOCUMENTARY SERIES	**TV SERIES**
CLASSIC (OLD) FILM SERIES	**VIDEO HYPNOSIS**
NEW RELEASES	**CHILDREN'S VIDEOS, FILMS, AND**
NOSTALGIA	**ANIMATED FEATURES**
TRAVEL VIDEOS	**FOREIGN FILMS**
EROTIC / ADULT FILMS	

PACIFIC ARTS PUBLISHING - public home video   **800-538-5856**
   the best of public television and other fine quality programs
TIME WARNERS VIEWER'S EDGE   **800-847-6753**
    Videos for under $10
MCA/UNIVERSAL PROPERTIES!   **800-487-4326**
   TV Show and movie merchandise
TIME WARNER'S SOUND EXCHANGE   **800-854-1681**
   Music, videos and collectibles
MOVIES UNLIMITED   **800-523-0823**
   688 page movie catalog, 30,000 titles
FUSION VIDEO COLLECTION   **800-959-0061**
   Hard to find TV & film videos
CRITIC'S CHOICE VIDEO   **800-544-9852**
    a variety of over 2,200 videos under $15
DIRECT BOOK SERVICE   **800-776-2665**
   dog & cat catalog - over 2,000 books & videos
VIDEO PROJECTS - computer training videos   **800-453-9002**
THE "BETTER SEX" VIDEO SERIES   **800-888-1900**
    (3 tapes) $30 each
THE VIDEO CATALOG   **800-733-2232**
NATIONAL GEOGRAPHIC VIDEO CLUB   **800-638-4077**
    PIONEERS & EXPEDITIONS, SCIENCE & DISCOVERY, CREATURES
GREAT & SMALL, ENDANGERED WILDLIFE, PREDATORS   **$20 / tape**

_____

is hereby awarded

An Evening On The Town

This Gift Certificate entitles you to a fabulous evening on the town. Including chauffeur service, fine dining, entertainment, and the after hours destination of your choice.

PRESENTED BY
_____

ON THIS ____ DAY OF _____ , 19 ____

– *TRAVEL* –

*T*ravel Related Gifts are so thoroughly fulfilling to give and receive, we've devoted a whole section to it. There are virtually an endless number of hotels, travel destinations, and travel related activities and ideas. Sorting through all of this, we have attempted to list only the most interesting, unique and creative selection. Hopefully, you'll find the ideal travel related gift to give. At the very least, we hope to spark your imagination to come up with your own uniquely tailored gift idea.

"Every charitable act is a stepping stone towards heaven."

HENRY WARD BEECHER

— TRAVEL —

QUICK REFERENCE LIST

Vacation / Travel Ideas

EXOTIC PLACES	TROPICAL DESTINATIONS	LIFETIME ADVENTURES
Galapagos Islands	Hawaii	Scientific Expedition
The Amazon Jungle	Aruba	Archeological Dig
Egypt	Virgin Islands	'Round-The-World Trip
Israel	Bermuda	Nile / Amazon Cruise
Africa	Saeschelles Islands	Motorhome Europe
Russia	Mexico	Rail Through Asia
Antarctica	Greece	Himalayan Trek
Bangkok, Thailand	The Caribbean	African Safari
Hong Kong / Singapore	Tahiti	Space Shuttle Flight

Travel Publications

SPECIALTY TRAVEL INDEX   415-459-4900
   magazine filled with hundreds of unique, creative travel ideas
CONDE NAST TRAVELER - magazine   800-777-0700
CRUISES & TOURS - magazine   800-317-5700
CRUISING WORLD - magazine   800-978-7477
AMERICA'S GREATEST RESORTS - catalog   212-807-7100
TRAVEL LEISURE - magazine   800-888-8728
TRAVEL HOLIDAY - magazine   P.O. Box 5233, Harlan, IA 91593

Major Airlines

SOUTHWEST	800-435-9792	UNITED	800-241-6522
AMERICAN	800-433-7300	ALASKA	800-426-0333
AMERICA WEST	800-247-5692	US AIR	800-428-4322
CONTINENTAL	800-525-0280	DELTA	800-872-7786
TWA	800-221-2000	CONCORD	800-876-2200
HAWAIIAN	800-367-5320	CANADIAN	800-426-7000
BRITISH AIR	800-247-9297	IBERIA	800-772-4642
KLM	800-777-5553	LUFTHANSA	800-645-3880
NORTHWEST	800-441-1818	QANTAS	800-227-4500
SWISSAIR	800-221-4750	VIRGIN	800-862-8621
AIR COURIER	800-822-0888		

TRAVEL HOTLINES

AIR COURIER ASSOCIATION   800-822-0888
travel inexpensively on a whim by escorting business documents
CLUB MED   800-CLUB-MED
DIVE ADVENTURES - Australia & Zoolife Travel   800-234-2585
OCEANIC SOCIETY EXPEDITIONS - Alaska   800-326-7491
NATIONAL AUDUBON SOCIETY - gift membership   800-365-6142
   travel programs from **$2,760 - $4,770**   212-546-9140
AFRICAN SAFARI CLUB   800-544-0934
   Nile cruise and Kenya **(14 days, $2,000)**
JOURNEYS - Himalaya Trek, 2-35 days   800-255-8735
VOYAGERS - African safaris   800-633-0299
AFRICATOURS   800-23-KENYA
GALAPAGOS TRAVEL   800-969-9014
WILDLAND ADVENTURES - Galapagos Islands   800-345-4453
HIMALAYAN TRAVEL   800-225-2380
TAHITI VACATIONS   800-553-3477
TRAVEL WILD   **$1,800 and up** 800-368-0077
   experience the gathering of polar bears in Manitoba
ARCTIC ODYSSEYS   206-455-1960
   Canada, North Pole, Greenland, dog sledding, wildlife trips
ALASKA WILDLAND - senior safaris, sportfishing   800-334-8730
BUSHTRACKS - African Safaris   800-995-8689
SCIENTIFIC EXPEDITIONS   619-450-3460
   join marine biology and archeology projects around the world
BIOLOGICAL EXPEDITIONS   800-548-7555
   whales and wildlife journeys
INNER ASIA EXPEDITIONS   800-777-8183
   Eastern Europe & Asia
BAJA EXPEDITIONS   800-843-6967
   whales and other wildlife adventures in the Sea of Cortez
HOLBROOKS TRAVEL WORLD   800-451-7111
   safaris, cruises and exotic adventures
INTERNATIONAL EXPEDITIONS   800-633-4734
   travel adventures around the world
THE HIDDEN COAST OF CALIFORNIA (guidebook)   415-601-8301
PASSPORT - undiscovered & interesting places   800-999-9006

AIR COURIER: THE ONLY WAY TO FLY...CHEAP

How about a trip to Hong Kong or Singapore for a weekend of dining and shopping for less than $400 round trip, or maybe Australia for $700, Europe for $200. Sound too good to be true? There are a select number of travel agencies throughout the country that specialize in booking last minute air fares for 50 - 75% off...or even free in some cases. They are able to do this with the help of companies who need your allowable baggage space to ship things to any number of destinations. You are actually doing them a favor by acting as a messenger, although you never actually see what you are escorting and have no responsibility to it. You will most likely fly on an airplane chartered for air freight. This doesn't mean you'll be flying on some broken down aircraft sitting on boxes across from a noisy, stinky Lama and a guy named Akbar. You'll fly regular coach class and receive all the normal perks (or lack there of) as you would with any other airline. The one drawback is that you will have to fit into their schedule, which means being spontaneous. Once you put your name in for a destination, you might be called in a moment's notice...and be in Hong Kong 48 hours later. Individuals with a loose schedule and a spontaneous nature benefit the most through this offer. Enjoy, you world traveler you.

AIR COURIER ASSOCIATION   **303-279-3600 800-822-0888**

AIRPLANE/JET CHARTER

If you've been fortunate enough to accumulate enough money and time, an airplane charter for one or as many friends as you can afford, to any destination near or far, could be an exciting, adventuresome party trip, leaving you wanting to repeat the experience year after year. Prices range dramatically for each person depending on where you are going and which private airline service you have selected. Your best source would be to check your local directory under *aviation, airline,* or *airports* and if they can't service you, they'll be sure to know who will. Most aviation companies will fly just about anywhere for their hourly fee. If it sounds like a great idea but out of reach financially, plan in advance and call one of the major airlines to reserve a block of seats for the dates you intend to travel, then have everyone pitch in their fair share for the party /

vacation of the decade. $70 - $100's / person
See also **AIRPLANE RIDE / TRIP**

AIRPLANE TICKETS

A simple airplane ticket, whether by itself or as part of a vacation package, always makes for a wonderful surprise and an enjoyable escape. The thought of opening up an envelope, box or bag to discover airplane tickets is truly an exciting notion. That fleeting thoughtful moment of what worldly adventure lay ahead...Europe, the tropics, Asia...memories to last a lifetime. Check with your newspaper's travel section, your travel agent, or call the airlines directly for destinations, travel, and vacation packages & prices.

AIR COURIER ASSOCIATION   800-822-0888
   travel internationally for cheap to nothing on a whim by escorting business documents

See also *MAJOR AIRLINE listings, TRAVEL SECTION, AIRPLANE RIDE, VACATION PACKAGE, AIR COURIER*

ARCHEOLOGICAL DIG

Imagine being the first to discover King Tut's Tomb, the Dead Sea Scrolls, The Shroud of Turin, a new dinosaur species or even an ancient civilization...or the missing link, although I think it's my brother. The hands down find of the century would have to be Noah's Ark, possibly still hidden somewhere on Mount Arrarat in Turkey. Keep in mind it is expensive, hard, boring work with little reward usually, much like digging for gold, it's either all or nothing. Good luck Indiana.   **$2,000 + (some pay or expenses may be covered)**

SCIENTIFIC EXPEDITIONS   619-450-3460
   join marine biology and archeology projects around the world

CROW CANYON ARCHAEOLOGICAL CENTER   800-422-8975
   long-term research projects and excavation

ARCHAEOLOGICAL TOURS   212-986-3054
   worldwide archaeological tours led by noted scholars

BEVERLY HILLS HOTEL STAY

Be pampered and enjoy the life of a royal or celebrity guest for a night or two. Bee-bop and hob-nob with the stars in the Polo Lounge. Bask in the sunshine of your own cabana at poolside. If you book way in advance, you might just see an Oscar nominee or two around Academy Award's time.

BEVERLY HILLS HOTEL   **310-276-2251**
$270 - $5,000 / Night (not including airfare)

BRANDO'S ISLAND

Tetiaroa is a group of atolls that make-up part of the South Pacific's Tahitian islands. What makes this island so unique and special other than its awe-inspiring beauty is that it is owned by the one and only Marlon Brando...and, it is accessible and available by just about anyone, provided you have the budget and reserve it far enough in advance. Brando's house is situated close to the landing strip next to the handful of other huts that make up the only accommodations on the island. The island itself takes about an hour to walk around the entire circumference and inhabits only a few natives that are all employed by the small island resort. If your looking for complete privacy, wade the 100 yards or so across the lagoon to your own 50 acre atoll. Brando himself is known to show up from time to time unannounced, as does his daughter, Cheyenne. At the very least, you'll get to know Brando's very friendly Bull-Terrier dog, Gus, as he follows you around the island or sleeps beside your mosquito-netted bed. Have Matt, the tahitian native with the one-in-a-million smile, take you by boat to one of the other near-by atolls that make up the group. Visit world famous Bird Island to see a variety of South Pacific birds and their nesting grounds. Only one place to eat, and only one item on the menu each meal, but the primarily french prepared cuisine is absolutely exquisite. Not many activities. It's definitely the place to go to enjoy...and relax. Beware the rum punch.

$1,200 - $3,000 / person (4 days, including airfare)

HOTEL TETIAROA   **011-689-42-63-02 & 03**
TAHITI VACATIONS   **800-553-3477**

CRUISE VACATION

Anybody and everybody is familiar with cruises to the Mexican Riviera, the Bahamas, Caribbean, and the Mediterranean, and you can find a million brochures about it. Gaining in popularity are smaller, more intimate cruises to more exotic destinations. A cruise on a small ship, sailing yacht, or cargo ship to places off the beaten...channel...can be a vital part of an interesting, unpredictable, and truly stimulating vacation gift package. Here are a few creative choices regarding this gift idea. If your on a budget, check out the sources below offering the same cruises for as much as 60% off normal rates.

CREATIVE ADVENTUROUS CRUISE IDEAS
AMAZON CRUISE, SOUTH AMERICA
NILE CRUISE, EGYPT
WINDSONG SAILING SHIPS, TAHITIAN & HAWAIIAN ISLANDS
CHARTERED YACHT, VIRGIN ISLANDS
STEAMBOAT THE MISSISSIPPI
See also *FREIGHTER TRAVEL (ocean freighters, riverboats & barges)*

CRUISE HOTLINES

CRUISES, INC. - a cruise directory	800-762-7447
CRUISES & TOURS - magazine	800-317-5700
CRUISING WORLD - magazine	800-978-7477
CRYSTAL CRUISES	800-999-CRYSTAL
Trans-Atlantic, N.Y. to London (9 days)	$2,400+ / person
South Pacific, Tokyo to L.A. (16 days)	$5,324+ / person
CARNIVAL CRUISES	800-327-7276
COMMODORE CRUISE LINE	800-832-1122
CUNARD LINE	800-221-4770
NORWEGIAN CRUISE LINE	800-327-7030
PREMIER CRUISE LINE	800-327-7113
PRINCESS CRUISES	800-LOVEBOAT
ROYAL VIKING CRUISES	800-426-0821
WINDJAMMER BAREFOOT CRUISES	800-327-2601
WINDSTAR SAIL CRUISES	800-258-7245
THE MOORINGS	800-437-7880

500' - 100' sailing yachts complete with crew & cook to the most exotic destinations in the world

QUEEN ELIZABETH 2 (QE2) - Cross the Atlantic   800-352-3800

THE DELTA QUEEN STEAMBOAT COMPANY   **800-543-1949**
Take a romantic trip down the Mississippi on the *MISSISSIPPI QUEEN*
or the *DELTA QUEEN* - video & catalog **$760 - $6,790, 3 -12 nights**

CRUISES AT A DISCOUNT

SHORT NOTICE CRUISE CLUB	**800-432-3491**
CRUISES OF DISTINCTION	**800-634-3445**
WHITE TRAVEL SERVICES	**800-547-4790**
THE CRUISE LINE	**800-327-3021**
CRUISES INTERNATIONAL	**800-ALL-SHIPS**
CRUISE SPECIALISTS	**800-544-AHOY**
THE TRAVEL COMPANY	**800-367-6090**
SHORT NOTICE CRUISE CLUB	**800-432-3491**

FOREVER HAWAII

Remember that unforgettable trip you took to Hawaii that one year?
Wouldn't it be nice to go back? Give to somebody a taste of paradise
and a sense of their tropical desires. If you can't afford to get them
all the way to Hawaii, bring Hawaii to them. We've gone through the
trouble and the agonizing task of actually going there to research this
gift idea just for you. I guess we enjoyed it a bit too, just a
little...actually we almost didn't leave. Share with somebody that
magical essence of Hawaii...They'll never forget it.

TAKE MAUI HOME   **800-545-MAUI**
Hawaiian foods gift baskets: **$53 - $89**, pineapples: **$36 / 2 - $90 / 10,**
Maui onions: **5 - 50 lb bags (market price)**, papayas: **$60 / 10 lb box,**
Macadamia nuts: **1/2 case (5oz cans) $40, case $63,** chocolate mac
nuts: **12 - 1/2lb boxes $88,** also available: Maui chips, Protea blossoms,
Mac nut brittle, Kona coffees, syrups, dressings, jams & more

COFFEE TIMES - Kona coffees direct from the big island   **808-326-7637**
5 kinds Kona coffee: **$11 - $17 / lb**
Mac nuts: **$11 / lb,** Hawaiian honey: **$5 / lb**

MRS. BARRY'S KONA COOKIES   **800-862-KONA**
personally sampled by ourselves for quality and safety...and they are
delicious. Choose between Mac nut chocolate chip, shortbread, white
chip, peanut butter, oatmeal, coconut shortbread and more
$3.50 / bag, gift boxes: $18 - $35

DAN'S GREENHOUSE   808-661-8412

    tropical indoor Bonsai trees grown into hand-sculpted lava rock
        Octopus / Umbrella Bonsai's, date palms, Schefflera: **$27 - $129**
                Antheriums - Hawaiian love bouquet: **$28 - $32**
    Orchid plant: **$30,** Plumeria plant: **$22,** sprouted coconut: **$22**

BIG ISLAND FARMS - rooted mature seedling plants   **800-323-2767**

    Antheriums, Ginger mac nut, Kona coffee, Bird of Paradise, orchids,
    Plumeria, Hawaiian tree fern, Ti plants and more   **$4 - $11 each**
    all kinds of Hawaiian seeds: **$3 / bag,** Bonsais: **$30 - $100,** sprouted
    coconut: **$30**

THE BAD ASS COFFEE CO - Kona coffees from the source **808-329-8871**

    many different grades & flavors to choose from   **$12 - $20 / lb**

HOT ISLAND GLASS   808-572-4527

    glass-blowing sculptures and decorator pieces from up-country Maui,
    Makawao

DREAMS COME TRUE ON LANA'I   808-565-6961

    bed & breakfast, house rentals on the secluded island of Lana'i

FREIGHTER TRAVEL

Throw caution to the wind, hop on board a freighter / cargo ship and travel the high seas to destinations unknown. Travel through the Norwegian Fjords, across the Atlantic, through the Panama Canal and on to Tahiti over the span of a 5 month circumnavigation.

DRAWBACKS: Cargo comes first...times, schedules and stops change frequently...No fancy food, no entertainment, only movies on VCR.

ADVANTAGES: About $50 cheaper per day then on a regular cruise ship, inexpensive alcohol, plenty of meat & potatoes, large cabins, lots of reading & quiet time, interesting people...and quite possibly the greatest adventure of your life.

Think it through before jumping on board. Cruises last longer then the standard 7-day loop. You are guaranteed to meet the most interesting people you've ever met before between the captain, crew and 12 or so other passengers. There is no pool, no activity director, only a long flat deck full of cargo. If you'd like to warm up to one of the long runs, try a short run on a riverboat or barge first. One must have a loose schedule and an open mind to really enjoy and appreciate this experience. People tend to either try it once, and never again, or swear by it and come back year after year...to see the world from a different perspective.   **approximately $150 / day**

FORD'S FREIGHTER TRAVEL GUIDE - everything you need to know about booking a trip on ocean freighters, riverboats & barges. Check bookstores or your local travel agent

TRAVEL TIPS - FREIGHTER WORLD CRUISES	**800-872-8584**
THE CRUISE PEOPLE	**416-444-2410**
CAROLYN'S CRUISES	**415-897-4039**
VAN DYKE CRUISES & TOURS	**800-282-5151**

GIFT EXOTICA

Next time you find yourself in an exotic foreign land for whatever reason, be conscious of the people in your life that you care about, seize the moment and take the time to find something truly unique, and interesting to bring home with you. Sometimes the most memorable gifts come from places you've never been, but dream of going some day.   **$1 on up**

SERRV - African Handcrafts   **800-423-0071**
COLLECTOR'S ARMORY   **800-336-4572**
  Replicas of weaponry from the past
WORLD OF PRODUCTS   **800-289-2869**
  over 3,500 decorator items and unique gifts
SUNDANCE   **800-882-8827**
  Founded by Robert Redford: unique southwestern gifts
CHEYENNE OUTFITTERS   **800-234-0432**
  Various Southwestern inspired fashions and gifts
SIMPLY SOUTHWEST   **800-447-6177**
  everything southwest, fashions, jewelry, & decor
MUSEUM REPLICAS LIMITED   **PO Box 840 Conyers, GA 30207**
  authentic weapons, battle gear and period clothing (catalog)
THE MYSTIC TRADER   **800-637-9057**
  old world and new age gifts from exotic places around the world
OXFAM AMERICA TRADING CATALOG   **800-426-3282**
  a non-profit hunger relief agency offering hand-crafted gifts from Asia, Africa and the Americas
HOUSE OF TYROL   **800-443-1299**
  gifts and collectibles from around the world from beer steins to cuckoo clocks and more

— TRAVEL —

See also **THE PERFECT GIFT'S INTERNATIONAL CATALOG COLLECTION, COLLECTOR'S CORNER, FOREVER HAWAII,** and **THE SPICE OF LIFE: EXOTIC FOODS**

HOUSE BOAT VACATION

A wonderful gift for the whole family or group of friends. Spend a few days on a floating house with a ski boat and jet ski attached to its side. Ski, fish, tan, sleep, party, and dive (not necessarily in that order) your way to a healthier, happier you. If you're not familiar with your local summertime water-recreation areas, talk to a ski boat or jet ski dealer, they'll know. You can also check your directory under *Houseboats*.

HOUSEBOAT RENTALS	$600 - $2,000 / week
SEVEN CROWN RESORTS	800-752-9669

LONDON...IN STYLE, ON THE CONCORD

A four-day all inclusive package featuring a flight on 'The Concord.' Fly from Washington D.C. or New York's JFK Airport and spend three lavish nights in London at The Cranley, Hampshire, The Ritz, or the Grosvenor House. Includes chauffeur driven transportation.

	$4450-$5553
BRITISH AIRWAYS HOLIDAYS	800-876-2200
CONCORD ROUND-TRIP AIRFARE (without package deal)	$7200 - $8500
ABERCROMBIE & KENT	800-323-7308
a vintage train ride from L.A. to New York, Cruise to London on the QE2 then return on the Concord	**starts at about $12,000 / person**

MOTORHOME AMERICA...THE WORLD

Whether you're retired or not, why wait to explore the great outdoors one mile at a time with all the comforts of home. Do like Charles Kuralt or John Madden and see this great land of ours...or a foreign land for that matter...by motorhome. Stop where you want. Stay as long as you like. You're the boss. If you receive a motorhome rental as part of a vacation package, the first thing you'll look into upon you're return is purchasing one of those baby's of your own...a forty-footer.

RV CENTER - Motorhome, Camper Rentals   800-367-3687
5 locations in California

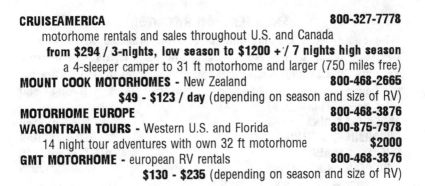

CRUISEAMERICA   **800-327-7778**
motorhome rentals and sales throughout U.S. and Canada
from $294 / 3-nights, low season to $1200 +/ 7 nights high season
a 4-sleeper camper to 31 ft motorhome and larger (750 miles free)
MOUNT COOK MOTORHOMES - New Zealand   **800-468-2665**
$49 - $123 / day (depending on season and size of RV)
MOTORHOME EUROPE   **800-468-3876**
WAGONTRAIN TOURS - Western U.S. and Florida   **800-875-7978**
14 night tour adventures with own 32 ft motorhome   **$2000**
GMT MOTORHOME - european RV rentals   **800-468-3876**
$130 - $235 (depending on season and size of RV)

ROAD TRIP SURVIVAL KIT

For kids and adults, include all the appropriate time-killing games for those long journeys on the open road. Include cards, word-play games, crossword puzzles, trivial pursuit cards, and any other fun, time-consuming stuff you can think of. Wrap it up in a cooler or picnic basket along with some favorite snacks and drinks. Perfect for the family leaving on a long road trip, the college freshman driving off to school for the first time or for those zany kids itching to take the car cross-country.   **$15 - $60 +**
WORLD'S BEST TRAVEL GAMES - book (found in bookstores)   **$5**
JUST FOR KIDS - traveling games & more   **800-443-5827**

SKI BAG

A perfect gift around Christmas time. Put together in a nice ski or tote bag all those accessories the ski fanatic has longed for. For the price of a pair of skis...or one ski for that matter...you can fill a nice ski bag with quality ski accessories. Take the following ideas as a suggestion, mix it up and put together a combination for the person you have in mind.   **$60 - $400 +**

SKI BAG & ACCESSORIES

SKI BAG	SKI BOOTS	AFTER SKI BOOTS	SWEATER
GOGGLES	SKI PANTS	GLOVES / MITTENS	SUN GLASSES
SKI JACKET	SKI HAT	SUN SCREEN	FANNY PACK
LIFT TICKETS	PLANE TICKETS	LONG UNDERWEAR	SKI POLES
A BOUTTA BAG	A LITTLE GAS MONEY / TRAVELER'S CHECKS...and ?		

SKI VACATION PACKAGE

Who could resist a combination set of airline and lift tickets to Vermont, Park City, Aspen, Lake Louise, Canada or certainly Zermatt, Switzerland. Even a bus trip to a local resort will suffice for the young ski fanatic. Could be a costly gift, think it through and price before committing.

ASPEN SKI TOURS	800-525-8955
SUGARBUSH, VERMONT	800-53-SUGAR
QUEBEC, CANADA	800-363-7777 ext. 279
EUROPEAN SNOW SAFARI	800-551-2085
6 famous ski areas in 3 countries	
THE ALPS	800-343-9676
AUSTRIA, SWITZERLAND, FRANCE	800-U-CAN-SKI
BIG ISLAND, HAWAII	(call travel agent)

SUMMER SKIING

MOUNT COOK LINE - Queenstown, New Zealand	800-468-2665
LAS LENAS, ARGENTINA - the Andes Mountains	(call travel agent)

SPIRITUAL JOURNEYS:
OFF...AND BEYOND...THE BEATEN PATH

Is there life out there? Find out for yourself. No need to jump on the space shuttle. It doesn't go that far...terrestrially speaking. Right here on planet earth you can journey to the world's most powerful places and explore the phenomenon first hand. Investigate the mysterious Crop Circles in and around England or camp out with a U.F.O. investigative team and wait for a probable sighting. There are also the older, great mysteries of Stonehenge, the great Egyptian pyramids, and the ancient Mayan ruins...or perhaps you can discover one of the newer power places closer to home such as Sedona, Arizona. If you start this journey, don't look for its conclusion, for there is no definite end or any questions answered, there is only belief...and the experience of a lifetime.

POWER PLACES TOURS	800-234-TOUR
conference / trips to study and explore the power places	
TAI CHI IN PARADISE RETREATS	619-259-1396

    Learn Tai Chi with national champion, Chris Luth. Tropical Beaches, Rain forests, Hot Springs - Gourmet Food

SACRED SIGHT JOURNEYS   **707-987-0243**
    contact Glen McTavish for journeys to Sedona, Mayan Mexico & Canada
SUNDOOR FOUNDATION   **800-755-1701**
    for Transpersonal Education Amazon excursions, Andean treks, Machu
    Picchu & Mystical Peru Adventures.
OUT OF BODY ADVENTURES (book) by Rick Stack - Astral Travel
    30 days to the most exciting experience of your life
See also *PAST LIVES REGRESSION*

TRAVEL KIT / BAG

Everybody should be so lucky to receive as a gift a brand new set of
necessities to travel with. One never seems to have an extra set, or
even a complete set, of anything. It can be a little frustrating packing
for a trip when you suddenly realize you're missing a few
essentials...with no time left to get them. Find a nice attractive carry-
on size bag with a smaller bag to match for all their bathroom stuff.
Continue to fill the bags with as much or as little as necessary...or
that you can afford. Go to your local discount supermarket, drug
store or 99 cent store and fill the smaller bag with that vital second
set of bathroom goodies. Then, if you have the time & expense, go
on to fill the carry-on bag with everything one loves to travel with.
Tailor the gift to the person's needs, then throw in something a little
personal. If you're a woman giving to an intimate male friend, throw
in a piece of your lingerie for him to remember you by. A note, a
picture or a cassette taped letter are all highly appreciated additions.

$15 - $100 +

CARRY-ON BAG & ACCESSORIES

INEXPENSIVE CAMERA	**FILM**	**A WALKMAN**	**MUSIC TAPES**
A GOOD MAGAZINE	**A GOOD BOOK**	**CASH**	**SUN GLASSES**
LETTER WRITING KIT	**HAND-HELD COMPUTER GAME**		
CLOTHES NECESSITIES & ACCESSORIES		**TRAVELER'S CHECKS**	

BATHROOM BAG / KIT & ACCESSORIES

TRAVEL SIZE SOAPS	**SHAMPOO**	**TOOTHPASTE**	**LOTION**
CONDITIONER	**TOOTHBRUSH**	**HAIR BRUSH**	**A NAIL SET**
A MAKE-UP KIT	**ELECTRIC RAZOR**		

See also *GREAT EXPLORER, BON VOYAGE: letter writing kit, CAMPING*
    SURVIVAL PACK

TRAVELOGUES

A travelogue is an entertaining travel / nature documentary shown at a local auditorium or movie house, sometimes narrated live by the host / film-maker. Often times they are put on by local Kiwanis clubs. You can purchase tickets for a series of travelogues which show consecutively every week or every other week. Each time you'll experience a different destination. A good travelogue has to be seen to appreciate this gift idea. The vivid pictures combined with good story-telling leave you almost believing you'd been there. For family members, relatives or friends who dream of exotic lands, who love to watch PBS & Discovery, and who love the great outdoors...a perfect gift. Pre-empt the person's future vacation with a travelogue on the same destination, or add the travelogue as part of a vacation package, but of course this will take some timely planning. If the travelogue itself is too much trouble as part of a vacation package, there are travel videos you can purchase. For upcoming travelogues in your area, call your local Kiwanis Club or ask at your local sporting goods store or even your travel agent.

Call your local Kiwanis club   **$5 - $25 / travelogue**
                                                 $49 - $175 (series of five)

TROPICAL VACATION

What could be better than escaping for a week to the romantic tropical destination of your choice. See Jamaica in the moonlight. Have a "Frozen Mudslide" at poolside in Aruba, a Pina Colada in Cancun, a margarita from Juanita in Los Cabos, or a rum punch that just might knock you out on Marlon Brando's Tahitian Island of Tetiaroa. Sip A Chi Chi from your balcony overlooking Waikiki or Lahaina. Wherever you go...Relax!...and enjoy...   **$100's - $1,000's**

CRUISES, INC. - a cruise directory   **800-762-7447**
AMERICA'S GREATEST RESORTS   **212-807-7100**
TAHITI VACATIONS   **800-553-3477**
See also beginning of *TRAVEL SECTION* for Ideas, sources & details

Vacation Account

Plan several months or even a year in advance for this gift idea. For your parents, the one you love or a close friend, secretly save a little each week or month for a fabulous vacation. Have a specific destination and details in mind, including a price range. Set goals to save little by little. Set that money aside in a hidden jar or box at home or in a separate "Vacation Account" at the bank. Plan for the gift to be presented before you have to actually pay for tickets, hotel stays and such, then make a creative "Vacation Package." Include the last deposit slip showing the balance to be utilized for the vacation or go so far as to withdraw the cash in one dollar bills. Load up a briefcase or travel bag along with the vacation plans and other accessories. Your creativity here will only add to your brilliant planning.

$15/week - $ 60/month - $ 720/year
$25/week - $100/month - $1,200/year
$50/week - $200/month - $2,200/year

See also **VACATION PACKAGE, TRAVEL KIT / BAG**

Vacation Package

This idea as a gift is always welcome and appreciated. Who could resist the thought of escaping to a wonderful destination to experience the events and stimulating surroundings that will create memories to last a lifetime. When putting together a vacation package as a gift, use your creativity and imagination. Go the extra mile and add that personal touch to create a truly unique and special gift for someone you care about. Put their plane tickets, traveler's checks, books, guides, maps, and any other travel related documents or necessities into a carry-on bag. Wrap the bag with a map of their designated destination and then with regular wrapping paper (so as to not immediately give away the surprise), then watch their eyes slowly widen and their smile broaden as the exciting possibilities race through their mind, while they unfurl the two layers of wrap. A concern that may come with this and other gift ideas is that they require specific dates to purchase tickets, make reservations, etc. If you are not able to make definite arrangements when planning a gift, enclose a cashier's check, traveler's checks, or American Express gift check, in the amount that will cover many of these costs...or whatever you can afford. This gives you and the individual or couple a little flexibility to do their own vacation scheduling. A great gift also for that group of friends or family members who can make better use of their gift-giving budget by pooling their money to really come up with something phenomenal.

VACATION PACKAGE NECESSITIES, ACCESSORIES & SUGGESTIONS

TRAVEL VIDEOS	MAPS	GUIDES	BROCHURES
CAMERA	FILM	CASH / CHECK	SUNGLASSES
AIRPLANE TICKETS	TRAVELER'S CHECKS		

See also *TRAVEL KIT / BAG, GREAT EXPLORER & beginning of TRAVEL SECTION for ideas, sources & details*

Congratulations !

You, _____ , are the recipient of a fabulous

VACATION PACKAGE

Entitling you to the vacation of your dreams!

DESTINATION: _____

(see attached for details herewith)

TRAVEL DATES: _____

PRESENTED BY _____

ON THIS _____ **DAY OF** _____ **, 19** _____

SPORTS & HEALTH

Sports related gifts can be a wonderful, welcome escape both physically and mentally from the pressures of daily responsibilities. After all, what is the point of working so hard to make your money? Hopefully to spend as much time as possible enjoying life's simpler, more enjoyable pleasures. What could be better than taking a young girl or boy to see their favorite professional sports team play, or perhaps to a gymnastics meet or tennis match.

"If there be any truer measure of a man than by what he does, it must be by what he gives."

ROBERT SOUTH

SPORTS & HEALTH

QUICK REFERENCE LIST

Sports & Sporting Events

FOOTBALL
SEASON	Aug - Jan
HOME GAMES	8
SEASON TICKS.	$100 - $400 +
INDIVID. TICKS.	$10 - $50 +

BASKETBALL
SEASON	Nov - April
HOME GAMES	36
SEASON TICKS.	$300 - $4300
INDIVID. TICKS.	$5 - $100

BASEBALL
SEASON	April - Oct.
HOME GAMES	81
SEASON TICKS.	$400 - $1000
INDIVID. TICKS.	$5 - $15 +

HOCKEY
SEASON	Sept - April
HOME GAMES	43
SEASON TICKS.	$1000 - $3500
INDIVID. TICKS.	$10 - $25

TENNIS
SEASON	year round
INDIVID. TICKS.	$5 - $500 +

Check your local tennis venue for upcoming events

TRACK & FIELD
SEASON	Jan - Summer
INDIVID. TICKS.	$5 - $50

Check with your area University or track stadium for upcoming meets

GYMNASTICS
SEASON	March - Nov

Check with your local University or college for details & prices

EQUESTRIAN POLO
Check with your local equestrian center or polo grounds for details & prices

WINTER OLYMPICS
NEXT	1998
WHERE	Nagano, Japan
INDIVID. TICKS.	Free - $100's

SUMMER OLYMPICS
NEXT	1996
WHERE	Atlanta, GA
INDIVID. TICKS.	$5 - $100's +

COLLEGE FOOTBALL
SEASON	Sept - Jan 1
HOME GAMES	6
SEASON TICKS.	$50 - $150+
INDIVID. TICKS.	$5 - $30

COLLEGE BASKETBALL
SEASON	Nov - March
HOME GAMES	18
SEASON TICKS.	$150 - $300+
INDIVID. TICKS.	$5 - $30

ATHLETIC / FITNESS INSTRUCTION

...To a person's favorite sport or other physical activity could be the revitalizing change that leads to new horizons. Better physical health and mental vitality is a gift surpassed by few. For the youngster, a great start that could ultimately lead to one of our olympic hopefuls... or a seven digit income with a professional sports team. This gift combines beautifully with a **sport bag** filled with all the accessories relating to that particular activity, including, of course, a gift certificate for the athletic / fitness instruction of their desire.

$15 - $100 + / month
(depending on the activity, frequency and quality of instruction**)**
any sport   martial arts   aerobic classes   dance / movement

FRISBEE GOLF

...Is free! And a guaranteed day of fun in the outdoors. A perfect gift for the person who <u>expects</u> a minimum dollar amount from you. This will open their eyes and they'll see that a good time or happiness from friends doesn't necessarily have to have a price tag. And, if they don't appreciate the thought of a great time together, free of any materialistic value..? Who needs 'em. This may be the perfect opportunity to make a positive change in one's life...by finding some better friends. There aren't many frisbee golf courses around the country. If you find one, it's an event to try at least once...although I've never met anybody who's tried it...only once. It's a Saturday addiction.   **FREE**

HEALTH CLUB / WORK-OUT BAG

Put together a package consisting of a sports bag, complete with towel, work-out gloves, aerobic/athletic wear, sports bottle, energy bars, nutrition supplements, gym membership and/or any other appropriate accessories for an individual's particular needs.

$25 - $250 + (including membership)
See also *HEALTH CLUB MEMBERSHIP*

HEALTH CLUB MEMBERSHIP

A health club membership, a home gym, a personal trainer, Martial arts, aerobics, step, jazzercise, funk, gymnastics, and yoga classes. Ultimately, a truly rewarding gift, as the results of their efforts, will pay off with a healthier heart, body, and soul...but be tactful, you don't want anybody thinking they're overweight and out of shape (even though they are). If looking into a health club membership or any of the services they offer, don't feel obligated to accept the first price they offer, more often then not you'll probably be able to haggle the price down 30 to 50%. Check your local directory for these popular clubs located in your area.

LIFETIME MEMBERSHIPS: $150 - $1000 or more
YEARLY MEMBERSHIPS: $75 - $150 + (not incl. iniation fee)
MONTHLY MEMBERSHIPS: $15 - $80 / month (not incl. iniation fee)

WORLD GYM	**800-779-4862**
GOLD'S GYM	**800-457-5735**
FAMILY FITNESS CENTERS	**800-300-7000**
NAUTILUS & AEROBICS PLUS	**800-846-8943**
BALLY'S HEALTH & FITNESS CENTERS	
JACK LALANE'S	
YMCA	

MEDITATION CLASS

Many people swear by it as being a powerful tool for a more rich, fulfilling, and happier life. Meditation is used to concentrate and focus on what someone may want for themselves, other people or the world in general. It could be for success, health, love, peace or virtually anything else one may desire. Not used as part of, or even considered a religion by most, but utilized rather for personal faith, belief, and confidence in one's self.   **$10 - $100's / session**

MIND GEAR   **800-525-6463**
   to reach a higher meditative state of mind through sight & sound sync technology
ZYGON - The Supermind, mindware   **800-865-7575 800-925-3263**
MIND LAB   **800-388-6345**
   light / sound technology sync with audio tape, also downloads software
See also MIND GEAR

OLYMPIC TICKETS

...to the 1996 summer Olympics in Atlanta, Georgia. Give to somebody a once in a lifetime experience with Olympic tickets to his or her favorite Olympic sporting event. The thrill of seeing such a history making event is unsurpassed. Many people end up revolving their lives around the Olympic phenomenon after they've experienced it in person...it's that good. Depending on how generous you are, you might want to let the recipient cover the travel expenses. Listed below are some of the more popular venues to attend. Ticket prices range dramatically depending on which event you are seeing and at which time. Keep in mind also that once these tickets go on sale the demand is very high. Tickets are usually sold by lottery, so mail in your ticket requests on the proper application along with a healthy check, then wait and pray you get what you want.

$8 - $100 / ticket (direct), $50 - $100's (scalped / private ticket service)

POPULAR SUMMER OLYMPIC EVENTS & VENUES

SWIMMING	TRACK & FIELD	GYMNASTICS	CYCLING
BASKETBALL	WRESTLING	ROWING	DIVING
WATER POLO	VOLLEYBALL	BOXING	TENNIS

OPENING AND CLOSING CEREMONIES...among many other events

U.S. OLYMPIC COMMITTEE - tickets and information   **404-224-1996**
GEORGIA TOURIST BUREAU   **800-847-4842**

PERSONAL TRAINER

A good personal trainer will do just about everything for you...except the hard work. Perfect for the person who needs help reaching their goals. They'll often design a good work-out program, motivate you through your routine of exercises, suggest a good nutritional diet and help refine and reach those goals. With their assistance and positive support you'll find it easier to push yourself harder. The results will be truly gratifying. Just be sure you are close enough to the recipient of this gift so they are not offended by the insinuation. Good personal trainers will be easy to find at any local gym, just check the bulletin board, work-out floor or ask at the front desk. Some fitness centers will even have their own staff of trainers that may go with a membership package.   **$5 - $40 / hour (or per session)**

PROFESSIONAL MASSAGE

...For a client, co-worker, boss, secretary, a friend or anybody, a phenomenal gift and a revitalizing experience, if the person is receptive to such an idea. Usually a more personal gift. A gift very appropriate for any individual you feel close enough to and confident they would appreciate such personal treatment. One wouldn't want to be falsely accused of sexual harassment...you never know.

$25 - $65 / half hour
$35 - $80 / hour

SKI LIFT TICKETS

By themselves, enclosed in a nice card, or given as part of a gift package, lift tickets are an invaluable gift that any ski fanatic would enjoy & appreciate...every run they make. Call the ski resort or ticket agency of your choice for tickets.   **$18 - $45 / day**

See also SKI SEASON PASS

SPA WEEK / WEEKEND

Enjoy, relax and be pampered in mineral pools & spas, mud baths, and sunshine. Most reputable spas also provide therapeutic massage, facials, and other beauty, relaxation & revitalizing treatments. Give someone the gift of spending a week, weekend, a day, or even a part of a day rejuvenating their physical and mental well-being. The stressed out parent, burnt out executive, or simply a deserving friend, will reap the rewards of this gift with better productivity, more energy and a more positive disposition. Also a very worthy investment for yourself. Many hotel/spas will have packages from an hour to a half day and longer, with or without a room depending on the length of stay. Makes a great part of a vacation package as some of the best spa/hotels are found at popular travel destinations around the world. Call your travel agent for their recommendation either near home or abroad. Prices do range dramatically as do the services offered, but don't be intimidated by these resort prices. Many spas offer individual services, half day treatments and such for under $100 in many cases.

CALISTOGA MINERAL SPRINGS
LA COSTA RESORT & SPA - Carlsbad, CA   **800-854-5000**
$390 / couple / night

SONOMA MISSION INN & SPA, Sonoma, CA   707-938-9000
    $20 - $35 and up per daily visit (not including room)
CANYON RANCH - Tuscon, AZ   800-742-9000
    Lenox, MASS   800-726-9900
    a spiritual retreat, quit smoking, lose weight, relax, exercise, whatever
    $300 and up / night
CALISTOGA HOT SPRINGS   707-942-6269
HAWAII REJUVENATION RETREAT   800-238-5788
    relax and unwind at a private estate on the island of Maui for health &
    adventure   **$1400 / 7 nights (not including air)**
SPA GRANDE - Maui, Hawaii   800-233-1234
GREEN VALLEY SPA - southern Utah near Grand Canyon   800-237-1068
    spectacular hiking, sensory relaxation and super pampering, reduce
    stress   **$1,800 - $2,200**
EL DORADO REJUVENATION & LONGEVITY INSTITUTE   800-460-4400
    $4,600 fee includes 2 night stay, 3 month supply of growth hormones
MAHARISHI AYUR-VEDA HEALTH CENTER - MASS   508-365-4549
    THE RAJ - IOWA   515-472-9580
    Combined western medicine and ancient Indian healing art
    $2,700 - $4,000
POLAND SPRING HEALTH INSTITUTE - Maine   207-998-2894
    complete physicals, diagnostic tests, vegetarian treatment spa
    $745 - $950
PRITIKIN LONGEVITY CENTERS - Santa Monica, CA   800-421-9911
    Miami, FL   800-327-4914
    concentrates on heart and blood ailments, minimum 2-week stay**$6,300**
STRUCTURE HOUSE - North Carolina   800-553-0052
    Weight loss spa, behavioral modification   **$1,400**
THE GREENHOUSE - Arlington, TX   817-640-4000
    Spa with mind and body connection weeks   **$3,800 - $4,050**
THE HEARTLAND - near Chicago, IL   800-545-4853
    wellness / fitness spa (28 guest limit)   **$1,900 - $2,200**
IHILANI RESORT & SPA - West Oahu, Hawaii   800-626-4446
    7-day revitalization program - connecting with nature **$2,750 - $3,650**
MAINE CHANCE - Phoenix, AZ   602-947-6365
    woman's spa - skin care, pampering, stress mgmt.   **$3,250 - $4,500**
THE PHOENIX - Houston TX   800-548-4700
    Woman's spa - stress reduction, meditation, exercise **$1,350 - $1,550**
SPA INTERNAZIONAL - Fisher Island, Florida   800-537-3708
    private island, 10 guests, fitness & nutrition   **$3,240 - $4,300**

GREEN MOUNTAIN - Vermont	802-228-8885
women only, weight loss, anti-diet	$1,100 - $1,800

CARIBBEAN SPAS

OASIS AT LESPORT - St. Lucia Island	800-544-2883
	rooms start at $400
JALOUSIE PLANTATION - St. Lucia Island	800-392-2007
	$480 and up / day (all inclusive)
PORT DE PLAISANCE - St. Maarten	800-732-9480
	$220 and up / night
CIBONEY OCHO RIOS - Jamaica	800-333-3333
	$380 and up

SPA SHIPS

NORWEGIAN CRUISE LINE	800-327-7030
	$1,300 - $5,300 (including air) 7 days
CUNARD LINE	800-221-4770
	$2,700 - $38,000 (including air) 11 days
COSTA CRUISES	800-462-6782
	$795 - $3,000 / 7 days

SPORT BAG

Put together a gift package associated with the person's favorite sport. If they're a golf enthusiast, fill a golf bag with clubs, balls, tees, a club membership, shoes, etc. If they're a ski nut, fill a ski bag with gloves, sunglasses, any other skiing accessories they may need, and don't forget some lift tickets or a season pass to their favorite ski resort. A tennis fanatic...you get the idea. A gift certificate to their favorite sporting goods store is also an appreciated addition. You might want to also include a health club membership, some peanuts, a beer mug, a Sports Illustrated subscription, etc.   **$35 - $100's**
Manny's Baseball Land - sports apparel   **800-776-8326**
See also *GIFT BASKETS, PACKAGES & SURVIVAL KITS, HEALTH CLUB / WORK-OUT BAG, HEALTH CLUB MEMBERSHIP*

SPORT / HEALTH MAGAZINE SUBSCRIPTION

A sports related magazine subscription makes a nice gift by itself or as part of a gift package. Check your local news stand for a suitable magazine.   **$12 - $32 / year**

MEN'S FITNESS	
MUSCLE FITNESS	800-276-4514
SELF	800-274-6111
SPORTS ILLUSTRATED	800-528-5000
LONGEVITY MAGAZINE - health & staying young	800-333-2782
MENS HEALTH	800-252-0800 800-666-2303
HEALTH	800-274-2522
INSIDE SPORTS	800-877-5893
AMERICAN HEALTH	800-898-7779
RUNNER'S WORLD	800-666-2828
WOMEN'S SPORTS AND FITNESS $20 / year	800-877-5281

See also *SPORTING GIFT BAG*

SPORT VIDEO PACKAGE

Sports related instructional videos and highlight films can be an ideal gift by themselves or as part of a gift package. Check your local video libraries for an appropriate selection.   **$12 - $100**

See also *SPORT BAG*

SPORTING EVENT FINALS

Tickets to the finals or playoffs of a sporting event have the potential to make an unforgettable gift. There is of course the Superbowl (Football), World Series (Baseball), NBA Championship series (Basketball), and the Stanley Cup (Hockey). There are also Collegiate sporting event finals as well as Track & Field, Gymnastics, Auto Racing, Tennis, and certainly don't forget the Summer Olympics (1996, Atlanta, Georgia).

SUPERBOWL TICKETS	**$100 - $1,000 / ticket**
WORLD SERIES TICKETS	**$75 - $1,000 / ticket / game**
NBA CHAMPIONSHIP TICKETS	**$100 - $1,000 / ticket / game**

See also *SPORTING EVENT TICKETS, SEASON TICKETS, OLYMPIC TICKETS and SPORTS & SPORTING EVENTS at the head of this section*

SPORTING EVENT SEASON TICKETS

...Is a fantastic gift for any sports fanatic. They'll appreciate this gift week after week for months...as long as their team keeps winning. Just be sure that the person will appreciate and utilize this type of gift. Sticking a person with a couple of tickets is bad enough, but a whole set of 'em... Keep in mind that one must plan far in advance for this gift and that the recipient may not benefit from it until months later when the season starts. Check your local paper for upcoming seasonal sporting events or call the person's favorite professional, collegiate, or amateur sports team or event facility. Check also the classifieds for fare-weather fans trying to get rid of a portion or all of their season tickets. Keep in mind that it's lonely going to a stadium by yourself even if it is filled with 80 thousand people. This gift doubles in price when you realize that the designated recipient needs someone to go to the games with.
See *SPORTS AND SPORTING EVENTS* for ideas seasons prices & more
See also *SPORTS FINALS TICKETS, SPORTING EVENT TICKETS*

SPORTING EVENT TICKETS

Still a creative gift idea, although often overlooked. A set of tickets to one's favorite sporting event is always a gift of a good time that is not soon forgotten. Whether it's basketball, football, baseball, hockey or any other sporting venue, the combination of good friends, a foot long hot dog, beer, soda, popcorn, peanuts and of course the exciting entertainment is the stuff that life's made of...Makes you wanna stand up and cheer.   **$10 - $60 / set of regular season tickets**
See *SPORTS & SPORTING EVENTS* at the head of this section for details,
see also *SPORTS FINALS, SEASON TICKETS, SPORTING GIFT BAG*

SPORTS MEMORABILIA

The desire and certainly the demand for sports collectibles has exploded in just the past five years, making this a huge industry. Just about every mall in the country has a sports memorabilia store. For that kid or adult that fortunately never grew up, an autographed ball, photograph, rookie card or article of clothing could be the gift to top all gifts in their eyes. Just be sure you know what they would want and that they don't already have it...or have something better. It can be a little competitive giving this gift. Who knows, you might just score. **prices range dramatically from new baseball cards to Babe Ruth's last home run bat**

THE SPORTS ILLUSTRATED STORE   800-274-5200
official championship sports clothing and memorabilia

UPPER DECK AUTHENTICATED   800-873-7332

JOHNSON SMITH CO.   813-747-2356
things you never knew existed catalog, all kind of sports collectibles from sports cards to autographed balls and more   **$8 - $150**

BASEBALL BARONS SPORTSCARDS - all sports   800-437-7814

MID-ATLANTIC SPORTS CARDS - posters, cards, sets   800-542-5345
flags, boating apparel, wetsuits, water skis and more

HERRINGTON   800-622-5221
the best in accessories   **autographed baseballs: $60 - $369**

LEGENDS OF THE GAME   800-265-4218
all sports: cards, autographed pictures, bats & balls

SPRING TRAINING BASEBALL FANTASY

Here's your chance to finally live that life long dream. Spend a week with the big boys...real, all star major-leaguers. Join such baseball greats as Steve Garvey and Larry Bowa for a whole week of nothin' but baseball. You'll field balls and swing for the fence during real games right along side these legends. You'll warm up, do drills and get coached by major league coaches. Live the "Dream Week." If you're good, maybe they'll recruit you...but it's not likely.

DREAM WEEK   800-888-4376
    Next: January 15 - 22, 1995, St. Petersburg, Florida   **$4,500**
Package includes: "Rookie" hotel accommodations transportation, club house meals, practice sessions with the legends, professional coaching, daily "big-league games, custom / personalized all star uniform, all star team jacket & hat, clubhouse locker, personal club house staff & trainers, big-league equipment & facilities, all star "welcome" party, personalized baseball cards...Of yourself, and a professional video tape of the entire event...Not to mention a lifetime of memories.

$ Inbestment $

Certainly, money doesn't buy happiness, but in our monetary based society it does buy time and a certain amount of freedom for you to choose to do with it what you want. So, for the practical minded professor, these gifts may lack a little heart and soul, but it does have the potential of being a powerful investment tool that leads to a bright future. And, between you and me, the thought of not receiving another "bad" decorator item that you feel obligated to display, is quite comforting. With the following list we've attempted to put back a little heart and soul lost with just cold hard cash.

> *"Behold, I do not give lectures or a little charity. When I give I give myself."*
>
> **WALT WHITMAN**

QUICK REFERENCE LIST

INVESTMENT INFORMATION

STOCKS - shares of investment in a company that has gone public and are usually purchased through a brokerage account. When a company succeeds...their stock increases. When they have difficulty or fail...their stock decreases or hits bottom. Stocks are traded on all major U.S. exchanges and the over-the-counter market. There are thousands of companies to choose from.

BONDS - corporate and municipal bonds can be purchased from corporations from around the country and overseas or from municipalities across the country, respectively. They are available in many denominations, maturities and quality ratings.

CD's - Certificates of Deposit are issued by banks and other financial institutions. They offer a fixed rate of interest for a specified period of time, ranging from three months to ten years.

TRUSTS - UIT's or Unit Investment Trusts are portfolios of selected corporate, U.S. government or municipal bonds. There is a fixed rate of return, regular income, and principal back upon maturity.

PRECIOUS METALS - Gold, silver, platinum coins and bullion can be purchased through most brokerage accounts. Storage or delivery is available.

Prices (as of publication):

GOLD, $ 378 / Oz
SILVER, $5.28 / Oz
PLATINUM, $ 399 / Oz

T-BILLS - Treasury Bills, notes and bonds are issued by the U.S. Treasury and are considered the safest of all securities. They are bought well below their face value and redeemed at face value at maturity. (see chart below)

TREASURY	MINIMUM	DENOM'S.	MATURE IN
T-BILLS	$10,000	$5,000	3, 6 & 12 mos.
T-NOTES	$ 5,000	$5,000	2 or 3 year
" "	$ 1,000	$1,000	4 to 10 year
T-BONDS	$ 1,000	$1,000	11 to 30 yrs

INVESTMENT SOURCES

PACIFIC COAST STOCK EXCHANGE   213-977-4500
NEW YORK STOCK EXCHANGE - 11 Wall St   212-656-3000
COMEX - Commodity Exchange, Inc   800-333-2900
LEXINGTON GOLDFUND - $1,000 min. investment   800-526-0057
FIDELITY STOCK REPORT SERVICE   800-847-7272
    in-depth reports and recommendations on nearly 4,000 companies   **$6 for each 7-page report**
THE WALL STREET JOURNAL   800-568-7625
    the standard for business & investing
FINANCIAL TIMES   800-628-8088
FORT KNOX SECURITY PRODUCTS - safes   800-821-5216
LIBERTY SAFE - security products and safes   800-247-5625

LARGE INVESTMENT BROKERAGE HOUSES

MERRIL LLYNCH   800-237-7403
DEAN WITTER   800-843-3326
PRUDENTIAL   800-862-3344
FIDELITY INVESTMENTS - discount brokerage   800-544-6262
DREYFUS MUTUAL   800-373-9387   800-645-6561
E.F. HUTTON   800-223-3019

GIFT INVESTMENT PLAN
(assuming an annual fixed investment return of 8%)

YEARS	MONTHLY INVESTMENT		
	$ 100	$ 300	$ 500
5	$ 7,348	$ 22,043	$ 36,738
10	$18,295	$ 54,884	$ 91,473
15	$34,604	$103,811	$173,019
20	$58,902	$176,706	$294,510
25	$95,103	$285,308	$475,513

AMERICAN EXPRESS GIFT CHECK

...Is a somewhat classy, more tasteful way of giving a cash gift. Perfect for almost any occasion, for anybody...weddings, showers, Christmas, bar mitzvahs, birthdays, relatives, co-workers etc...to be utilized in any matter they choose...almost anywhere. What could be more perfect then that, practically speaking. You can pick up one or more beautiful gold certificates in increments of **$25, $50,** and **$100** denominations. Ask your local bank branch if they carry them, call American Express directly, or stop by one of their many offices.
Available at:
   All **GREAT WESTERN, WELLS FARGO, 1st INTERSTATE BANKS, AAA,** anywhere AE Traveler's Checks are sold, **AMERICAN EXPRESS offices** or by calling: **AMERICAN EXPRESS**   800-553-6782

COLD HARD CASH

Not exactly a creative gift idea, although the kids in the family might argue the point...and they'd find a million creative ways to spend it. Each year I give my nieces & nephews a little spending money for Christmas, their birthday, etc., but I don't just give it to them, I give the gift creatively. Half the fun, especially for kids, is the excitement and anticipation of opening a gift. I think I'm guilty of enjoying this gift as much or more than they do as I watch them contemplate a twenty dollar bill stuck frozen in a small block of ice, or search for the hidden treasure buried somewhere in the back yard or neighborhood with the help of a treasure map. There are a million fun creative ideas to give this gift. All it takes is a little thought and creative energy.   **$10 and up**

GIFT TRUST

Set up for a youngster, family member or close friend a trust account for their future financial security, or personal investment purposes. Try to give this gift with "no strings attached" as long as you know the individual is responsible and trustworthy. Of course they must be if you know them. Try to avoid conditional gifts..."I'll give you this, if you do that." There are always limits. I suppose you could hardly justify a trust meant for a college education spent on Europe, debts or drugs. Make it easy on yourself. See an investment counselor at

a financial institution to see what you can safely afford, then have a predesignated amount transferred each month.   **$100 - $1000's**
or even millions (let me know if you need my account # for a deposit)
See the GIFT INVESTMENT PLAN at the head of this section

GOLD, SILVER & COMMEMORATIVE COINS

This gift can be a great monetary investment as well as a genuine keepsake for kids, family members or friends. Many banks and savings institutions issue U.S. gold & silver commemorative coins, and foreign coins & currency for investment purposes. They can usually be purchased in weights of 1, 1/2, 1/4 & 1/10 troy ounce. Prices fluctuate daily depending on the per oz. price of the precious metal set be the Commodities Exchange Commission. Check also some jewelry stores, and coin shops. It could start someone on a valuable coin collection. This investment gift, among all the ideas in this section, may be the best option for most of us on a budget.

PRICE: Fluctuates
See also RARE COIN / COIN COLLECTION, GOLD & SILVER BARS, PENNY STOCKS and the INVESTMENT SECTION

GOLD & SILVER BARS

A little more costly than a coin. Gold and silver bars are made in different weight increments. Prices for these precious metals are based on a per ounce cost set by the Commodities Exchange Commission each business day. Gold fluctuates just under **$400/ounce** while the less expensive silver stays around **$5/ounce.** A one-pound bar of gold, which isn't very big, will run somewhere around **$6,000,** while a one-pound bar of silver will cost around **$130.** Many of the larger investment brokerage houses can handle precious metals commodities, but will usually require a minimum buy-in of about **$10,000.** Your best bet is to go through a smaller brokerage house or bullion reserve company. Don't ever let a broker intimidate you if you or they think you're investing too little. After all, it's your money. If they don't handle smaller sums of money, they'll certainly be able to refer you to someone who will.
See INVESTMENT INFROMATION & SOURCES at head of this section

INVESTMENT PORTFOLIO

A great gift to start anybody on their future investments, from children, to your wife, husband, or co-worker. This might include Stocks, Bonds, CD's, T-Bills, precious metals and a whole world full of other investment options. Call or walk in to a local banking, investment institution or brokerage house for any help or information. Make the investment something the individual is interested in. If a friend has an obsessive interest in large commercial aircraft, get them a couple of shares of Boeing or McDonnell Douglas Stock...You get the idea. Check also the business section of any major paper including the Wall Street Journal for all current trading prices on "public" companies that sell stock and any other investment information you may need. Keep in mind that most of the larger investment brokerage houses require a minimum investment of about $10,000 for commodities, stocks & bonds, and about $2,500 for mutual funds and the like. Minimums will vary. The more you have to invest the more options you will have. On large investments, brokerage fees are around 1% and less of your total investment, and up to 5% on smaller investments. If you're like me and this is slightly out of your price range, contact a discount or smaller brokerage house and let them know the amount you plan to invest and in which direction. If they can't help you, they can most certainly point you in the right direction.   **$50 on up**
See also **PENNY STOCKS, INVESTMENT INFO. & SOURCES, BUSINESS / FINANCE MAGAZINE SUBSCRIPTION**

PENNY STOCKS

...Can be a great, fun way to begin one's education in the world of investment, business & finance. Also a good start on someone's investment portfolio, without a heavy financial risk. Penny stocks are just what they imply, ranging from a few pennies to a few dollars per share of stock. These are usually companies of a more risky nature that have gone public to finance their efforts. These often include gold, silver, and diamond mines, oil wells, and almost any other high-risk or new business you can think of. Giving a couple of shares of stock from a major company for fifty dollars a share may not seem like a worth while investment. With that same hundred dollars you might be able to buy literally thousands of shares of a penny stock. Keep in mind that companies such a Kodak started as Penny Stocks. Anybody holding a thousand dollars worth of their stock as they grew, are undoubtedly multi-millionaires now. Many a risk-taker made a fortune in penny stocks, but the odds are stacked against you. The name of the game of Penny Stocks is RISK. They usually explode...one way or the other. Through the following sources you'll find information on "hot" and "not" companies as well as brokers who will buy and sell for you.   **$50 minimum investment on up**

THE LOW PRICED STOCK SURVEYS   **219-931-6480**
                                                      $82 /year (bi-weekly)
UNITED & BABSON INVESTMENT REPORT   **617-235-0900**
                                             $215 / year (weekly newsletter)
OPPENHEIMER & CO. - N.Y. City brokerage   **800-626-6853**
    "Stocks under $10, under book, in the black and paying dividends" list
S & P's STOCK COMPANY REPORTS - financial data on more than 4,000 companies, available at brokerage houses & libraries
VALUE LINE INVESTMENT SURVEY   **800-634-3583**
    follows 1,700 stocks, at libraries or...   **$65 / 10 weeks subscription**
THE SPECULATOR   **800-444-3190**
                              $50 / 3 months (once every 3 weeks)
BOWSER REPORT   **804-877-5979**
                                              $48 / year (monthly)
See also **INVESTMENT PORTFOLIO, STOCK & BONDS, and the INVESTMENT SECTION**

PRECIOUS METALS INVESTMENT

Gold, Silver, Platinum and other precious metals can make an interesting creative gift for a family member, co-worker or friend. For a young person it can start them in the right direction by educating them about investments and the all-mighty dollar and its less than all-mighty fluctuations. A person learns best when he or she is interested or impassioned with the subject. Investments are just investments if you don't have any. Where is the incentive to learn? Now, if you have an investment, it personalizes it, creating interest. See my point? Who knows, maybe they'll even make a few bucks. Gold has climbed up to over $800/ounce before, more than double its current rate. Other good investment ideas are coins, penny stocks, and other stocks

& bonds. If purchasing precious metals, you can request to have the actual coins, bar or bars (depending on how much you buy) sent to you, or the recipient, rather than just holding on to a piece of paper. For a young kid, the notion of having a bar of solid gold or silver in a safe or safe deposit box, is very exciting. Call an investment broker to help you.

See INVESTMENT SECTION for other ideas, and INVESTMENT SOURCES at the head of this section
See also PENNY STOCKS

STOCKS / BONDS

Stock in a favorite and hopefully upwardly mobile company, will give a girl or boy of the right age, or an adult for that matter, a welcomed start or addition to their investment portfolio. If you've invested in them wisely over the years, you may have even helped pay for their college education, a new car, or a down payment on a house...who knows.

see also INVESTMENT PORTFOLIO, BUSINESS / FINANCE MAGAZINE SUB.

SWISS BANK ACCOUNT

More of a fun gift than to be taken seriously...unless you're planning to launder some money. Switzerland has always been known as a safe haven for large sums of money. Their banks offer anonymity, which means you are known as a number rather than a name. Nobody, and I mean nobody, is allowed access to your name or money through one of these accounts, except you of course.

"Yes, I'd like to deposit a large sum of money."
"...And your account, Sir?"
"...Bond, James Bond...007..."

CREDIT SUISSE PRIVATE BANKING	**212-238-5100**
	new account minimum: $500,000
BANK OF SWITZERLAND - Geneva	**011-41-22-391-2111**
JOHNSON SMITH CO.	**813-747-2356**

things you never knew existed catalog, millionaire's club membership, anyone can join, includes authentic certificate **$20**

STOCK CERTIFICATE

is hereby awarded _____ shares of stock

an Investment for Your Future Endeavors

Presented by _____

On This _____ Day Of _____, 19 _____

To be given in person, in the form of cash or check, or to be deposited in a personal savings account or trust **(each share of stock is equivalent to one U.S. Dollar)**

S.E.A.L.

Fantasy

*L*et this section be your motivation to acquire just about anything you want within your lifetime. John Goddard of Pasadena, California, while still a teenager, wrote out a list of seemingly impossible goals to accomplish. He's achieved almost all but a few including canoeing the Nile, flying a jet and reading the bible, among many other amazing feats and adventures of which most of us only dream about. I believe he still has yet to have walked on the moon...but there's still time.

"If one is lucky, a solitary fantasy can totally transform one million realities."

MAYA ANGELOU

QUICK REFERENCE LIST

ACADEMY AWARDS TICKETS

There are only five different ways we can think of to get in to see the Oscars...live. You cannot buy tickets and you can't sneak in:

1. Nominated for an award
2. Invited because you're a big star or an academy member
3. As a guest of someone who's invited
4. Work for the theatre or production crew
5. Be a seat filler

Since most of us don't fall into the first four categories...unfortunately, that leaves number five. Seat fillers are needed to sit in the vacated seats when stars and their guests leave to go to the bathroom, accept an award, etc. Production does this to make it appear to the TV viewing audience that the place is jam packed and everyone is having a great time. Just a little more wool TV likes to pull over our eyes. The odds are, you're likely to get a part-time front row seat next to a big celebrity and probably get your face on television. To become a seat filler you'll probably have to wait around most of the day and go through a screening process. Call the network or production company for details. Truly a once in a lifetime experience. Hob nob all evening with the biggest stars in the business. You'll mingle with icons, producers, and movie moguls as you see in person the biggest event of the year. Put on your best black tie or dress, roll up to the red carpet in your own personal limousine and enjoy the attention as the paparazzi try to guess who you are. If you're lucky enough to attend this event, pull out all the stops. Make a whole day out of it. Have your hair, nails and face done. Get a professional massage so that all your senses can be alive to completely take in the experience. You're sure to leave with a couple of good stories you can tell your grandkids about. Just be sure to get lots of proof. Get pictures before and after the event of you and all your new found friends. Enjoy and good luck...however you get in. **FREE - a few hundred (not including travel, wardrobe and limo)**
DOROTHY CHANDLER PAVILLION - Los Angeles   213-972-7211
ACADEMY OF MOTION PICTURE ARTS AND SCIENCES   310-247-3000

CONTROLLING COMPANY STOCK

If you happen to have a company that has gone public, are a major stock holder in a company, or plan a hostile takeover, give someone you truly care about that controlling stock...as long as you have three or four other companies you can still play with. If you have it, be generous. After all, you can't take it with you. If you have the money to play this game there's no need to refer you to the right sources for this gift idea...not that I could.   **100's of thousands - millions**

DREAM HOUSE

Buy for your parents, your spouse or someone you really, really like...their dream house. One of the most important things to an individual's health and well being is a comfortable home, a place that gives them security and an identity...a place they can always go to...a place they can call home. Wouldn't it be nice to help somebody else fulfill their dreams. Sometimes even a down payment will do.

$150 - MILLIONS

FANTASY SHOPPING SPREE

How would you like to do just as Julia Roberts did in *PRETTY WOMAN* and take all the time you need to shop Beverly Hills' golden triangle, of which at the center lays Rodeo Drive. Even window shopping will cost you some money here, but if price is no object...and if you have good taste, you can buy the best wardrobe, fashion accessories, art, gifts, jewelry and decorator items & collectibles, found in the world. Rodeo Drive, being the most famous upscale shopping street in the world, has attracted the most exclusive designers and their boutiques from Armani, Valentino, Montana, Gucci, Polo, Ralph Lauren, to Ferragamo, Christian Dior, Fred Hayman, Hermes and many others. Some stores are so exclusive (or pretentious) you have to make an appointment just to walk in the door. And don't forget to pick up that 5 million dollar diamond and gold bracelet at Cartier or Tiffany & Company. Department stores include I. Magnin & Co., Neiman Marcus, and Saks Fifth Avenue. Enjoy !   **Price: Incalculable**

LUNCH IN SAN FRANCISCO, PARIS, OR ROME

An event to be experienced at least once in your lifetime. Be spontaneous with a financial windfall and take off with the one you love or good friend to the destination of your choice, have lunch or dinner and return the next day. You may find it hard to stay less than a couple of days, but to do something totally frivolous and illogical is a healthy experience and it may just lead to a richer more fulfilling life.

San Francisco: $150 - $250 per person (including lunch)
Paris & Rome: $750 - $1,200 + per person (including lunch)
See *AIRLINES & ROMANTIC DESTINATIONS*

PARTY SPECTACULAR

Follow in the same tradition of the late Malcolm Forbes and throw the party of the decade for someone truly special. In this section of the guide you don't need to stress and pull you hair out trying to pull off the perfect party. Why bother with the headache? Enjoy the party as much as your guests. Hire a company or team of people to do all the work. Make sure they include a great band complete with a stage, dance floor & lights, complete catering with three open bars. If your place isn't suitable, contact a real estate or property management company to rent out a nearby estate for the occasion. Make sure it has a heated pool & jacuzzi. Have valet service for convenient parking. Check your local directory under Party Services or Party Planning & Consultants. There, you'll find many companies eager to help.   **$100's - 100's of $1000's**
See *CREATIVE PARTY IDEAS* for more details

PICASSO PAINTING

You'll be able to get your mitts on this gift idea by one of three ways. One, you'll have to do what's never been done; take one home with you after visiting the Louvre Museum in Paris. With this method, which is not advised and highly illegal, it may take you 10 to 20 years to return home. Two, you can travel in all the right circles for a few years, purchasing a painting here and a painting there for a few million each until you're invited to attend an auction offering such a treasure. Lastly, you can garage sale hop until you find one of his lost masterpieces for about 10 bucks...then you can retire. **10 bucks to...Ohhhh...30 - 40 million**

A PRIVATE JET

...is not difficult to get ahold of provided you have the funds to purchase it, not to mention, operating expenses, such as a pilot, a parking spot, gas and continuous upkeep. Once you get past all that you can fly off into the sunset. Imagine being able to fly just about anywhere you want at a moment's notice for business or pleasure. No more dealing with travel agents, airlines, or public airport terminals...and most importantly, no more waiting. I envy the person who receives this gift. See you in Aspen...or was it Switzerland. Have an experienced technician or pilot help you with finding and purchasing a private jet. Private airline companies may be able to locate one for you, or you can contact the manufacturers directly. You can also inquire with a high-end business sales agent. A select few may even be obtained for a below market price from a governmental agency as a drug related seizure or forfeiture. Check the governmental auctions around the Florida area.

FALCONJET **201-393-8056**

'ROUND-THE-WORLD TRIP

Take 2 to 3 weeks or even a month or more to circle the earth by plane, boat and/or train. And don't forget to make several stops along the way through Europe, Asia, Africa, the South Pacific, and South America. Travcoa offers what they call "The Ultimate Journey," a 'round the world trip via private jet that picks you up in your own home town then continues to Los Angeles, Hong Kong, Bali, Australia, Mauritius, Dubai, Istanbul...then you get on a luxury cruising ship from Turkey to the Agean Islands, Peloponnese, the Ionian Islands, Malta...and finally home. Everything is done first-class over 28 days. **all for only $42,000**

Call your travel agent, favorite airline or check the travel section for less expensive trips. **$3,000 - $10,000 + per person**

AMERICA'S GREATEST RESORTS **212-807-7100**

TRAVEL CONNECTION - 'round the world trips **800-637-3273**

TRAVCOA - "The Ultimate Journey" 'round the world trip   **800-992-2003**
FIESTA WEST - around the world holiday   **$17,420 800-993-4378**

SURGICAL AESTHETIC ENHANCEMENT

Plastic surgery performed exclusively to improve your appearance is thought of by some as stupid, vane, ridiculous, an unnecessary risk, and even immoral. Others claim that along with improving appearance, it rejuvenates the soul, improves self-esteem, and generally adds quality to life. Whichever you believe, it is all a matter of opinion, and not for us to pass judgement. It is, however, something for the individual to think through thoroughly and to consider all the positives and negatives before making a finale decision. Here are some of the more common areas to have enhanced: The nose, breasts, eye-lids, face lift, lipposuction, the chin, cheeks, lips, and virtually anywhere else, but we won't get in to all those areas.   **$1,500 (for something minor) - 10's of $1000's**

A SOUTH PACIFIC ISLAND

Your own tropical island. Aaah...how nice. Do as Marlon Brando and a select few wealthy individuals have done. Purchase your own tropical island complete with coconuts, reefs, white sand beaches and blue lagoons. Believe it or not, you can purchase a salt water island for as little as $100,000 or even less. As you're probably aware, they're not making islands anymore, so there are a limited number available. Worldwide, you might find as many as 300 offered for sale at any given time. Find one of these islands closer to home off the coast of Seattle or Vancouver on the west coast and from Maine to Florida on the east. There are sandy coral atolls in the Bahamas, or how about something a little more exotic off the coast of France, Spain, Italy, Scotland or even Greece. Try down south off Brazil's Atlantic coast for an island covered with lush tropical hardwoods. Aaah...the South Pacific. The South Sea Islands in Fiji have a few available, or try off the coast of New Zealand. Your options are open and the prices seem reasonable, but don't let the paradise-like image you hold in your mind, cloud your vision. The reality is that you have to be very careful with what you purchase. Buying an island requires intense research. In many cases there are foreign ownership restrictions, a lack of fresh water, harsh weather conditions, vandalism and pirating among other things. And try to avoid those low-laying atolls in the Pacific. They're here today...gone tomorrow, after a good hurricane.

	$100,000 - $5,000,000 +
PREVIEWS INC. - Palm Beach FL	**407-832-7131**
BLAIR DUFFY & ASSOCIATES - Honolulu, Hawaii	**808-538-1418**
VLADI PRIVATE ISLANDS - Hamburg, Germany	**011-49-40-33-8989**
COLLIERS MACAULAY NICOLLS - Vancouver, B.C.	**604-681-4111**
ISLANDS MAGAZINE - check classifides	
FINANCIAL TIMES **$428 / year (daily)**	**800-628-8088**
WALL STREET JOURNAL - Real Estate Section	**800-568-7625**

A SPANISH CASTLE

Just as with a tropical island, you might be rather surprised at how affordable these foreign beauties really are. A 3-acre rustic farmhouse might run you about $100,000. If you're looking for an updated "old Europe" feel, try a 17th-century french chateau starting at a half million, or a 15th-century Italian palace on the Venice canal for under 3 million. If you want something a little warmer on the outside, but colder on the inside, check out a modest medieval estate on Mallorca. Spain lately has become one of the easiest and most affordable places to buy as a foreigner, from a beautiful Spanish castle to renaissance farmhouses. On the down side of foreign ownership you have to deal with a lot of red tape, traveling distance, and of course taxes & fees...from both countries. The reality may never meet the fantasy, but if you've got money to burn...why not!

FEDERATION OF OVERSEAS PROPERTY DEVELOPERS, AGENTS &	
CONSULTANTS	**P.O. Box 981, Brighton BN2 2FT**
FINANCIAL TIMES **$428 / year (daily)**	**800-628-8088**
WALL STREET JOURNAL - Real Estate Section	**800-568-7625**

WHITE HOUSE DINNER INVITATION

Like the Academy awards or buying an island, it is difficult to obtain. To receive a dinner invitation to the White House you must fall into one of the following categories:

COST: Taxes...every day of your life

Be on a championship sports team
Be a sports hero or legend
Be a well known, recognizable actor / entertainer
Be a diplomat or leader of a foreign country
Be a Mayor, Governor, Senator, Congressman, or other
   government official
Ba a personal friend to the first family
Be a personal friend, spouse, or date of any of the above
Date the President's daughter
Be a little girl or boy who wrote a touching letter
Become the President of the United States

I think most of us fall into one of those categories...don't we?

A YACHT

It's often been advised to resist the temptation to buy a boat, as they are typically more pleasurable and less trouble to look at from a distance. But if you're in this league, it should be no trouble to hire people for yearly upkeep...at about 50K a year. It'll probably be more a gift for him than for her, but if you do purchase a 50-footer for your honey, make sure to have her name painted across the stern (that's the back). Enjoy!   **$10,000 - $2,000,000 +**

YOUR OWN SMALL TOWN

Do like Kim Bassinger and purchase yourself a small midwestern town. It is actually possible, although if all the inhabitants are not happy with being bought by an outsider, you won't be well received. If a whole town is on the market, usually all the property owners are in cooperation with the sale. Many small towns have simply gone bankrupt as generations change and so does the local economy. A somewhat risky investment might be to buy a deserted town complete with all the acreage, stores, farmhouses and the like, restore it to its original working condition then either retire there or rent it out or resale it to one of the movie studios.   **$300,000 - Millions**
FINANCIAL TIMES   **$428 / year (daily)**   **800-628-8088**
WALL STREET JOURNAL - Real Estate Section   **800-568-7625**

CREATIVE GIFTS & YOUR BUDGET

~ 161 ~

Priceless Gifts UNDER A PENNY ⊘

~ 163 ~

NO-BUDGET *TO*

LOW-BUDGET $5 - $25 $

~ 165 ~

- AFFORDABLE - $25 AND UP $$

~ 167 ~

PRICE IS NO OBJECT $$$

BABY !

Priceless Gifts

UNDER A PENNY

*G*ifts that require virtually no financial investment were probably the single greatest motivation to create this guide. If one had a thousand dollars to shop with for a gift, the ideas are almost endless. It is when there simply isn't a budget that your desire and imagination overcome this obstacle to really come through to create something...simply priceless.

> *"The human race built most nobly when limitations were greatest, and therefore when most was required of imagination in order to build at all."*
>
> ### NAPOLEON HILL

QUICK REFERENCE LIST

NO-BUDGET

TO

LOW-BUDGET

$5 - $25

$

• • • And then there are those of us...about 95%...that fall into this category. We've pushed and pulled, scrimped and saved, but it still seems almost impossible to get ahead, leaving us little left to give outside of a heart-felt smile. Well, have no fear...stress...or pressure, because this is exactly why we've made an extra creative effort to put this section together, to relieve those undesirable feelings often attached to the process of gift giving. With the following ideas we've provided, you'll be able to give just as brilliantly and creatively to your heart's content...without leaving your pocketbook bone dry.

"Teach us to give, and not to count the cost."

LOYOLA

QUICK REFERENCE LIST

- AFFORDABLE -

$25 AND UP

$$

If you have found yourself in this section, you're in luck! Here, you'll find more choices and the most flexibility. When there isn't the looming pressure of finances, your spontaneity and creativity is allowed to flourish. One idea will lead to another and this will lead to that in your search for the perfect gift. Soon you've put together something quite unique and extraordinary. Just as long as you don't go too crazy...financially speaking that is. We'll save that for the next section.

> *"Not what we give, but what we share, for the gift without the giver is bare."*
>
> *J.R. LOWELL*

QUICK REFERENCE LIST

ADOPT-A-PET	197
ADULT TOY BOX	47
AIR COURIER: FLY CHEAP	111
AMERICAN EXPRESS GIFT CHECK	144
BATHROOM IN A BASKET	198
BEACH BAG	173
BUD CLUB GIFT CERTIFICATE, THE	193
BUNGEE CORD JUMP	76
BUSINESS / FINANCE MAGAZINE SUBSCRIPTION	273
CHOCOLATE CLUB, THE	49
CLASSES, COURSES, SEMINARS	200
COAT-OF-ARMS FAMILY FLAG	201
COFFEE LOVER'S / TEA-TOTALER'S DELIGHT	202
COLD HARD CASH	144
CUSTOM TIES	203
DAVID WINTER COTTAGES	21
EDUCATIONAL / GIFTS TO LEARN FROM	238
EVENING ON THE TOWN	177
EVENING ON THE TOWN GIFT CERTIFICATE, AN	105
EXOTIC PLANT	204
FINE WINES, CHAMPAGNE & SPARKLING WINES	285-286
FIRST BANK ACCOUNT	240
FISH TANK...WITH FISH	240
FISHING CHARTER: OCEAN	78
FISHING POLE & EQUIPMENT	241
FORT / TREE HOUSE KIT	242
GARDENER	212
GIFT BASKET DELECTABLES	294
GIFT BASKETS, PACKAGES & SURVIVAL KITS	292-293
GIFT CERTIFICATES	309
GIFT COUPONS	311
GIFT THAT GIVES TWICE, A	22
HAND CARVED YACHT & ESTATE NAMEBOARDS	32
HEALTH CLUB / WORK-OUT BAG	130
HIGH PERFORMANCE KITES	245
HOBBY SHOP, THE	246
HOLLYWOOD STUDIO STORE GIFT	99
HONEYMOON KIT	63
HONORING PLAQUE, AWARD, TROPHY	279
IMAGINARIUM	247
LEATHER BRIEFCASE / ATTACHE	280
LEATHER NOTEBOOK	281
LEATHER-CRAFTING KIT	23
LINGERIE	66
LINGERIE OF THE MONTH CLUB GIFT CERTIFICATE	69
LIVE PERFORMANCE TICKETS	100
LIVE TREE	216
MAID / HOUSE CLEANER	217
MAPLE TREE / SAP BUCKET LEASE	28
MOTHER EARTH: ANIMALS, NATURE & THE ENVIRONMENT	29
MOVIE SCRIPT LIBRARY, THE	101
MURDER MYSTERY DINNER THEATRE	102
NATIVE AMERICAN-INDIAN: HANDMADE GOODS & JEWELRY	30
NAUTICAL FLAGS, DECORATIVE ITEMS & COLLECTIBLES	31
ORGANIZER/DAY-PLANNER	283
PENNY STOCKS	146
PERSONAL JIGSAW PUZZLE	34
PERSONALIZED CALENDAR	219
PERSONALIZED / MONOGRAMMED GIFT	183
PHONY CELEBRITY, A	102
POLAROID CAMERA & FILM	256
PROFESSIONAL MASSAGE	133
PSYCHIC READING	37
RARE COIN / COIN COLLECTION	257
RC - REMOTE CONTROL STUFF	258
ROMANTIC GIFT PACKAGE	61
SHOOTING STAR	39
SKI LIFT TICKETS	133
SPORT BAG	135
SPORTING EVENT TICKETS	137
STOCK CERTIFICATE: AN INVESTMENT IN YOUR FUTURE ENDEAVORS	149
SWEET TOOTH: DESSERTS	289
TENT, A	262
TOY STORE / HOBBY SHOP GIFT CERTIFICATE	264
TRAVEL KIT / BAG	121
U.S. MINT / PRINTING & ENGRAVING BUREAUS	266
WEDDING GIFT BASKET, THE	63
WINE CONNOISSEUR'S CLUB	285
WINEMAKING KIT / HOME BREWERY	42
WOOD CARVING & WOOD WORKING KIT	44

PRICE IS NO OBJECT
BABY !

"Whatever you want, Babe! No, really! Look...the next 48 hours is yours. For this special occasion we can fly, dine, be driven, entertained, catered to and be pampered in the finest hotel...You name it, whatever you want...Price is no object, Babe!"

Now, if only good looks accompanied the individual who made such a statement, you'd really have it all...maybe.

> *"The spirit in which a thing is given determines that in which the debt is acknowledged; it's the intention, not the face-value of the gift, that's weighed."*
>
> *SENECA*

QUICK REFERENCE LIST

CREATIVE GIFTS FOR THE PEOPLE WHO HAVE... ALMOST EVERYTHING

SIMPLY FRIENDS

What can you say about friends? If you're one of the lucky ones, you might have three or four truly great, close friends...soulmates, in your entire lifetime. Friendships with family, relatives, and co-workers often seem forced upon you because our social structure says they must be a part of our lives. Because of this, gift-giving can sometimes become more of a chore or an inconvenience. With friends, on the other hand, gift giving is most likely to reach its most pure form, coming from the heart, giving unconditionally because one truly wants to...an expression that might simply say, "I like you. I appreciate our friendship. I enjoy the wonderful times we have shared together. Thank you!" A small token in return for the intangible and immeasurable gifts a friendship has given.

> *"The greatest pleasure I know is to do a good action by stealth, and to have it found out by accident."*
> *CHARLES LAMB*

QUICK REFERENCE LIST

ADOPT-AN-ACRE

Through The Nature Conservancy you can save an acre of threatened tropical rain forest in the name of someone truly special. Each gift recipient will receive a personalized honorary land deed suitable for framing. Do something wild and natural this season.   **$30 / acre**
THE NATURE CONSERVANCY   **800-628-6860**
See also ADOPT-A-TREE, ADOPT-A-WOLF, ADOPT-A-WHALE

BEACH BAG

For the tropical traveler, a friend, kids, brother, sister, or virtually anyone who gets their feet wet or face tanned. Put together in a colorful cotton or canvas, Aztecian print, draw-string, shoulder-strapped bag, an assortment of water, beach and sun necessities and accessories. This gift can range dramatically in price depending on where you shop. There are the larger sun and surf chain-stores found in malls that can supply you with just about everything, or you can pick through your larger discount stores or even your local supermarket.   **$25 - $100** (not including jeep)

BEACH BAG ACCESSORIES & NECESSITIES

SUN TAN LOTIONS & SUNSCREENS	**TOWEL**	**SUNGLASSES**
SPORT RADIO & HEADPHONES	**FRISBEE**	**SWIMSUIT**
BEACH CRUISING THONGS	**PADDLE BALL SET**	**WATER BOTTLE**
CHAIR UMBRELLA	**BEACH BAG**	**MAGAZINES**
AND IF A JEEP DOESN'T FIT...GET A BIGGER BAG		

BEST FRIENDS, FRIENDS FOREVER, OR SWEETHEART PENDANT / CHARM

...can be a somewhat less expensive gift idea than a ring or bracelet. Pick something out for a best friend, your girlfriend or your boyfriend. If you're shopping alone, know the person's taste, otherwise try to pick something out together. Take a look at the "friends forever" or "sweetheart" two-piece charm. One for each of you. When the pieces come together they make a full circle or complete heart...becoming one. Have the back personalized with a note of love, friendship or perhaps a future meeting date. If the person loves a particular animal, or a particular shape, you'll be sure to find it at a good jewelry wholesaler who would normally have hundreds of charms to choose from.   **$8 - $60**

JOHNSON SMITH CO.   **813-747-2356**

things you never knew existed catalog

FRIENDS FOREVER PENDANT - two pieces of a heart when fitted together hearts become one, each with its own chain   **$8**

SWEETHEART / BEST FRIENDS PENDANTS - when together two halves join together to become a full circle as a symbol of being one, each with separate chain and gift box   **$15**

many other interesting and unique gift pendants   **$4 - $13**

See also *FRIENDSHIP BRACELET, RING, JEWELRY*

BIG COMFORTABLE PILLOWS

For apartment dwellers on a budget, the college student living away from home, the bachelor, the better half of a recent break-up, or as a house-warming gift, these big cuddly, comfortable pillows could easily become their new best friend, sleeping companion...punching bag, or...whatever. A simple yet versatile gift that's always needed and always appreciated.   **$12 - $65 each**

BON VOYAGE PEN-PAL KIT

Say "Bon Voyage," not "Good-bye." Give to somebody who's departing, a gift to keep in touch. Put together an attractive, handy letter writing kit. Include pens, paper, pre-addressed envelopes, foreign stamps and/or currency, a journal, a photo, a mini-cassette recorder & tapes, a handy little zip-bag or notebook to keep it all in and anything else you might think is useful.

$20 on up (not including recorder**)**

See also *GREAT EXPLORER, TRAVELER'S KIT*

BOOZE CRUISE

Organize this gift for a group of friends, family members, co-workers, or just the two of you to party as the sun goes down or party the evening away afloat a large yacht, cruiser, party boat or party barge. Prices range dramatically depending on where you are and whether or not it's a private charter or public cruise. Check with your local water recreation area or your local directory under "boat rental/charter," "yacht charter" or similar heading.

private charter (day): $60 - $200 / person (min. 6 or more people)
public party cruise: $12 - $45 / person (not incl. dinner & drinks)

CARE PACKAGE

Who needs a reason to give to someone a bag of groceries, a basket of baked goods or a box of necessities. A gift always appreciated by son or daughter, or the mature folks who don't get out much. A friend in need will forever be indebted. There are really no rules with a care package. It can include any number of things from cash, food, clothes and other necessities. Just be aware of the persons likes and needs. It's a thoughtful inexpensive gift that can be given anytime for any reason...even if it's as simple as a fresh batch of homemade cookies. It's a gift that says...you 'Care.'   **FREE - $100 +**
See also *THE SPICE OF LIFE* and other food *GIFT BASKETS & PACKAGES*

CREATIVE CARDS...THE GIFT OF UNSPOKEN WORDS

A card or note expressing a word or thought could be considered even more important than the actual gift. The gift is only a representation of those feelings shared. With that understanding, put your true thoughts, feelings and creativity into the card. The more personal the better. Try to avoid pre-fabricated "love lines" unless it's absolutely appropriate. And remember when putting your thoughts on to paper that sometimes less is more. Don't feel that it's necessary to wait for a particular occasion. A gift of unspoken words given any time is always appropriate and a most powerful gift...to be heard again and again, whenever one chooses to open it up again.

HOMEMADE - It's almost easier to make your own card than it is to go out and buy one. It's more personal. It costs less. It may not be as pretty, but it will certainly be beautiful to the recipient. Use a photograph or your natural talent with paints, pencils and cut-outs. Add an original poem, a reminiscent line or a note of love. If that's a little too much to handle, you can always meet us half-way with a "blank inside" card...although you still have to come up with the creative words yourself.

ON YOUR BODY - with a washable marker or body paints, let the one you love know exactly how you feel about them...and maybe what you plan on doing about it. Let them follow the trail of words down your body.

PERSONAL AD - let the whole world know how you feel about someone by placing an ad in the local paper. You'll probably have to point the ad out, especially if you're on a budget. Ad spaces of any size can get pretty expensive. If price is no object, consider **a full-page ad**, **a billboard,** or even **sky writing.**

PERSONALIZED / CUSTOM MADE - These custom card-making machines are sweeping the country. You'll probably find one in your local mall stationery or card store. Through this source, you can select from a variety of occasions and different set-ups. All you have to do is tell the machine whose name and what dates to graphically print in the appropriate spaces. It'll look as if you're either incredibly talented, or had a card company print one up just for that person...all for about $3.50, in about 3 minutes.

OF NO OCCASION - For whatever kind of card you give, who needs an occasion. A card expressing love, caring friendship, well wishes or erotic thoughts & feelings, can be given spontaneously without any occasion at all.

INSPIRING WORDS - In life we often hear or run across an inspiring word, feeling, thought, poem or song that leaves a powerful impression in our lives. Something we can truly identify with. It's only natural to want to share the same feelings we experienced at the discovery. If you couldn't say it better yourself...copy it! Just be sure to give credit to the original source.

CREATE-A-BOOK - Put together for your parents, children, close friend or the one you love a personalized book, scrapbook or photo album of your lives. Get as involved or go as deep as you like. Include photos, memorable papers, cards and other items, original thoughts or the real life story to go along with it. Create captions and put quality into the construction so that it will last for years and perhaps generations. The gift of a memory is an unbeatable gift.

FANTASY CARD / BOOK - Create a book or card detailing a romantic or erotic fantasy. Use your creativity. Cut out some pictures to paint them a more vivid picture. Use it to plan a future occasion with a specific date, time, meeting place and as many details as you plan to let them in on...maybe just a couple of clues to heighten the anticipation...or rip the last page out, only to be given back after certain obligations are fulfilled.   **FREE - a couple of bucks**

TRUMBLE GREETINGS - fine art cards and gifts   **800-525-0656**

ANITA BECK CARDS   **800-328-3844**

EARTH CARE PAPER   **800-347-0070**

Environmental cards, stationery, gift wrap and more

BRAINSTORMS   **800-621-7500**

write & illustrate your own 12-page hard-bound book   **$25**

PAPER JOURNEY   **800-827-2723**

Journals, scrapbooks, albums, notecards and more

See also *FANTASY LETTER, MEMORY CARD*

EVENING ON THE TOWN

Create a gift certificate or state in a card: One "Evening on the Town." And go on to describe what it all involves...or simply let it be an evening full of surprises for the recipient. The evening might include any of the following: Limousine service, dinner, a movie or theatrical experience, a sporting event or musical concert, and dancing. You might even start the evening with a new outfit for the individual...or if you'd like to get really extravagant, watch their expression as you approach the airport. After all, you didn't say which town.   **$40 - $250 +**

See also *WEEKEND AWAY, FANTASY GIFT PACKAGE, EROTIC GIFT PACKAGE*

EXOTIC HAIR STYLE and CUT

What's all the hub-bub over these "hair-stylists of the stars"? Before you risk your 'do with somebody who cuts hair with a blow-torch or razor, send in one of your friends. It's bad enough to have your appearance temporarily ruined, but to pay 200 big ones for it? They're actually pretty tame if you just tell them generally what you want, show them a picture out of a magazine, or listen carefully to their suggestions. Just make sure two inches means two inches in their language. Most likely, the recipient of this gift will be forever indebted and you'll probably be right on their heels into the salon. A new style has the potential to change one's life by bringing a renewed confidence through their outward appearance and the reaction of others. When making an appointment or purchasing a gift certificate at one of the big salons, you may not be able to get the main stylist that everybody's crazy over. You'll most likely be able to set something up through one of the top associates. After several appointments the main 'do dude might be able to squeeze you in. I guess it takes time to be somebody.

JOSE' EBER   **224 N. Rodeo Dr. Beverly Hills: 310-278-7646**
  5 locations: 4 in California including Palm Desert, and Dallas, TX
  Jose' doesn't take new clients, but does do consultations
                    Basic cut: $55 (men), $74 (women)
JESEPPE FRANCO   **350 N. Canon Dr. Beverly Hills: 310-274-8967**
  no prices given over phone, consultation with Jeseppe himself
VIDAL SASSOON   **405 N. Rodeo Dr. Beverly Hills: 310-274-8791**
  Vidal retired   **$49 (men), $70 (women)**
CRISTOPHE'S SALON   **348 N. Beverly Dr. Beverly Hills: 310-274-0851**
  $175 1st, $125 thereafter (men), $250 1st, $175 thereafter (women)

FINDING THE PERFECT GIFT: THE ULTIMATE GUIDE

If you find this guide useful as well as enjoyable, why not give a copy to a friend, family member or someone at the office. Help us share and spread the traditional values of gift-giving with a creative edge. In a small way it might just make the world a better place.
                                    $12.95
send check or money order to: **DOG GONE BOOKS, P.O. Box 4054-11**
  (See order form on last page)   **Malibu, CA 90264**

FRIENDSHIP

A gift that costs nothing. A gift you can't buy, but always a perfect gift...and a priceless one. One of the greatest gifts you could give or receive.   **FREE**

FRIENDSHIP BRACELET

The style of this gift changes as much with an individual's personal taste as it does with the trends. Aside from the more expensive gold and silver bracelets there are the more trendy bracelets found at African artifacts stores, new age, and bead shops, some jewelry stores, and swap meets among other places. They can be made of

silver, copper, turquoise, horse hair, brass, bone, bead, leather and the popular Indian/Aztecian cotton weave. If you decide to go the traditional route with a gold or silver bracelet, have it engraved with an inscription, a name, initials, or a date.   **starting at $2**
See also FRIENDSHIP CHARM, RING, MONOGRAMMED GIFTS, JEWELRY

FRIENDSHIP RING

Any of these tokens of friendship or love make an irresistible gift and goes much deeper than its materialistic value. It has the potential of strengthening a bond, creating a sentimentality, and in the future it will become a symbol that opens a flood-gate of wonderful memories. A gift that will last a lifetime...and held in the heart forever. Try to find your city's wholesale jewelry district for more down to earth prices. Decide on something together. Perhaps a gold, white gold, silver, or platinum ring with a small diamond or two, a birth stone, or even a pearl...or look for something more trendy from an African artifacts store, a new age shop, or even a swapmeet.
See also FRIENDSHIP BRACELET, CHARM, JEWELRY $10 - $200 +

GAMES PEOPLE PLAY

Some of the best laughing and enjoyment I've done has come after dinner, playing one of these games with a group of friends or family members. You'd be surprised what you'd find out about the people closest to you....and you thought you knew them. It's more than a game. It's spending quality time with people you care about. It's one of those little moments in life that we need to recognize as "happiness," that state of being we spend our lives struggling to achieve...and it was right there all the time. A gift definitely not to be overlooked. I can't tell you how many good games we've lost to friends who have borrowed them. Let your guard down, open up your mind, let go...and go wild. It's just...Fun!   **$8 - $35 +**

THE FAIL-SAFE CLASSICS

TRIVIAL PURSUIT	**THERAPY**
PICTIONARY	**MONOPOLY**
POKER SET: CARDS, CHIPS, ETC.	**SCRABBLE**

MONOPOLY - collector's edition **Franklin Mint, Franklin Center, PA 19091**
  hardwood gameboard with gold and silver game pieces **$495**
TIMELESS EXPECTATIONS **800-622-1558**
  electronic games including scrabble, chess, bridge, backgammon, gin,
  cribbage, regular board games, books & gifts
CONSTRUCTIVE PLAYTHINGS **800-448-7830**
  toys, novelties, games, puzzles, books and more
JUST FOR KIDS **800-443-5827**
  games, traveling games and more
WINDMILL HOBBIES **800-333-5963**
  games & accessories
WORLD WIDE GAMES **800-243-9342**
  casino games, outdoor games, kites & games from worldwide sources
F.A.O. SCHWARZ **800-426-TOYS**
  the world famous toy department store found in most major cities
  Known for the "animals & toys" Christmas window display

GLAMOUR PHOTO SESSION

Give the gift of a make-over, complete with wardrobe, hair-stylist
and make-up artist, then capture the finished product on film with a
professional photographer. The fantasy of living the life of a high-
fashion model for a day can be an exhilarating, rewarding, and
confidence building experience...and at the very least, you'll have a
set of the most flattering photographs you had ever taken. Who
knows, the spark may touch off a fire within someone that may burn
out of control. Ask around for a reputable photographer who also
shoots real fashion layouts for magazines and catalogs. Be careful not
to get ripped off by an overpriced, poor quality, factory, modeling
school photographer. Ask to see previous work. Bring in examples
and an idea of what you like and what you want. If you and the
photographer are not speaking the same language so to speak,
chances are you won't get what you want. Keep looking. Remember,
you are the one hiring them. **$50 - $250 (including prints)**
See also **BUDOUR PORTRAIT**

HAPPY BIRTHDAY !

Birthdays, birthdays and more birthdays. This guide might as well be
called "The Birthday Book" since virtually all of these gifts could be

given for birthdays. The category itself is too large to encompass, so we'll just give you a few creative sources that specifically relate to dirthdays, birthdates and other special days.

HISTORIC NEWSPAPER ARCHIVES   800-221-3221
   newspapers on the day you were born
WAY IT WAS - original back issue newspapers   213-374-1766
PERSONAL CREATIONS - personalized gifts   800-326-6626
   personalized bottle of wine that says, "Happy Birthday!," personalized
   birthday decorations, birthday news certificate, LIFE Magazine from the
   week you were born, historic newspapers from the day you were born,
   and lots and lots of other great personalized ideas

HORSEBACK RIDE

If your friend, mate, or child loves animals, the outdoors, and is somewhat athletic, a horseback ride on the beach or in the mountains could be just the ticket to enhance a beautiful weekend. A much smaller commitment and responsibility than buying or leasing a horse. On the other hand, there aren't very many healthy, vibrant rental horses out there, since they are constantly ridden...seven days a week. You could get lucky. Either way, you'll probably have an enjoyable experience. Call your nearby stable or equestrian center for details and prices. Decide also if you want an escorted "group ride" or a non-escorted ride on your own, then ask the stable which they offer.

See also HORSE LEASE $8 - $12 / hour

MALE REVUE

Tickets to the hottest "all male" show in town could have the makings for an unforgettable night...for the right person, although you might be surprised to see Aunt Bessy being restrained by the bouncers because she had a hard time squeezing that dollar into his micro-shorts. For some reason, these shows have a tendency to bring out the animal in the most mild-mannered women. Let your hair down and go for it! Also an ideal, somewhat safe place for baccalaureate parties. Be advised though that these institutions have ruined more marriages...even before they started. Ask around at some local clubs or check your local entertainment guide to see if there's one in your town. You'll be sure to find them in most major cities with the best being in Las Vegas and Los Angeles.

$12 - $40 / person

Music mix

Music can be a most powerful gift...It awakens the heart and inspires the soul. A personal selection of music from a dear friend can turn out to be a rich, rewarding gift filled with hours and hours of inspiration and enjoyment. In our western culture sight tends to be most people's strongest sense, while for a select few, sound can be the more powerful and vivid sense...and they are aware of it. They are musicians, and lovers of music. They often close their eyes while listening. There aren't many gifts of sound to be given. The few that you can give are great. Much can be learned about an individual through their taste in music. Here are a few and ideas and suggestions for this gift: **$2 - $10 for blank tapes**
$5 - $19 + / tape or CD (already recorded)

1)   Put together a tape of your favorites
2)   Put together a tape of their favorites
3)   Introduce an individual to a whole new type of music they're not familiar with.
4)   Mix together a tape of memorable tunes surrounding an event, a time, or a relationship.
5)   A tape of Love ballads
6)   A tape of Pure Country
7)   A tape of Classical favorites
8)   A tape of New Age - relaxing sounds of nature, inner-harmony music
9)   A collection of hits from a particular decade or era: the 40's, 50's, 60's, 70's, etc.

ADVENTURES IN CASSETTES   800-328-0108
      music, self-help and kids CD's & tapes
AMERICAN ACCOMPANIMENT TRACK TAPES   800-525-7155
      karaoke sing-a-long cassettes
COLUMBIA HOUSE LASER DISC CLUB   800-538-2233
WARNER CUSTOM MUSIC   415-592-1700
      you pick the songs they make the tape
TIME WARNER'S SOUND EXCHANGE   800-854-1681
      music, videos and collectibles

BOSE EXPRESS MUSIC   800-444-2673
   world's most complete music source
SOUND CHOICE - karaoke sing-a-long tapes & CD's   800-788-4487

PERSONAL POSSESSION / TRINKET

One of the most precious of gifts is a possession of personal value, something of meaning, given unconditionally to someone special you care about. The material worth, quality or taste should be of little importance. Read the introduction again to fully comprehend the meaning of gift-giving and its true purpose. One should not give for the sake of giving for some special occasion or holiday simply because you're supposed to. Give because you want to...from the heart. A personal treasure which can carry more value and meaning than the most expensive gift listed in this guide, should never be given for the wrong reason. Give a personal possession when you want to, for the right reason, whether or not you have sufficient funds in the bank. When it's right...or wrong, you'll feel it in your heart. Something personal might be a piece of jewelry, a watch, a necklace, bracelet, ring, a painting or other decorator item, a piece of clothing, a book...just about anything you personally possess that caries some meaning with it, yet would mean more to give it to someone you care about. Sometimes a person will unknowingly drool over something you have which is of little importance to you. Know what the person would like, then give...freely and honestly.   **FREE**
See also *SIGNET RING, FAMILY HEIRLOOM*

PERSONALIZED / MONOGRAMMED GIFT

Adding a personal touch to a creative gift can make an otherwise ordinary present into a hands down favorite. Some monogramming and engraving services also offer many gifts in store that they can personalize, or, you can always bring something of your own in. Think about it, just about anything can be personalized. Monogramming, engraving, embroidery services can also be found in specialty stores in most malls throughout the country, or you can check your local directory under *"monogramming / engraving services."*   **$4 - $100's**

PERSONALIZED CREATIVE GIFT IDEAS

1) Have a message or name stitched or embroidered into **a bathrobe, pair of panties, boxers,** or other **lingerie.**

2) Engrave or etch a message, date or names into **a silver heart shaped box, music box,** or **crystal box** for a loved one or family member for any special occasion. (also wood, rock, glassware or ceramic)

3) Have a message, date or names engraved or etched into **a piece of jewelry: a watch, ring, charm, pendant** or **bracelet.**

4) Personalize for the family member executive, or co-worker **a briefcase, wallet, organizer / day-planner, desk clock, money clip** with a name, initials, company name and logo, etc.

5) For the graduate, executive co-worker or associate, a personalized **Mountblanc pen for $10,000** (personalizing service included)

6) A brass, bronze or wood **name plate** for the home or office

7) See also *AWARDS, PLAQUES & TROPHIES, FAMILY CREST FLAG, FAMILY CREST / COAT OF ARMS, COMPANY STORE*

THE BIG THREE
(the best three "personalized gifts" catalogs)

1) **PERSONAL CREATIONS** - personalized gifts   800-326-6626
Personalized wedding & birthday gifts (frames, plaques, bottles of wine, champagne flutes), celebration accessories, kitchen accessories / housewares, fashions & accessories, acrylic keepsakes, bronze name-plates, office accessories, photo albums, wood signs, door mats, mailboxes, toys & accessories for kids & babies

2) **THINGS REMEMBERED** - engraved / personalized gifts   800-274-7367

3) **INITIALS** - personalized / monogrammed gifts   800-444-8758

CUSTOM IMPRINTED BASEBALL CAPS   800-535-5030
For a company, group of friends, family - caps, t-shirts, aprons, jackets, tote bags, coffee mugs, pens, key chains, athletic wear, calendars, and more.   **starting at $2 each**

LILLIAN VERNON - personalized items and various gifts   800-285-5555

NAUTICAL FLAGS - nautical / U.S. / custom flags   800-536-4002

HAND CARVED - yacht and estate nameboards and more   203-642-6008

COWBOY CHUCK CO.   800-378-6400
unique, charming cartoon pictures personalized with the names of your choice, 200 picture choices for all occasions

ADVERTISING IDEAS CO.   800-323-6359
luggage, desk accessories, caps, t-shirts and other promo novelties

AMSTERDAM PRINTING   800-543-6882
   advertising novelties with custom printing
B & F MAXAM   214-333-2111
   promotional merchandise: luggage, knives, cameras, briefcases, more
BEST IMPRESSIONS CO.   815-223-6263
   advertising promotions, incentives, gifts
CRESTLINE CO.   800-221-7797
   badges, ribbons, buttons, portfolios, pens, gifts and other novelties
LUCKY DUCK FORTUNE COOKIES   617-389-3583
   custom made Chinese fortune cookies
SUPERGRAM - giant banners   800-3-BANNER
NAMARK CAP & EMBLEM CO.   800-634-6271
   custom screen-printed emblems caps, t-shirts, jackets
HUDSON INCENTIVES & IMPRINTS   800-942-5372
   advertising novelties with custom printing
NOVELTIES UNLIMITED   800-647=1652
   advertising novelties with custom logos
PRESTIGE PROMOTIONS   800-328-9351
   pens, mugs, buttons, calendars and other novelties
ENGRAVING PLACE - engraved solid brass nameplates   800-828-4378
LANDMARK BRASS   718-499-0984
   custom-engraved brass architectural plaques
TAILOR GRAPHICS   800-777-1836
   award & recognition plaques, desk & doorplates, paperweights, brass I.D.
   plates, photo charm products, nameplates, business card cases
SALES GUIDES   800-654-6666
   promotional merchandise: pens, desk top items, foods, executive gifts,
   time pieces and more
N.G. SLATER CORP.   212-924-3133
   advertising novelties: t-shirts, bags, pens, coins & medallions, buttons,
   jewelry and more
CARTOUCHE   800-AT-EGYPT
   handmade pendants with your name in ancient Egyptian hieroglyphics
JOHNSON SMITH CO.   813-747-2356, Fax: 813-746-7896
   things you never knew existed catalog, custom street signs   **$40**
PHOTO LOGO   800-887-3087
   have any photograph printed on fun and useful products from hats,
   keychains and mugs to buttons and special frames   **$4 - $13 / Item**
See also *AWARDS, PLAQUES, TROPHIES, and COMPANY STORE*

THE BIG BASH !

This is it! The big THREE-O, FOUR-O, graduation day, engagement party, bon voyage, house warming...or whatever other reason you can think of to throw a party. Actually, who even needs a reason to throw a party?...And, as a successful party-thrower, don't hesitate to solicit help from your friends. Spread out the responsibility...and the financial burden...a bit. This way, you can enjoy the party as much as your guests, instead of worrying about being an efficient host. We have always found our friends to be of great help, always adding creative ideas to theme, attire, games and even food. With a shared responsibility you and your friends wind up enjoying the process of planning a party as much as throwing the actual party.

Add a few vital elements to ensure the party's success. Start with a dynamite invitation that sets the tone, mood and says, "This is going to be a great party." Good food and drink are always a plus, and be sure to invite that friend with endless energy and that one-in-a-million personality to keep the momentum and theme going.

As you sit down with your "planning committee" or jump on the phone to plan the big event, you'll be surprised at how fast creative ideas flow. We'll start you off with the right idea. All you have to do is pick your committee, plan, then add your personal touch and style to leave you and your guests with something to reminisce about for months and years to come. So exercise that creative imagination and plan your next BIG BASH!...and enjoy.

CREATIVE PARTY IDEAS

THEMES AND IDEAS

YACHT PARTY
KARAOKE PARTY
COSTUME PARTY
HYPNOSIS PARTY
PSYCHIC PARTY
MURDER MYSTERY PARTY
BYO / POT LUCK PARTY
LINGERIE / PAJAMA PARTY
ELVIS PARTY
TACKY / BAD TASTE PARTY
    (with tacky awards)
TOGA PARTY
PERIOD PARTY:
    40's, 50's, 60's, 70's etc.
HAWAIIAN LUAU
ROAST 'EM
THE SNOWMAN THEME

PARTY ADDITIONS

LOOK-A-LIKES
MODELS
GO-GO DANCERS
GAMBLING TABLES
VALET PARKING
LIVE MUSIC / D.J.
CATERING
OPEN BAR(S)
PARTY GAMES
    & AWARDS

PARTY LOCATIONS

HOUSEBOAT /
    PARTY BARGE
AN ESTATE PARTY
A TRAIN CAR
CRUISER / YACHT

PARTY IDEAS & SOURCES

THE WEDDING FANTASTIC   800-527-6566
THE CELEBRATION FANTASTIC   800-527-6566
GAMES MAGAZINE - Fun games   800-886-6556
AMTRAK - TRAIN CAR RENTAL   800-872-7245
    Hitch up your own private train car and roll anywhere for about
    $30 per person...provided you can come up with about 84
    friends
WORLD'S GREATEST GAMING CATALOG   800-282-6666
    gambling products, equipment and games
SUPERGRAM - giant custom banners   **800-3-BANNER**
ADVANCED GRAPHICS   510-370-9200
    free-standing life-size cut-outs of your favorite celebrities
PERSONAL CREATIONS   800-326-6626
    personalized celebration accessories
LUCKY DUCK FORTUNE COOKIES   617-389-3583
    custom fortune cookies

PET LOVERS GIFT PACKAGE

Next to their stomach, the quickest way to a person's heart is through their pet. If a dog, cat, bird, fish, horse or other pet is the center of one's world, you can never go wrong with this gift. It's fairly easy and inexpensive to put together a pet gift basket or package. Just include a likeable mix of snacks, toys (fish not included, fish don't play with toys) and maybe an accessory or two...and if you love this guide that much and would like to show your appreciation, our dog, "Betty" (a black lab) loves to get toys in the mail. She requests "no fruitcakes, please." **Gift Package: $5 - $50 and up**

PET OWNERS RESOURCE BOOK   **800-562-7169**
    for the health and happiness of your pet

R.C. STEELE - wholesale pet equipment & supplies   **800-872-3773**
ANIMAL TOWN - pet supplies   **800-445-8642**
PERSONAL CREATIONS   **800-326-6626**
        personalized gift products for your pet and everyone, pet bowls, bandannas, even a slate-rock memorial etched with pet's name for when they travel to a better place...that big backyard in the sky
TURNER ENTERTAINMENT   **800-887-3737**
    celebration of people & their pets (dogs & cats)   **$20 2 (videos)**
J-B WHOLESALE PET SUPPLIES   **800-526-0388**
OUR BEST FRIENDS PET CATAL. - food, supplies, clothing **800-852-PETS**
PET WAREHOUSE - dog, cat, bird, fish supplies   **800-443-1160**
WHOLESALE VETERINARY SUPPLY - all animals   **800-435-6940**
CAL-FORMED PLASTICS CO.   **800-772-7723**
        two-piece interlocking dog house with 5-way flow through ventilation
PET LOGS - cedar log dog houses   **800-334-5530**

PHOTO COLLAGE OF MEMORIES

If you happen to be camera happy, put together a creative collection of memorable photos in the form of a collage. Use photos either from an event or simply a medley of memories from several different occasions. Use a store bought collage set-up, or make one yourself. Put a little careful time, effort, and quality into it. Make it something they would truly want to put on the wall. The gift of warm, happy memories is priceless...and timeless.   **0 - $40**

KELLY COLOR - photo montages, composites   **704-433-0934**
See also *PHOTO ALBUM* **for sources,** *VIDEO MEMORIES, CAPTURED MOVIE MOMENT, RESTORED PHOTO*

SHOPPING SPREE

This gift idea should contain a strong warning to those giving their credit card or wallet to their spouse or kid, then dropping them off at the local mall. Set a dollar limit, not a time limit...then, and only then, it's safe to let them go wild. Allowing someone, especially kids, to pick out what they want for themselves is a gift rivaled by none. They'll know exactly what they want...and use every penny of their limit, trust me. But they'll certainly love you for it...until tomorrow!

$15 + (for children)
$20 - $100's (for kids, spouses & friends)

SPIRITUAL AWAKENINGS
BOOKS...BOOKS...& MORE CREATIVE GIFT BOOKS

There is a message in the sounds of silence. The sound is vivid and the message is clear. I am speaking of empowering books and written words. One should never underestimate the potential received from such written works. A book can take you on a distant journey, make you fall in love, cause you to laugh...and cry. Books somehow bring people, and the world, a little closer. The written word may be printed in many different languages, but it reads the same...its meaning universal. Although the people may have distinct and different religious beliefs and cultural differences, we all share the common goal of...perhaps peace, a higher understanding of self...and of God. That is what generates the serene sounds of silence...Unity. A book given as a gift or as part of a gift has the potential to serve as an incredibly powerful tool. A gift that could enable one to reintroduce themselves to the world in many different capacities. A gift of empowerment to nourish the seeking mind and to cultivate earnest desires. In such a gift could be found courage and confidence...and faith...an intangible gift that will last a lifetime. A small inexpensive gift by itself (in most cases), and can add beautify to any gift package. You may be able to find a few good selections listed through this guide, but the world of books and other written works is vast and numerous and requires as many different tastes. We recommend that you take some time out to visit your local library or bookstore to find a selection that better suits your recipient's needs.

$5 - $80 + / book

BOOKS AS GIFT ACCESSORIES & STOCKING STUFFERS

LIFE'S LITTLE INSTRUCTION BOOK   *THE FAR SIDE...ANYTHING*

DREAM INTERPRETATION - ASTROLOGY - MOTIVATIONAL BOOKS - SELF-HELP BOOKS - FAMILY COOKBOOK - EASY TO READ BIBLE OR BIBLE INTERPRETED - A PERSONALLY SIGNED AUTOBIOGRAPHY - DOCTOR'S HOME REMEDIES BOOK

SUCCESSORIES   **800-535-2773**
  The most attractive and powerful supply of motivational products and visuals, including $6 motivational quote books: *GOAL QUOTES & BEST OF SUCCESS*

DIRECT BOOK SERVICE DOG & CAT CATALOG   **800-776-2665**
  over 2,000 books & videos

AUDIO EDITIONS   **800-231-4261**
  Books on Cassette: from mysteries to self-improvement

PYRAMID BOOKS AND THE NEW AGE COLLECTION   **800-247-1889**
  new age / mystical books and stuff

SEND-A-BOOK   **800-793-SEND**
ANY AND ALL BOOKS   **800-ALL-BOOKS**
BOOKCASSETTE - all types of books on cassette   **800-222-3225**
WEEKLY READER BOOKS - Science & Nature for kids **800-487-1236**
EASTON PRESS   **800-367-4534**
  order a library collection of your favorite books in hard bound leather

CROSSINGS - book club for Christians   **6550 E. 30th St.,**
                          P.O. Box 6335, Indianapolis, IN 46206

BES ENTERPRISES - Personalized children's books   **800-76-STORY**
  your child becomes the star of the story, 16 titles to choose from

See also **THE WRITTEN WORD, NEW AGE, MOTIVATIONAL / SELF-HELP, ROMANTIC BOOKS, PERSONALIZED ROMANCE NOVEL**

STRIPPER

Male and female strippers come in all shapes and sizes with as many different talents. Good as a gag gift or "bare" entertainment for birthdays, bachelor & baccalaureate parties, showers, co-workers, friends, and sometimes family members. As our culture slowly approaches true equality, women can hire and enjoy a stripper just as men can. If you've ever witnessed an all female audience at a male strip revue, women definitely put men to shame. strippers are always loads of embarrassing...and/or exciting fun. Strippers, male and female, will often show up in the uniform or costume of your choice...to start. Make sure to inform all the party goers to bring lots of dollars for tipping...they're not there for their enjoyment...although it could happen. They'll pretend anyway. Just be sure to always use discretion when planning this event. Keep your audience in mind. You don't want to offend anyone.

See also MALE REVUE   **$50 - $350 (not including tips)**

SUNDAY BRUNCH

Their favorite meal of the week for many people. Who could pass up brunch at their favorite restaurant. A great opportunity for family, friends, and couples to spend a glorious Sunday together. Contact your favorite local restaurant or eating establishment, that is known for their fabulous brunch, for reservations and gift certificates.

$10 - $30 / person

VIDEO / CASSETTE TAPE LETTER

Under the right circumstances, a homemade video tape can be a fantastic, original gift idea. For a far away friend, or the family back home whom you are close to in spirit but not in miles, it may be the next best thing to being there. If the person you have in mind isn't familiar with your lifestyle or surroundings, put down on video where you live, your neighborhood, your friends, anything you think they might find entertaining as well as touching. Just be sure not to go on too long. We wouldn't want to bore them with the neighbor's cat. On the other hand, who needs a good reason to make a video. Maybe all the kids want to get together to wish mom and dad a "Happy Anniversary" or "Merry Christmas." They'll have fond memories to look back on in years to come of a specific place and time in their lives...and they'll laugh and cry as they see how much things really do change. Let these be a guide to stimulate your own imagination. Create a little movie. Let yourself go, and have some fun. You can always rewind and tape over it. The point is to not stop yourself before you start. Once you have started, you'll be surprised how one clever or humorous idea will lead to another. You'll probably have as much fun creating it as the recipient will watching it.

$4 - $10 / tape (Including postage)
CUSTOM SONG - Songs for Special Occasions   **213-396-5706**
Have a song made with custom lyrics and music   **$500**

WRIST WATCH

...And other creative time pieces. This may not sound like an overly creative, unique, or even an exciting gift, but quite simply...it is. Wrist watch styles have exploded in recent years to make this fashion accessory the hottest, hippest, most identifying accent a person could wear, whether for the conservative, subdued professional, or the loud, trendy punk, biker. The creative subtleties cannot be described in words, nor can they be seen at a department store. Your best bet is to check out the wholesale jewelry area in your city, or even swap meets and flea markets. Even cheap copies from the Orient have better quality than previous years...and look fantastic. If you find the right source, you're not likely to walk away with a bare wrist.

$10 - $80 for neuvou, wholsale and good copies
$100 up to $1000's for quality vintage

THE TWO BEST WATCH STORES IN THE COUNTRY

WEST COAST: WANNA BUY A WATCH?   **213-653-0467**
vintage & new edition Hamiltons, Swiss Army, Gruen's from **$175 - $350,** 40's Rolexes starting at **$1000,** high grade tiffany's starting at **$2200**   **Melrose Ave, Los Angeles, CA**
EAST COAST: FINE TIMES   **Boston, Mass 617-536-5858**
a great selection of vintage time pieces from the 1950's and later
$250 and up

WORLD TIME WATCH CO.   **800-327-7682**
Name brand watches at a discount
MARCUS & CO. - large fine watch and jewelry discounter   800-654-7184
catalog available
SHOPPER'S ADVANTAGE   **800-TEL-SHOP**
best buys on name brand products   **Watches: $19 - $70**
WATCH DEPOT - over 1,000 styles   **800-469-2824**
name brand watches at a discount, includes gift boxes
ROSS-SIMONS - the finest jewelry, watches and more   **800-521-7677**

A panel of German beer drinking experts and connoisseurs have unanimously voted _____ into their esteemed organization "B.U.D.," "Bier Und Deutschland," meaning "Beer of Germany." You are now a charter member in

THE BUD CLUB

You are required to consume a designated amount and selection of exotic gourmet brews from around the world each month. Membership will be revoked if beer consumption is irresponsible. DO NOT DRINK AND DRIVE !

AUTHORIZED BY _____

ON THIS _____ DAY OF _____ , 19 ___

MOM, DAD, SISTER SUZY

UNCLE BOB

You're pretty much stuck with your parents and relatives as long as either you or they are around. Be careful not to let gift giving with them get old. Don't just give a list of material possessions back and forth every holiday or special occasion. Cut yourself away from the old traditions. Set a new standard. Soon, your own brothers and sisters may be outdoing you when it comes to gift giving...It could happen. At any rate, one's family could always use a hug and a smile. It only takes one person to change the lives of many. You only got one family...you might as well enjoy 'em.

"It is more blessed to give than to receive."

JESUS CHRIST (Acts 20:35)

MOM, DAD, SISTER SUZY & Uncle BoB

QUICK REFERENCE LIST

ADOPT-A-PET

Dogs, cats, birds, fish and a select group of other animals can make the perfect gift for the right person. Although, this gift idea should be thought through thoroughly before acting on. It is an unfortunate thing for an animal to be given as a gift only to be given back, given away to someone else, or worse, brought to the pound...it happens. As good as your intentions may be, the potential recipient should be a perfect candidate for such an animal. As far as animals are concerned there are two types of people, those who appreciate, respect and love animals...and those who don't. When selecting an animal, especially a dog or a cat, please try to avoid pet stores and breeders. Not only are the animals expensive, but it continues to promote breeding for profit when there are literally thousands of animals in shelters around the country in need of a good home. If you go to a local pound or shelter, you'll probably be out the door with an adorable, loveable pet for under fifty bucks. They'll have had their shots...and be forever greatful through loyal companionship for rescuing them. Check your local paper under *"pet adoptions"* or visit your local animal shelter.   **FREE - $65**

See also *ADOPT-A-HORSE, ADOPT-A-WHALE, ADOPT-A-WOLF*

ADOPT-A-WOLF

Wolves around the globe and especially here at home are fighting for their lives as the human element crowds in on their territory. The following organizations help protect the wolf and fight against aerial wolf hunts, predator control programs and no-limit wolf trappings. American Indians as well as many other people who have a great deal of respect for animals and the land they live in, regard the wolf as being a mystical, higher being and should be revered and looked up to rather than needlessly destroyed. Help save a beautiful creature. A generous gift never goes unrewarded.

WOLF HAVEN INTL.   **800-448-9653**
   adopt-a-wolf program: **$20**, includes certificate, photo and biography
   Wolf Tracks catalog, unique gifts from jewelry, note cards, books, toys
ALASKA WILDLIFE ALLIANCE   **907-277-0897**
   info & merchandise catalog to help stop the illegal killing of wolves
See also *ADOPT-A-HORSE, ADOPT-A-WHALE, ADOPT-AN-ACRE*

BABY / TODDLER PHOTO SITTING

A simple, easy gift to give for Christmas, or for the child's birthday or christening. A nice alternative from the typical teddy bears, rattlers and clothes. Choose a studio chain found at one of the larger department stores or malls throughout the country. They tend to run quite a bit less expensive than independent studios and photographers...and they grow so fast. Soon it will be time for their next set of pictures.

SEARS PORTRAIT STUDIO   **$15 - $150** (including all prints)

BATHROOM IN A BASKET

Body & skin care, replenishing bath oils, herbal extracts and other soothing, luxury bath & body products make an irresistible gift for anyone who loves to be pampered. A gift to be appreciated again and again to revitalize the body. Many bath & body shops and catalogs already have prepackaged gift baskets & gift sets, making it easy for the man shopping for the one he loves to spoil.

$25 - $100 + for a basket of suds, scrubs, lotions & more

BRAINSTORMS - SOOTHING SCENTS & SOUNDS KIT   **800-621-7500**
   for a soothing & sensual bath experience, includes classical music, bath
   oils and more all in a beautiful gift box   **$20**
BAUDELAIRE FINE IMPORTED COSMETICS   **800-327-2324**
   European therapeutic bath oils, herbal extracts, essential oils
THE BODY SHOP - toiletries & cosmetics   **800-541-2535**
BORLIN INDUSTRIES - non-ecotoxic nat. body care prods.   **800-825-4540**
THE FLORIST SHOP - soaps, bath oils, body milk & more   **800-J-FLORIS**
VICTORIA JACKSON COSMETICS   **800-392-9250**
   body, bath, hair care and other cosmetic & skin care items
KEY WEST ALOE   **800-445-2563**
   cosmetics, skin care, hair, bath products for women, toiletries & personal
   care products for men
KATHERINE MARCH, LTD.   **800-876-2724**
   European soaps and luxuries for the bath
LA COSTA PRODUCTS INTL.   **800-LA-COSTA**
   hair, skin & body care products for men and women

BED & BREAKFAST STAY

Some people say, "It's the only way to travel...but let's keep it a secret." Put together a gift certificate or vacation package for a stay at one or more of the growing number of Bed & Breakfast's... everywhere. Contact your travel agent, tourist information bureau or a good B&B guide for recommendations and details for a particular area. **$40 - $200 + / night**

BED & BREAKFAST INTERNATIONAL   **800-262-4630**

AMERICA'S WONDERFUL LITTLE HOTELS & INNS by Sandra Soule (guide)

THE BED & BREAKFAST GUIDE FOR THE U.S. & CANADA

DREAMS COME TRUE ON LANA'I   **808-565-6961**

    bed & breakfast, house rentals on the secluded island of Lana'i

See also *VACATION PACKAGE, WEEKEND GETAWAY & TRAVEL SECTION*

CAPTURED MOVIE MOMENT

If your family has a collection of old 8mm, Super 8, or even 16mm family films of the past, you can have a still photograph taken from a single frame of film as if you'd taken it as a single still photograph. The quality will be every bit as good as if it were taken with a still camera. Get creative and have prints made from a strip of consecutive frames. As familiar as any of the family members might be with their collection of photographs, they'll be gloriously surprised with these new treasures. Don't let the video age intimidate us photograph lovers. I have overheard more than one person say that video camera fiends of the recent past are reverting back to their hobby of choice...still photography. Prints can also be made from video, although the affordable technology in this area will still not produce a good quality duplication. A photograph of a video frame is like comparing a professionally shot photograph to a polaroid. Film will always be...film.   **$5 - $50** (depending on size of photo)

See also *PERSONALIZED CALENDAR, RESTORED FAMILY PHOTOS, VIDEO TRANSFER, PERSONAL POSTER*

CHRISTMAS EVE

Where does one begin when trying to encompass the gift giving day of the year for many people? Virtually all of the gifts in this guide qualify as great Christmas presents, but for our purposes we'll narrow it down to the best of the best, the cream of the crop...keepsakes, conversation pieces and memories to last a lifetime. Christmas more than any other occasion for many people is a time for family and close friends to come together to not only exchange gifts, but to share thoughts, feelings and memories. Our objective is to provide you with the winning gift ideas that add to the sentimentality and the love shared for such special occasions.

See also

HOMEMADE CHRISTMAS ORNAMENTS	**FAMILY COOKBOOK**
FAMILY RESERVE	**CHRISTMAS TREE**
THE COMPANY STORE	**PERSONALIZED CALENDAR**
FAMILY PHOTO SITTING	**FAMILY VIDEO PRODUCTION**
PICTURE THIS...PICTURE THAT	**FAMILY HEIRLOOM**
VIDEO PHOTO ALBUM	**DAVID WINTER COTTAGES**
FAMILY TREE / GENEALOGICAL RESEARCH	

ASSOCIATED PHOTO CO.   513-421-6620
   custom photo Christmas cards with name imprint
EMERALD, BALLIN GEARY   County Cork, Ireland
   Christmas and religious items and lots of other great buys
GENERAL TRADING CO.   144 Sloane St., London SWIX 9BL, England
   Christmas catalog, gifts of all kinds
UNIVERSITY OF TEXAS MD ANDERSON CANCER CENTER   800-231-1580
   children's Christmas cards made by cancer patients, brochure
CRAFT TIME CATALOG   211 S. State College Bl, Aneheim, CA 92806
   ready to paint plastercraft, ready to paint Christmas village
HOT OFF THE PRESS   1250 NW, 3rd, Canby, OR 97013
   "Christmas Village" How to paint 32 plaster buildings
NASCO - arts & crafts supplies, ceramics & more   800-558-9595
See also CHRISTMAS ARTICLE

CLASSES, COURSES, SEMINARS

...To a person's hobby, interest, career or passion. Check at a local Community College. You'll probably find courses to interest just about anyone and for a very reasonable price. A new interest or hobby in one's life can revitalize the spirit and awaken the soul. I once read an article about a woman who had suffered from deep depression for some twenty years. When she began painting as a hobby she miraculously came out of her depression and continues to have a successful career as an artist. Changes in one's day to day life are very important for health & happiness.

COMMUNITY COLLEGE TUITION for classes   about $10 / unit

CLASS, COURSE & SEMINAR IDEAS

SINGING LESSONS   COOKING SCHOOL   PHOTOGRAPHY CLASS
ACTING CLASS / SCHOOL   ANIMAL TRAINER   MAGIC LESSONS
DETECTIVE ACADEMY   SKETCHING TECHNIQUES
PIANO & other music LESSONS

SORCERER'S SHOP - witchcraft lessons   **213-656-1563**
TICKET TO ADVENTURE   **800-929-7447**
   get a job on a cruise ship, guidebook listing cruise ship employment
   sources   **$17**
SEATTLE FILMWORKS PHOTOGRAPHY SCHOOL   **800-445-3348**
   Photography learning program
CREATEX - Learn how to airbrush   **800-243-2712**
HOLLYWOOD FILM INSTITUTE   **800-366-3456**
   2-day film school   **$280**
INTL. COMMERCIAL DIVING INSTITUTE (SCUBA)   **800-964-ICDI**
NEW YORK INST. OF PHOTOG. - guide / study catalog   **800-336-NYIP**
THE SCHOOL OF ANIMAL SCIENCE   **800-223-4542**
   at home study course to be an animal care specialist
NATIONAL AUDUBON SOCIETY   **207-293-2985**
   expedition institute for environmental education degrees
SCIENTIFIC EXPEDITIONS   **619-450-3460**
   join marine biology and archeology projects around the world
CROW CANYON ARCHAEOLOGICAL CENTER   **800-422-8975**
   long-term research projects and excavation

COAT-OF-ARMS FAMILY FLAG

My grandfather once gave his son, for Christmas, a cleverly designed, brightly colored flag with our family name and coat-of-arms embroidered onto it. The gift stood out as something more than just an ordinary gift. It carried with it, somehow, a symbol of strength, pride and integrity. It carried our family name perhaps a little higher and gave it a little more significance. Family, it will be argued by many people, is the single most important thing anyone might be privileged enough to have. In creating a family flag, you will give these qualities to family members for generations to come. It will create great pride, unity, and a bond between family members, past, present and future. If your ancestry or family tree is not too well defined or known, now might be a good time to start.

$25 - $115 and up / custom family flag
CROWDMASTER FLAGS   **800-352-4776**
   nautical, patriotic, sports teams, company and custom flags, banners

a couple of bucks - $2000 (30' x 60')
NAUTICAL FLAGS - nautical / U.S. / custom flags   **800-536-4002**
See also FAMILY TREE, FAMILY CREST / COAT OF ARMS

COFFEE LOVER'S / TEA-TOTALER'S DELIGHT

Have a subscription of exotic coffees or teas from around the world, including Africa, India, Indonesia, the Pacific, Arabia, and North & South America, delivered right to their doorstep from one to four times a month, or every other month. Many walk-in coffee specialty shops also offer this subscription service. For coffee lovers as well as tea-totaler's, check your local listings under *coffee & tea specialty shops* or *gourmet coffee & teas*.

COFFEES

THE COFFEE CONNECTION   **800-284-JAVA**
   coffees from around the world   **$15 a shipment and up**
STARBUCKS   **800-23-LATTE**
   2 kinds, 2 pounds **$15 - $17 each shipment**
THANKSGIVING COFFEE COMPANY   **800-445-6427**
   award winning coffees and accessories
COFFEE TIMES - Kona coffees direct from the big island **808-326-7637**
   5 kinds Kona coffee: **$11 - $17 / lb**
THE BAD ASS COFFEE CO - Kona coffees from the source   **808-329-8871**
   many different grades & flavors to choose from   **$12 - $20 / lb**
GREEN MOUNTAIN COFFEE   **800-223-6768**
PEERLESS COFFEE COMPANY   **800-372-3267**
   coffees, teas, spices, gift baskets and more
GEVALIA KAFFEE IMPORT SERVICE   **800-678-2687**

TEAS

STASH TEA BY MAIL - teas and accessories   **800-826-4218**
O'MONA INTL. TEA CO. - 200 teas from around the world **914-937-8858**
SELFRIDGES   **44-71-629-1234**
   tea-time gift baskets direct from London; Teas, jams, shortbreads, biscuits, cake and pate   **$76 and up**

MACKINLAY TEAS - decaffeinated in exotic flavors   800-TEA-FOR-U
DESERT TEA - caffeine free wild herb tea   800-955-4832
STEAMER HOT COCOA - gourmet cocoa mixes   800-444-5860

CUSTOM TIES

Hand painted, personalized and custom made to your specifications. From a nautical flag tie to someone's favorite sport, hobby, or favorite dog, you're sure to find something unique or perhaps a little zany that only they could wear around their neck. You'll never buy another dull $85 tie again.   **$17 - $75**
CHIPP, LTD.   **212-687-0850**
ALYNN - custom mad ties for groups, organizations   **800-252-5966**
HIS FAVORITE TIE   **800-552-TIES**
    illustrating sports and hobbies
EXPRESSIONS - a musical tie   **800-624-8957**
CUSTOM CLOTHIERS AND FURNISHINGS   **212-687-0850**
    custom ties **from $35**

DAD'S STUFF

Tools, tools and more tools! What is it with men and their tools after they hit 35 or 40. Is it that mid-life thing? Men do have a particular kind of taste. They tend to like the odd, the old, the machines and sometimes the tacky. I suppose that's why women gave men the den for their lovely belongings and "decorations"...The darkest room at the furthest end of the house. When gift shopping for a man in your life, know his tastes, his likes and his dislikes. It's not too hard to figure out. If you've been around him long enough, you'll see that "thing" and know it's just perfect...for him.

OVERTON'S DISCOUNT BOATING ACCESSORIES   **800-334-6541**
    everything for your boat & more from barbecues, fish finders, flags, boating apparel, wetsuits, water skis and more
HERRINGTON   **800-622-5221**
    the best in accessories for motoring, video, golf, photography, travel, fitness and skiing and more. First aid kits: **$100 - $190,** car police scanner: **$200,** autographed baseballs: **$60 - $369**
THOMPSON CIGAR CO.   **800-237-2559**
    cigars, pipes, tobacco, hand gun replicas, decorative knives, swords and other collectable weaponry, a beer machine as well as other gift items, collectibles and novelties

REAL GOODS
800-762-7325

solar power goods, electric cars, natural gardening supplies, environmentally friendly goods, unique tools, safety products & more

NORTHERN
800-533-5545

home & outdoor accessories, equipment, tools and recreational products at great prices
inflatable boat with electric motor: **$50**
water balloon launcher: **$17**
motorized go-carts: **$500 - $900,** non-motorized go-carts: **$75 - $130**

HEARTLAND AMERICA
800-229-2901

best prices on name brands from leather backpacks, slot machines, home electronics, office equipment, personal accessories and more

BROOKSTONE - hard to find tools catalog
800-926-7000

tools and accessories for the home, yard and car
pitching horseshoes: **$30**
(4 steel shoes, 2 steel stakes, instructions & official rules)
Backyard croquet set: **$100**
Hammocks & accessories: **$100 - $300**

SHOPPERS ADVANTAGE
800-TEL-SHOP

best buys on name brand products:

CAMCORDERS	TOOLS	HOME ELECTRONICS
WATCHES	JEWELRY	HOME FURNISHINGS
OFFICE MACHINES & EQUIPMENT		COMPUTERS & ACCESSORIES
CD-ROM & MULTI-MEDIA KITS		SPORTING GOODS
LUGGAGE, BAGS & LEATHER GOODS		PHOTO EQUIP. & SUPPLIES
ELECT. GAMES & CARTRIDGES		MUSICAL INSTRUMENTS

LARGE & SMALL TOYS OF ALL KINDS
4-PIECE LEATHER ATTACHE SET: **$59**   POLICE SCANNER: **$89**
ORGANIZER / DAY PLANNER: **$29**   CAMERAS: **$39 - $359**
HAND-HELD COMPUTER ORGANIZERS: **$19 - $100**

EXOTIC PLANT

If you're going to get a co-worker or anyone else a healthy green plant to enhance their surroundings, why not put the extra effort and creativity into it and find something really unusual or exotic...something that does more then just look green. Here are a few good ideas and suggestions.   **$5 - $85 +**

EXOTIC PLANTS & IDEAS

VENUS FLY TRAP	MINIATURE PALM	BONSAI TREE
BANNANA TREE	MINIATURE BAMBOO TREE	CREATIVE CACTI
MINIATURE PINE	MINIATURE ROSE	DISH GARDENS
ROCK GARDENS	HERB GARDENS	TERRARIUM

EDIBLE LANDSCAPING - live fruitful and other edible plants 800-524-4156
JOHNSON SMITH CO. 813-747-2356
  things you never knew existed catalog, miniature tree garden seeds $12, sensitivity plant seeds $4, Hawaiian bamboo orchids (bulbs) $3, cactus seeds $2, giant vegetable seeds $10, venus fly trap bulb $5, miniature pines, spruces and other dwarf Bonsai trees $8
ENDANGERED SPECIES 714-544-9505
  bamboo, rare and unusual rock garden plants
DAN'S GREENHOUSE 808-661-8412
  tropical indoor Bonsai trees grown into hand-sculpted lava rock, Octopus / Umbrella Bonsai's, date palms, Schefflera: $27 - $129
  Antheriums - Hawaiian love bouquet $28 - $32
  Orchid plant: $30, Plumeria plant: $22, sprouted coconut: $22
BIG ISLAND FARMS - rooted mature seedling plants 800-323-2767
  Antheriums, Ginger mac nut, Kona coffee, Bird of Paradise, orchids, Plumeria, Hawaiian tree fern, Ti plants and more $4 - $11 each
  all kinds of Hawaiian seeds: $3 / bag, Bonsais: $30 - $100, sprouted coconut: $30
TRIPPLE BROOK FARMS - bamboo, exotic fruits and trees 413-527-4626
GARDEN WORLD'S EXOTIC PLANTS 512-724-3951
  bamboo, bananas, citrus trees, cacti and other tropical stock
GIRARD NURSERIES 216-466-2881
  Bonsai trees, evergreen seeds & trees and more
SPRING HILL NURSERIES 309-691-4616
  Bonsai, roses, small fruits, seeds, plants, gardening supplies
APACHA CACTUS - cacti for dish gardens 707-485-7088
Y.O. RANCH CACTUS CO. 512-367-5110
  rare/unusual plants from Texas, Mexico, S. America, S. Africa
CAROLINA EXOTIC GARDENS - carnivorous plants & seeds 919-758-2600
NEON PALM NURSERY 707-578-7467
  palms, rare and unusual plants for interior settings
MINIATURE PLANT KINGDOM 707-874-2233
  miniature roses, maples and other Bonsais
ABUNDANT LIFE SEED FOUNDATION 206-385-5660
  organic vegetable, grain, herb, wildflower, and other seeds

AMERICAN HORTICULTURAL SOCIETY   703-768-5700
  donated hard-to-find and heirloom seeds
THE BANANA TREE - rare seeds   215-253-9589
KARTUZ GREENHOUSES   619-941-3613
  miniature terrarium, rare and tropical, flowering and foliage plants
See also *LIVE TREE*

FAMILY COOKBOOK

Plan this gift well in advance. Call or write to all your family members and relatives to obtain as many original recipes as you can that have been in and come from the family tree, past and present. Compile it, organize it, and copy it...then distribute the new family cookbook as a great gift for Christmas, the next family reunion or family function. It's hard to top a gift that contains sentimentality, practicality, wonderful memories, and heritage...not to mention good food.   **$11 - $75** (paper, copying & supplies)
PERSONAL CREATIONS   800-326-6626
  personalized "Collected Recipes Cookbook"   **$24**

FAMILY CREST GIFTS / COAT OF ARMS

This gift, although more practical, closely relates to the Family Crest flag. Don't be so boring or impersonal as to give to somebody an ordinary set of wine glasses. Add something personal. There are many different sources where you can have glasses and almost anything else etched or monogrammed with initials, a name, a date, a crest or coat of arms, a saying...anything you want. Have a whole set of wine glasses, goblets or other bar glasses customized with a family crest or coat of arms. If you have a hard time coming up with something really original, ask the person who does the etching. I'm sure they'll be able to give you a whole list of interesting and exciting ideas that they've run across in their work, including a few bizarre ones, I'm sure.   **$25 - $100 +**
ROOTS RESEARCH BUREAU   **39 W. 32nd St., N.Y., NY 10001**
  coat of arms, ancestry chart, genealogical manuscript
PERSONAL CREATIONS   800-326-6626
  personalized and monogrammed gifts
INITIALS - personalized / monogrammed gifts   800-444-8758
THINGS REMEMBERED - Engraved Gifts   800-274-7367

LILLIAN VERNON - personalized items and various gifts   **800-285-5555**
NAUTICAL FLAGS - nautical / U.S. / custom flags   **800-536-4002**
THE GENEALOGY STORE   8405 Richmond Hwy., Alexandria, VA 22309
     genealogical software, preservation materials, coat of arms, and maps
HERALDIC IMPORTS   **212-719-4204**
     coat of arms drawings of names used most frequently in U.S.
See also FAMILY CREST FLAG, MONOGRAMMED GIFTS, FAMILY TREE

FAMILY HEIRLOOM

A family heirloom can be just about anything that caries a particular meaning, value, or history with it. It's not so much the practicality of the gift your giving. It is a symbol of caring, love, trust, and/or responsibility that will be carried on through the family or friendship. A gift that is appropriate almost anytime, for any occasion or even for no occasion at all. The following is a list of suggested heirlooms to give as gifts for particular occasions.

A **family watch** given upon graduation, moving out, new job, coming of age, Christmas.

A **Family ring**, a **wedding ring**, other **jewery** of special meaning, given upon engagement, wedding, graduation, moving out, friendship, coming of age, and any other occasion.

A **decorative item**, **a painting**, or a **piece of furniture** that has been a part of the family or your personal possession for years or perhaps generations. Given for such occasions as graduation, weddings.   **NO COST**

See also PERSONAL POSSESSION / TRINKET

FAMILY PHOTO SITTING

A great gift for your parents or the whole family. Organize your brothers and sisters and any other family members that you may want to include and plan a portrait sitting. Have the finished product given as a surprise for an anniversary, or Christmas, etc. If you'd like to include your parents in the sitting, simply give them a gift certificate for a family portrait with a date in the near future. Have a friend refer you to a good portrait photographer, or check the yellow pages. If you're on a budget, do shop around as different photographers will fluctuate greatly in price...and quality.   **$75 - $100's**

The Spirit Of

The spirit of Christmas means as many different things to as many different people. It can be a season, a warmth, and a closeness to be shared with friends, family, and just about anybody you may have contact with. It might start as the air gets colder, or when the stores start setting up their decorations, but whether you like it or not, you know it's here when you hear Bing sing, *White Christmas*...once again.

Our monetary based society has a tendency to influence and shape the way we live by inundating us with messages and advertising, causing us to lose sight of the true spirit of gift giving and the Holiday season. The economy thrives on all the buying and selling during the Christmas season, and most people, at least mentally, prepare for the financial impact Christmas will leave. Always give from your heart, not out of necessity or influence from outside sources. Make the financial investment your least important consideration, but don't spend more than you can afford, yet don't be afraid to spend too little. Gift-giving is not, and should not, be about monetary value, unless of course it's investment related.

Take the time and plan ahead to think about what you'd like to give to a particular individual. Let your creativity and imagination come up with something truly special. Don't just go to a store and pull the winning gift off the shelf. Add your personal touch. The saying, "It's the thought that counts" hasn't much meaning if not very much thought was put into it.

If your Christmas gift giving list becomes too long, remove all reasons for consideration. Take each person and

... Christmas

ask yourself if you would really give from your heart, and if you would derive pure satisfaction from giving to this individual. You might find that your Christmas list will be cut down to a manageable size, allowing you to spend more time and energy on the people you really care about.

Is it tradition in your family for everybody to get everybody a gift for Christmas? Does it seem that your family is growing exponentially each year as price limits are pushed higher and higher? If this is true and Christmas is starting to become more stressful and less enjoyable, don't be afraid to make the following suggestion. It might be easier on everyone if each family member chose only one name out of a hat at Christmas to shop for. Our family started this new tradition a few years ago and continues to be very successful. Much of the Holiday season gift-buying pressure is off, allowing everyone to relax and enjoy more thoroughly each other's company and the quality time spent with one another. Of course you wind up with fewer gifts, but the effort and time an individual is now able to put into that one gift surely makes up for it. Some families have agreed to cut out gift-giving around the Holiday season all together and have found it more satisfying. In a way it releases a certain amount of control society's influences may have.

Whichever tradition you decide to follow, old or new, try to keep the rules loose and at a minimum and always search your soul for what gift-giving and Christmas are all about and what it really means to you. Do what makes you happy first, then share that happiness with those you care about most. Oh yes...and Merry Christmas !

FAMILY TREE / GENEALOGICAL RESEARCH

There are several different sources to research information regarding your family, past and present. There are Companies that simply list all the people that share your last name, throughout the country...and/or the world, in a nice hard-bound volume along with their addresses and phone numbers. Then there are individuals who will do deep investigative work to trace your specific family roots and heritage...or, if you have the time, you can always do the work yourself and present it in an interesting legible format with as many details and/or stories as you had found. There is even computer software available to help you out. For some people it becomes a joyous never-ending obsession. If you have one of them in your family, you and your family will benefit greatly by their research. Although your greatest source of information may come directly from grandma or grandpa. If this thought enters your mind, don't hesitate. It would be unfortunate to let your grandparents pass along with their precious...and priceless memories. Some of our greatest novels and movies have been based on those very memories.

COST: minimal if doing yourself...supplies, copying, phone calls, etc.
$40 - $60 for a company to create a book of names
$100's if hiring people to do deep investigative work

THE WORLD BOOK OF NAMES　　　　　　　　　　216-945-8200
　　　　　　　　　　　　　　　　　　　　　　　$34.50 per book
COMPUTER SOFTWARE　　　　　　　　　　　　　　　$49
ROOTS RESEARCH BUREAU　　　　39 W. 32nd St., N.Y., NY 10001
　　coat of arms, ancestry chart, genealogical manuscript
GENEALOGICAL PUBLISHING CO.　　　　　　　　800-727-6687
　　genealogy books, manuals, how-to books, references, finding aids and state guide books
THE GENEALOGY STORE　　8405 Richmond Hwy., Alexandria, VA 22309
　　genealogical software, preservation materials, coat of arms, and maps
GENEALOGY UNLIMITED　　　　　　　　　　　800-666-4363
　　genealogy books, supplies, European maps
GODSPEED'S - genealogy books and publications　　617-523-5970
HERALDIC IMPORTS　　　　　　　　　　　　　212-719-4204
　　coat of arms drawings of names used most frequently in U.S.
HERITAGE BOOKS　　　　　　　　　　　　　301-390-7709
　　genealogy books and periodicals arranged by state and subject

NATIONAL ARCHIVES & RECORDS ADMINISTRATION   **202-523-3164**

GUIDE TO GENEALOGICAL RESEARCH IN THE NATIONAL ARCHIVES: a source of valuable information for genealogical research, includes census records, military service info., passenger ship arrival lists and other information   **book: $19**

NATIONAL GENEALOGICAL SOCIETY   **202-785-2123**

publications on local area history, biographical data, and heraldry information

FLY-FISHING ROD & REEL

Make sure to give this gift with an instruction video or class if they are not already skilled in this finesse sport. Why wait to give this as the perfect retirement gift. We work so hard all of our lives so that we can someday retire and do all of those things we once did as a child. But by the time you retire you are fully aware of life's little ironic trick of age and physical condition brought on by 40 or more years of hard work. It's almost a sad unfortunate thing that we have to grow up and be adults. Let's make the most of life and be who we want to be and do the things we want to do as much as possible right now. You don't have to be a child but you can be child-like. You can continue to see things with awe-inspiring curiosity and can experience things with zest and vigor...if we allow ourselves. It's your choice. Go fishing...as often as you want.

With instruction video on technique: **$45 - $150 +**

L.L. BEAN - fly-fishing supplies and much more   **800-221-4221**

BERKELEY - fishing equipment   **800-237-5539**

HOOK & TACKLE CO. - fly-fishing tackle and accessories   **800-552-8342**

K & K FLY FISHER'S SUPPLY   **800-821-5374**

ORVIS MANCHESTER - fly-fishing tackle and accessories   **800-548-9548**

FINGERHUT - catalog   **4404 Eight St N, St Cloud Minnesota 56395**

fishing package with 2 rods, reels, tackle, tackle box and more   **$80**

GARDEN KIT

For a girl, boy or adult of the right age, frame of mind and surroundings, a gardening kit can turn into a creative time-consuming project offering hours and hours of enjoyment. While the youngsters are out of school watching the seeds sprout and grow into amazing things, parents also benefit from this gift as it keeps the kids out of the house...and their hair. Just be sure to designate where the landscaping is allowed, otherwise you might have an attractive turnip patch where your roses used to be. Be sure to include in the package seeds, plants, garden gloves, tools, pottery, etc. You'll find all you need at your local, nursery, garden Center, or supermarket. **$1 - $60**

INDOOR GARDEN KITS & IDEAS

BONSAI TREE KITS	**DISH GARDEN KITS**	**ROCK GARDEN KITS**
TERRARIUM KITS	**HERB GARDEN KIT**	**ZEN GARDEN KITS**

JACKSON & PERKINS - Roses & gardens   **800-872-7673**
WHITE FLOWER FARM   **800-888-7756**
 bulbs, shrubs, strawberry plants, books, tools, gardening supplies
KARTUZ GREENHOUSES   **619-941-3613**
 miniature terrarium, rare and tropical, flowering and foliage plants
See also **EXOTIC PLANT & LIVE TREE** for a complete list of gardening sources

GARDENER

...For a day, week, month, year, etc. For dad, mom, best friend neighbor, or virtually anyone with a yard and a Chinese elm, this gift could be a welcomed relief, giving you back those hours and hours of free time that mysteriously dissipated on the weekends. Can make a great part of a gift package. Wrap up along with the gardener gift certificate, a hammock or set of golf clubs...you get the idea.
See also **MAID/HOUSE CLEANER, HAMMOCK** **$25 - $50 / day**

THE GIFT OF SAFETY & SECURITY

As far as this book is concerned, one of the less creative ideas, but an important one. It can be thought of as a practical safety mechanism or an insurance safety valve against life's unpredictable nature. Much like a lottery ticket, it's either all or nothing. You may never use or need one of these ideas, but if you do, it will be there...and you might just indirectly save a life. Ultimately it makes an ideal gift as most people would never buy for themselves, because it often provides no vital need or necessary service in the moment, where most of us live and think. This gift of safety & security should be given with the sole intention of providing that safe, secure feeling within knowing it's there, and with the hope that it will never be used.

EARTHQUAKE PREPAREDNESS KIT
EMERGENCY CAR KIT
ANTI-CRIME KIT / PERSONAL PROTECTION
CHILD'S SAFETY KIT
DISASTER PREPAREDNESS KIT
FIRST AID KITS
TOOL BOX

HERRINGTON   **800-622-5221**
the best in accessories   First aid kits: **$100 - $190**
RAND McNALLY GIFT ATLAS   **800-234-0679**
highway emergency kits   **$45**
THE SAFETY ZONE   **800-999-3030**
helpful products for safety & security, for children, home, car and self
SAFE-T-MAN - life-size, life-like male "dummy" for your travel companion
in your car or company at home for safety   **$120**
HAND-HELD EMERGENCY CB for the car (2-way radio):   **$70**
BREATHALIZER (personal alcohol tester):   **$150**
ALARM SYSTEMS FOR HOME OR AUTO: **$50 - $400**

WHISTLE:	**$13**	**MACE / PEPPER SPRAY:**	**$15 - $25**
FIRST AID KITS:	**$37**	**CAR EMERGENCY KIT:**	**$60**
WALL SAFE:	**$150**	**SURVIVAL KITS:**	**$40 - $90**
BOOK SAFE:	**$10**	**TRAVELER'S HEALTH KIT:**	**$50**

QUORUM SECURING LIFE   **800-745-1264**
security devises for home, car and personal use
See also KID'S SAFE

GOOD NEWS

This, unfortunately, with all the bad news we hear about or is manifested from TV news at home or around the world, is a rare gift. It is the telling of good news by you to a person who might benefit from it emotionally or otherwise. Telling your parents or your spouse that you are having a baby, announcing an engagement, a career success, a monetary windfall, are all good examples. Sometimes you may be able to plan them for specific occasions, or they may coincidentally fall on them, or it may just create an occasion all by itself.   **FREE**

GRANDPARENTS

Since they have seemed to have lived longer than most and have been there, done that and have had just about everything, grandparents are thought of as sometimes being difficult to shop for. Our word of advice is "don't be lazy." There are as many or more great gift ideas out there as there are years they have been alive. Grandparents, typically, may not care much about material, practical, useful possessions, but they will endear and treasure something personal from you to them. Whether it's a work of art from their grandchild, a personal possession, family heirloom, video memories, a night out on the town to their favorite restaurant or entertainment center, a trip to their favorite vacation destination, a picture album or even something so simple as a gift basket of their favorite goodies, they'll appreciate it far more than you'll ever know...and if all else fails, get them anything with their grandchild's picture on it.

GREAT ADDITIONS TO A GRANDPARENTS GIFT PACKAGE

BOOKS - *Unbelievably Good Deals & Great Adventures That You Absolutely Can't Get Unless You're Over 50, Grandmother Remembers, The Armchair Angler*

RECORDINGS FROM THE PAST - Glen Miller: *The Popular Recordings, 1938 - 1942, The Shadow Radio Show* by Orson Wells, *The Whistler:* 20 shows of the original broadcast available to fans of this popular mystery theatre on the radio from 1942 - 1955

VIDEO COLLECTIONS - *For Gardening Grandparents*

See also

BUNGEE CORD JUMP	WHALE WATCHING	SPA WEEK / WEEKEND
VIDEO GIFT PACKAGE	CRUISE VACATION	MOTORHOME AMERICA
TROPICAL VACATION	TRAVELOGUES	VACATION PACKAGE
DREAM HOUSE	CARE PACKAGE	EVENING ON / TOWN
FRIENDSHIP	MUSIC MIX	MAID/HOUSE CLEANER
FAMILY COOKBOOK	FAMILY PHOTO SITTING	FAMILY RESERVE
FAMILY TREE	GARDEN KIT	GARDENER
HAMMOCK	PHOTO ALBUM	FLOWERS
VIDEO MEMORIES	TRAIN RIDE	BOOKS ON TAPE
HONORING PLAQUE	POCKET WATCH	GIFT BASKETS
CAPTURED MOVIE MOMENT	'ROUND-THE-WORLD TRIP	
SPIRITUAL AWAKENINGS: BOOKS	ENTERTAINMENT GIFT PACKAGE	
LIVE PERFORMANCE TICKETS	PERSONALIZED CALENDAR	
RESTORED FAMILY PHOTOS	GIFT OF SAFETY & SECURITY	
THE PERFECT TASTY GIFTS	AMERICAN EXPRESS GIFT CHECK	

BROOKSTONE - hard to find tools catalog   **800-926-7000**
tools and accessories for the home, yard and car
Grandpa's favorite game: pitching horseshoes
        $30 (4 steel shoes, 2 steel stakes, instructions & official rules)
                        Backyard croquet set: **$100**
                Hammocks & accessories: $100 - $300

GYMBOREE

The nation's leader in parent / child play programs. 7 different age group programs from birth through 5 years old, available to give to those new parents in the form of a gift certificate to help them take their first baby steps in the right direction. Gymboree was developed out of a fundamental commitment to positive parenting with goals to play up the best parts of childhood, meeting others, laughing, learning, as well as understanding and appreciating their child's growth. Parties for your child can also be organized through one of the many services Gymboree offers, complete with Gymbo-the-Clown. Also, don't forget Gymboree's always fashionable wardrobe for the little ones, found in their stores throughout the country.
GYMBOREE   **800-632-2122**
        $135 / 13 classes (classes meet once a week, 45 minutes each)
$25 one-time enrollment fee & gym club membership (siblings half price)
                            $16 for single classes

HAMMOCK

A perfect gift for the workaholic or anybody who needs to or loves to relax in the sunshine. A necessary leisure activity for all moms and dads.   **$18 - $225**
SWING 'N' HAMMOCKS   **310-371-6667**
HANGOUT'S - Mayan / Brazilian design hammocks   **800-HANG-OUT**
TWIN OAKS HAMMOCKS - woven rope hammocks   **800-688-8946**
BROOKSTONE - hard to find tools catalog   **800-926-7000**
        tools and accessories for the home, yard and car
                        Hammocks & accessories: **$100 - $300**
CRATE AND BARREL   **800-323-5461**
        country-style indoor and outdoor housewares, furniture and more
        hammocks: **$100 - $150,** hammock-style swing chair: **$120,** the ultimate
        hammock: deluxe hammock with self-supporting stand, canopy, pillows,
        hammock caddie & pad   **$555**

KIDS-SAFE: HOME SAFETY KIT

Safeguard your home and keep your child out of harm's way. Choose between an assortment of cabinet, drawer & door latches, door knob covers, safety outlet plates, door stoppers, and a jillion other things that are available for home safety. If you're a parent, you'll have no trouble knowing what to include in this gift package.   **$25 - $75**

ONE STEP AHEAD - Helpful gifts for baby   **800-274-8440**

TOYS TO GROW ON   **800-542-8338**
   Educational toys for kids & toddlers

PERFECTLY SAFE - safe stuff; toys and products for kids   **800-837-KIDS**

THE SAFETY ZONE   **800-999-3030**
   helpful products for safety & security, for children, home, car and self

LIVE TREE

Years ago, my mother once took me on a tour of her old neighborhood where she grew up as a little girl in Pasadena, California. As we slowly rolled by the old house she used to live in, the one thing that still stood as a shining symbol of her youth, the one thing that put a tear in her eye and a smile on her face...was that little pine tree she planted with her folks...sixty years before. Not only did it outlast all the structural changes to the house and neighborhood, it flourished and grew one foot for every year...to a majestic sixty-feet high. If left untouched, it will last another sixty years. A healthy, growing tree is a miracle of nature...every day. A live tree or interesting plant can be a meaningful gift and a symbol of life, beauty and growth in a relationship. Just make sure you choose a hearty one...plant that is.   **$4 - $100 +**

AMERICAN FORESTS - famous and historical trees   **800-320-TREE**
seeds are collected from some of the most historical trees from the U.S. and around the world. They are grown, then shipped at a height of 1-3 feet. Includes a certificate of authenticity. Choose from George Washington Poplars, Mt. Vernon Maples and Sycamores, Roosevelt Pines and Magnolias, Napoleon Willows, Robin Hood English Oaks, Ponderosa Pine, trees from Thoreau's Walden Woods and much, much more. This source is on our top ten list of the best most creative gift sources.   **$35 any tree**

VANS PINS   **619-399-1620**
   evergreen, pine, oak, spruce, fir, cherry, walnut, ash, and poplar

WAYSIDE GARDENS   **800-845-1124**
   container-grown trees ready for transplanting

WESTERN MAINE NURSERIES - evergreen trees   **800-447-4745**
EDIBLE LANDSCAPING   **800-524-4156**
   live fruitful and other edible plants
JOHNSON SMITH CO.   **813-747-2356**
    things you never knew existed catalog, bonsai trees & kits   **$8 - $12**
TRIPPLE BROOK FARMS - bamboo, exotic fruits and trees   **413-527-4626**
DAN'S GREENHOUSE   **808-661-8412**
    tropical indoor Bonsai trees grown in sculpted lava rock, Umbrella
    Bonsai's, date palms, Schefflera: **$27 - $129,** sprouted coconut: **$22**
GARDEN WORLD'S EXOTIC PLANTS   **512-724-3951**
    bamboo, bananas, citrus trees, cacti and other tropical stock
GIRARD NURSERIES   **216-466-2881**
   Bonsai trees, evergreen seeds & trees and more
NEW ENGLAND BONSAI GARDENS   **800-457-5445**
   Bonsai's in ceramic pots, Bonsai supplies and more
SPRING HILL NURSERIES   **309-691-4616**
   Bonsai, roses, small fruits, seeds, plants, gardening supplies
MINIATURE PLANT KINGDOM   **707-874-2233**
   miniature roses, maples and other Bonsai's
THE BANANA TREE - rare seeds   **215-253-9589**
See also *EXOTIC PLANT, GARDENING KIT*

MAID / HOUSE CLEANER

...for a day, week, month, etc. What could be better for mom, a
family member, a roommate, or a friend who has a million chores to
do, than the services of a maid or house cleaner. A luxury expense
that usually doesn't fit into their budget...becomes a wealthy treat.
Ask a friendly neighbor if they can recommend someone. Otherwise
look in the local paper in the classifiedes under *services offered,* or
your local directory under *"Maid / House Cleaning Services."*
See also *GARDENER*   **$25 - $85 / day**

ORGANIZATION / CLUB MEMBERSHIP

More popular with men are the memberships to the country club,
yacht club or local men's club, but if you look, there are also a
number of women's groups, clubs and organizations. It just takes a
phone call to get involved. The most important and probably the best
reason for most people to get involved in a group is for that

intangible benefit you won't find anywhere in the brochure...friendship. No one actually likes to golf...it's an excuse to be with friends. No one likes to work either. We do it for the sake of friendship...or is it money? Think about someone who has some time on their hands and could use a few more friends in their life. It could make all the difference in their world.

YACHT CLUB $100 - $1,000's Initiation, $100 + / year dues
COUNTRY CLUB $100 - $1,000's Initiation, $100 + / year dues
JOHNSON SMITH CO. 813-747-2356, Fax: 813-746-7896
   things you never knew existed catalog, MILLIONAIRE'S CLUB membership, includes authentic certificate, anyone can join **$20**
NATIONAL GEOGRAPHIC SOCIETY MEMBERSHIP 800-638-4077
   $21 / year + magazine
SIERRA CLUB P.O. Box 7959 San Francisco, CA 94120
   membership: **$35 and up**
YMCA / YWCA, KIWANIS CLUB, ROTARY CLUB, THE ELKS LODGE

PERSONAL FILM / VIDEO PRODUCTION

Have a special event professionally videotaped, edited, and produced complete with music for the family, group of friends, or co-workers. Memories are truly one of God's greatest gifts. To be able to capture it on tape and relive it again and again is an amazingly wonderful thing...simply, priceless. Check your local directory under *"Video Production"* or ask at a professional video supply store for their referral. **$85 - $500 + (includes everything)**

SPECIAL OCCASIONS SUITABLE FOR A VIDEO PRODUCTION

WEDDINGS	**SHOWERS**	**ANNIVERSARIES**
BIRTHDAYS	**PARTIES**	**HOLIDAYS**
TRIPS	**A DAY IN THE LIFE...**	

See also *VIDEO MEMORIES*

PERSONAL POSTER

Have a favorite or forgotten photograph blown up poster size (20"X30" or larger) from your own personal collection of photographs. It's advised that the quality of the original should be as good as possible. The bigger you make a photograph, the less quality you will have. To complete the gift add a nice frame with glass and mounting, or have it mounted on gator-board or foam-core for a cleaner look.

Poster: $18 - $65
Frame (optional): $20 - $45
Mounting (optional): $10 - $$25

ACTION PHOTOS - color posters up to 20" x 28"   **713-556-5900**
GENERAL COLOR CORP. - custom prints up to 24" x 30"   **800-321-1602**
PRO PHOTO LABS - custom enlarging   **800-237-6429**
SHOOTERS OF U.S.A. LAB - custom color enlargements   **708-956-1010**
THE SLIDEPRINTER - color enlargements   **Box 9506, Denver, CO 80209**

PERSONALIZED CALENDAR

The only kind of calendar one should ever give as a gift. Ultra-creative and personal, beautifully combining practicality, warmth and memories...every day of the year. There are generally three different ways to go about creating this gift idea:

1) There are several different companies cropping up that make a business out of creating a few copies of a personalized calendar, using family photos, or any other pictures or written words you might want to include. Simply select the photos, special dates, captions and any other written dialogue and submit it to the company, printer, etc. with specific details. Be sure to allow plenty of time. An ideal gift for family or loved ones around the holidays. **$85 + $25 per calendar**

2) If you're on a budget, some companies will use stock photos of nature and other scenics while personalizing specific dates such as birthdays, anniversaries or anything else you wish to have printed in type. This may be an ideal gift for business promotion or to give out around the office to co-workers. Create an inspirational or motivational theme with famous quotes and sayings. It'll be a great way to kick off a new year. **$45 + $15 per calendar**

3) If you have the time and creative means, why not put together the whole thing yourself. Use your favorite calendar as a guide and format. Have a selection of pictures blown up to a uniform size. Use the actual calendar part of another calendar to add specific dates, captions, and other type written or computer generated words. Have it photocopied on nice paper, then mount the corresponding photo on the back of the previous calendar page. Have your local printer help you with any questions or other needs, including binding, laminating,

protective sleeves, etc.   **$110**
R.A. GRAPHICS   **800-959-1065**
Calendar - turn 12 color photos into a calendar / photo t-shirts
GRANDMOTHER CALENDAR COMPANY   **800-593-8888**
                                                       $15 each
FOTOFOLIO CALENDARS   **800-955-3686**

PHOTO ALBUM/BOOKLET OF MEMORIES

Put together for your parents, your siblings, other family members, or close friends for that matter, a photo album, or booklet of stored away and forgotten photos. You'll laugh and cry while you file through all the old photos as you organize this gift. Laugh and cry again when the gift is opened...and share all those wonderful memories...again.

EXPOSURES   **800-572-5750   800-222-4947**
     photo accessories, frames, albums, etc
LIGHT IMPRESSIONS   **800-642-0994**
     photo albums and storage systems
PAPER JOURNEY   **800-827-2723**
     journals, scrapbooks, albums, notecards and more
ALBUMS, INC.   **800-662-1000**
     wedding albums, photo mounts, plaques, frames
PERSONAL CREATIONS - personalized photo albums: **$32**   **800-326-6626**
ANTIOCH PUBLISHING   **513-767-7379**
     personalized book plates, albums, diaries, scrapbooks
MEMORIES, INC. - wedding books and albums   **800-462-5069**
MICHEL CO. - albums, photo mounts, frames   **800-621-6649**
PENN PHOTOMOUNTS - mounts, albums, folios   **800-228-7366**
See also *PHOTO COLLAGE, VIDEO MEMORIES, CAPTURED MOVIE MOMENT, RESTORED PHOTO*

PICTURE THIS...PICTURE THAT

In all our years of gift-giving, a picture project full of memories given as a gift always becomes a priceless possession. You can never go wrong by giving back a gift of a memory. It will be cherished again and again...every time they set their eyes on it. You don't necessarily have to go to a specialized professional photo lab, many large discount drugstores such as Osco or Sav-On, chain stores, one-hour photo labs and even copy centers offer a variety of creative picture projects from photo sculpture keychains, memo holders and magnets to photo clocks, watches, mugs, t-shirts, hats and buttons. The following are some of the more creative ideas. Just call and ask if their photo department might offer these services or ideas.

PERSONALIZED PHOTO-MEMORY IDEAS

RESTORED FAMILY PHOTO   PHOTO ALBUM / BOOKLET
PHOTO COLLAGE   PERSONALIZED PHOTO CALENDAR
PERSONAL POSTER   CAPTURED MOVIE MOMENT
PHOTO JIG-SAW PUZZLE   VIDEO MEMORIES
PHOTO PLAYING CARDS   PHOTO PLATE
PHOTO SCULPTURES   PERSONAL PHOTO POSTCARDS
PHOTO CHRISTMAS CARDS   PHOTO to OIL PAINTING

OSCO / SAV-ON DISCOUNT DRUG - personal puzzle, photo playing cards, photo plate and many other ideas including the following
photo sculptures - laminated onto acrylic, precision cut and mounted on a pedestal base   **as low as $10** (sizes 4" to 10" and larger)
Photo Playing Cards: $25
Photo Plate: $15
ASSOCIATED PHOTO CO.   **513-421-6620**
custom photo Christmas cards with name imprint
KELLY COLOR   **704-433-0934**
photo restoration, montages, composites and display transparencies
PERSONAL CREATIONS - personalized photo gifts & more   **800-326-6626**
quality photo transfers to t-shirts, sweatshirts and many other products
MASTER ART & FRAMING   **714-855-3003**
transfers photographs to art canvas that resemble oil paintings
POST-PIX - makes postcards from photos   **714-529-1152**
See also *PHOTO RESTORATION, PERSONAL POSTER, PHOTO COLLAGE / BOOKLET / ALBUM, CAPTURED MOVIE MOMENT*

QUALITY MAGAZINE SUBSCRIPTION

Give a gift that not only keeps one informed and involved but does so with belief, humorous entertainment and quality journalism that carries with it an unwritten sense of our traditional American values. Give a gift one looks forward to coming home to, curling up by the fireplace or in bed, and opening up to a new page of delightful discoveries...much like looking forward to resuming an enjoyable conversation with an old dear friend.

READER'S DIGEST	800-234-9000
	12 Issues / 1 year - $14
NATIONAL GEOGRAPHIC	800-638-4077
	12 Issues / 1 year - $21
LIFE	800-345-0900
	12 Issues / 1 year - $28
AUDUBON	800-274-4201
AMERICAN HERITAGE	800-777-1222
SATURDAY EVENING POST	800-289-7678

RESTORED FAMILY PHOTOS

Many good professional photo labs have the ability now to fully restore even badly damaged photographs. You'll be amazed to see the photographs you once thought would never look the same, restored and reproduced looking like new. Water damage, cracks, chips, colors, too light, too dark, faded, and even a blurred image can all be corrected. See samples before deciding on a photo lab and leave only a 50% deposit. Upon receipt of the restored photos, make sure the quality you expected, and they promised, is delivered. If you are not happy with one lab for some reason, don't be discouraged. Restoring pictures is an art form and some artists are better than others, so try again elsewhere. When you're happy with the restoration process, have a negative made, then duplicate enough pictures to be given as a wonderful, priceless surprise. Try to deal with only professional photo labs that have experienced restoration abilities and facilities.

$5 - $75 / picture (not including negs. and duplicates)

ALL PRINT IMAGES - restoration services	303-755-9509
DEVERAUX PHOTO RESTORATION	212-245-1720
MODERNAGE PHOTO SERVICES - photo restoration	212-227-4767
LEXINGTON LENSMASTERS - photo restoration	816-259-2171
ELBINGER LABORATORIES	517-332-1430
tinted reproductions, oil coloring, black & white	
KELLY COLOR - restoration and copy services	704-433-0934

SIGNET RING

...Is typically a ring that has the first letter of their last name die-stamped or etched onto it. Traditionally given by parents to son or daughter, or from one family member to another as they come of age. For graduations, moving out, moving away, significant birthdays, Christmas, etc. Engraving or die-stamping can be done through most jewelers or engraving specialty stores. This gift will grow with intangible value from year to year, generation to generation, person to person...until some special day it is yours to receive...and then some special day to pass along. Try to find a good wholesale jeweler to buy from as prices fluctuate dramatically between them and a national jewelry store chain found at a mall. If it's a hearty financial investment, have an expert check the quality.

$65 - $100's (including engraving)

See also **JEWELRY, FAMILY HEIRLOOM, PERSONAL POSSESSION**

SUBSCRIPTION FOR NEW PARENTS

What a nice gift of education and enjoyment for new parents...to be appreciated month after month. Great to give as part of a baby shower or newborn gift...or for anytime, really.

PARENTING	**415-546-7575**
WORKING MOTHER	**P.O. Box 5240, Harlan, IA 51593**
SESAME STREET PARENTS	**303-447-9330**

A publication for parents to assist them with the education through entertainment of their children

See also **BABY, BABY, BABY**

VIDEO MEMORIES

If one picture is worth a thousand words, a whole video will surely leave you speechless. Here's a chance to use your talent as a Director, Producer, and STAR! Get out your shoe box of old photos or dusty box of old films. If you don't already have these in your possession, obtain from your friends, loved ones or family members, their old 8mm films, photographs and/or slides. Organize the photos and/or films & videos chronologically, or by event, or person, so that it tells a story. Find a personal selection of music that fits the occasion. Have it all organized, edited, music added, and transferred onto video to make your own personal movie. Try not to give away your plans as this makes for a terrific surprise. Have copies made to be given to the whole starring cast. This ranks as perhaps one of our best gift ideas for sentimentality and stirring all those warm wonderful feelings. Memories are a large part of everyone's life and since our sight is typically our most powerful sense, the recipient will be able to relive those memories vividly, again and again. Find the right video transfer / production service that's right for you in terms of cost, ideas and technical ability & quality. You certainly don't want to spend a lot of money on something that defeats your purpose by diminishing those wonderful memories. Remember, you've hired them, which makes you the producer and director. They are your skilled technicians or "crew." If you've made someone laugh...and someone cry, you have succeeded. Check your local listings for *Video Production* or *Video transfer service*. Your local camera store may even be equipped. There are also some larger discount drugstore chains with a photo department that can handle it. Some nationwide services will do everything by mail. If you choose this route be sure to insure those valuable memories before sending them off, or better yet make duplicates.

$85 - $300 (initial production cost)
$5 - $20 each additional tape

SCATTERED PICTURES
800-879-0986
Video Photo Album: **$100**

PLAY IT AGAIN VIDEO PRODUCTIONS (stills)
508-655-2252

OSCO / SAV-ON DRUG STORES
$30 and up

See also **VIDEO PRODUCTION**

A WEEKEND AWAY

A weekend away, no matter how planned out, spontaneous, extravagant, or budgeted that it may be, is inconsequential unless you actually get up and go. Give to somebody, a loving couple, your parents or yourselves, the excuse to get up and go. If one lives in a big city such as Los Angeles or New York, it's easy to forget about what one is working so hard for. One will get more accomplished in a week after a weekend away then in a whole month in burn-out or gridlock. One of the healthiest things one can do for the mind, body and soul.

$85 - $100's (including hotel)

See also ***ROMANTIC WEEKEND***

The Greatest Father in the World

This award is given only once a year to the most outstanding father in the world for his continuing love, support, understanding and for making this world just a little bit more safe and sane to live in. Fathers are from where we derive our kindness and our gentleness. They are our rock, our comfort and our joy. Fathers are what make the real world go 'round.

Presented with Love, by _____

given this _____ _day of_ _____, 19 ____

Award of Recognition

Congratulations !

_____ *has just been unanimously named*

Mother Of The Year

This award is given only once a year to the greatest mother in the world for her continuing love, support, understanding and for making this world just a little bit more safe and sane to live in. Mothers are our rock and our joy. They are what make the real world go 'round.

Presented with Love, by _____

given this _____ *day of* _____ , 19 ____

Aaah...
the Little Ones

Children and kids can be the most fulfilling to shop for and give to. Their reaction to a gift they absolutely love is priceless. Kids are probably the easiest to shop creatively for. The world revolves around entertainment, fun, constant excitement and stimulation, which is a kid's job...until they have to get a real job. With children and kids, a little creativity is truly appreciated as they love the interesting, the different, and the one of a kind. It never hurts to help them learn, grow, and have one of the most precious of all things...a happy childhood...as often as possible.

"No person was ever honored for what he received. Honor has been the reward for what he gave."
CALVIN COOLIDGE

QUICK REFERENCE LIST

ADOPT-A-HORSE

Leasing or buying a horse for any period of time can be the best gift in the whole wide world...especially for the little ones, but please understand for the animal's sake that it takes a big commitment and much responsibility to properly take care of a horse...or any animal for that matter. This gift idea is not recommended if there is not plenty of free roaming acreage or sufficient skills or knowledge to care for such an animal. It also requires a considerable financially and time commitment. Carefully think this through before making this big decision. With all that said, the joy this gift could bring to the whole family could far out weigh any effort involved. Look in your local classifieds or ask around at the local equestrian center or horse stables. The Bureau of Land Management (BLM), a federal agency, performs periodic round-ups of wild Mustangs and burros in order to maintain an ecological balance in most of the western United States. These wild horses and burros can then be adopted for a small adoption fee. A fee is required mostly to cover shipping and vet costs.

BLM adoption: $125 (horse), $75 (burro)
To Buy: FREE - $1,000 and up
To Lease: $100 - $300 / month

BUREAU OF LAND MANAGEMENT - horse adoptions   **800-513-0927**

ADOPT-A-WHALE

"You can make a difference." and "Every little bit counts." are phrases we've all heard for years from charities or non-profit organizations...and it's true. You can make a difference! Many of our endangered animals, including many species of whales, are coming back in strong numbers, but it's only due to public awareness and financial help that support the efforts of the brave, kind-hearted souls on the front lines. Make a difference and help save a whale...or two.

WHALE ADOPTION PROJECT   **Dept 94GC, 70 E Falmouth Hwy**
   catalog of whale gifts   **E Falmouth, MA 02536**
   adopt-a-whale program, **$17** includes certificate, photo of whale, migration map and subscription

See also *ADOPT-A-WOLF, ADOPT-AN-ACRE*

AIR SHOW

An air show will give a youngster memories to last a lifetime. The Blue Angels and the Thunderbirds travel to most major cities throughout the country. Their uniform acrobatics will dazzle and mystify a young impressionable mind. Other types of aircraft will also be sure to impress as they perform death-defying stunts. Be sure to get a ticket, so that you can get onto the tarmac to view these magnificent works of engineering up close and personal. Who knows, the recipient may just be lucky enough to sit inside the cockpit of a fighter jet. Call your local military installation or airport for upcoming events.   **FREE IN MOST CASES**

AIRPLANE RIDE / TRIP

An airplane ride for a small child doesn't have to empty your wallet. There are many short, inexpensive commercial flights to fun, exciting local destinations. For a wide-eyed first-timer, the flight will definitely be the highlight of the trip...especially the take-off and landing. There are also small private planes from which you can make a quick hop, or do some sight seeing from God's point of view. Call your favorite airline or travel agency for prices, destinations, and other details.   **$35 - $100's / ticket, Round-Trip**
See also *TRAIN RIDE and MAJOR AIRLINES listings*

AMUSEMENT PARK SEASON PASS

What a perfect gift to keep the kids out of your hair...and you out of theirs...during those summer months. Amusement parks around the country are becoming the frequent hangout for teenagers. Use your discretion and don't let them hang with the wrong crowd, otherwise let 'em knock their socks off.   **$80 - $250**
See *THEME PARK listings*

ANIMAL PUPPETS

Many toy stores are now carrying a good supply of these adorable, expressive friends. Your hand and your natural acting ability will entertain and fascinate a youngster for hours and they'll soon learn to create and entertain for themselves...if they can get them away from you. These funny, furry friends have to be seen to be appreciated. You'll fall in love. **$12 - $85**

ARCADMANIA

The ultimate kid's toy might be to have a garage or den full of arcade games. For our purposes...and expenses...we'll just start with one. We're talking about coin-operated pinball machines, video games and all that fun stuff found at a public arcade. For cost and selection you might want to see if there are any arcade / video game auctions in your area coming up in the near future. Check your local newspaper under *"Auctions."* You might also want to get a padlock for the door so the kids don't start to live in one room...and hold the key, but don't lose it or you'll be buying a new door.

ARCADE GAMES   **909-598-9422**
    coin-operated video & pinball games

WEST COAST GAMES   **714-535-0100**
    all kinds of arcade games, jukeboxes & more

BABY, BABY, BABY...!

For that hard to shop for baby. Baby showers, newborns, christening, for their first couple of birthdays, here are some of the more creative ideas and sources.

LITTLE ONE - gifts for the newborn   **800-227-5451**
    shower and christening gifts, invitations, announcements, nursery accessories and unique toys

HAND IN HAND   **800-872-9745**
    innovative and traditional for the early years

GET SMART - the educational superstore   **800-726-7627**
    creative, educational toys

HANNA ANDERSON   **800-222-0544**
    Swedish cotton clothes for kids, infants and pre-teens

MUSIC FOR LITTLE PEOPLE   **800-727-2233**
    imaginative and unique music inspired products and more

STORYBOOK HEIRLOOMS - fashions for children   **800-825-6565**

A GENTLE WIND   **518-436-0391**
    music & story cassettes for children ages 1 - 12

VIDEO REVOLUTION   **800-342-3436**
    audio & video tapes for children

MUSIC FOR LITTLE PEOPLE   707-923-3991
   music cassettes, videos & instruments for children, including famous
   stories, favorite songs, lullabies and more

BIRTHDAY EXPRESS - the children's party catalog   800-685-4996
   themes and partyware, decorations and more

CHILDCRAFT   800-222-7725
   educational toys & games for babies & young children

GROWING CHILD   317-423-2624
   toys, games, puzzles, books, recordings, arts & crafts up to age 6

SENSATIONAL BEGINNINGS   800-444-2147
   toys & books for babies & children up to age 4

THE RIGHT START   800-LITTLE-1
   everything infants and children want and need

PERFECTLY SAFE   800-837-KIDS
   safe stuff: toys and more for kids & toddlers

See also **SUBSCRIPTION FOR NEW PARENTS, BOOK OF NAMES**

BATTING CAGES

A season gift certificate for the batting cages is a practical and much
appreciated gift for the family baseball star. You may just be
producing the next World Champion MVP. Not a gift to be pushed
on a kid who'd rather be doing something else besides baseball.

$4 - $8 / half hour
$150 - $300 / season pass (40 hours)

BATTING TUTOR - check sporting goods or toy store, portable pitching
   machine at home: fastballs, curveballs, sinkers & sliders, 10-60 MPH

THE BIG BACKYARD

Check out these "big stuff" toy stores for the backyard. From
swingsets, climbing gyms, slides, wooden playsets, modular units and
lots more, you can give to that monst...I mean, that lovely, adorable
child their very own "safe" playground.

BIGTOYS - playground equipment   800-426-9788

CEDAR WORKS - wooden playsets for the backyard   800-233-7757

FLORIDA PLAYGROUND - swings & backyard equipment   800-822-4456

GYM-N-I PLAYGROUNDS   800-232-3398
   modular playground structures, swing sets and other equipment

WOODSET - backyard structures   800-638-9663

WOOD BUILT OF WISCONSIN   800-475-5051
    hardware kits for swing & slide sets
WOODPLAY - redwood backyard play sets   800-982-1822
YARDS OF FUN   800-228-0471
    backyard wooden swing sets & climbing gyms

BOAT RENTAL

There are few things more fun then being on the water on a warm, sunny day. Teach the kids how to tack back and forth in a sailboat. Head out to the "calm" sea or lake to fish from a motorboat. Paddle around the bay, harbor, lakeshore or river in a paddle boat, rowboat or canoe. Make a trip, weekend or day gift package out of it, filled with fun, adventure and being together. Call to make reservations in advance at your local recreational body of water. Make sure the weather is favorable and that your sailing skills are in "tack" for safety purposes. The last thing you want with good intentions is a disastrous result.   **$12 - $45 / hour**
See also SAILBOAT RENTAL, WHITEWATER RAFTING

BOOK OF NAMES

A terrific gift or gift accessory, often overlooked, for baby showers and even part of a wedding gift basket. Check your favorite book store for a creative book of names...how about a book of Hawaiian names for something a little different.   **$4 - $25**

CD-ROM / MULTI-MEDIA KIT

Movies, sounds, pictures and more through your computer. A CD-ROM drive is a revolutionary piece of computer hardware that works in conjunction with your computer to play CD's. Slip in your favorite music CD, watch your favorite movie or educate through a picture encyclopedia. The future of computers is here. There are so many different set-ups and brands for computers and their accessories that we couldn't even begin to recommend one particular system. Your best bet would be to upgrade from a MAC or IBM compatible, whichever you feel most comfortable or familiar with. Check different sources and try out different systems until you feel happy and comfortable with something suited to your needs.

MAC WAREHOUSE - everything for the MAC   **800-255-6227**
     CD-ROM DRIVE   **$150 - $300 +**
     ENCYCLOPEDIA ON CD-ROM   **$100**

CLUB KIDSOFT'S MULTIMEDIA KID'S STORE   **800-354-6150**
     computer software / CD-ROM magazine & catalog for kids & parents - responsible, educationally based

SHOPPERS ADVANTAGE   **800-TEL-SHOP**
     best buys on name brand products, including CD-ROM & multi-media kits

See also *SOFTWARE, EDUCATIONAL*

CHALK BOARD AND COLORFUL CHALK

Don't overlook this simple old-fashioned gift. In this world where our minds are bombarded and our senses overloaded with the best this and the biggest that and ultra everything, a young mind can develop a warped sense of reality and miss out on one of the most beautiful gifts given to us at birth...creativity and imagination. Give them the simple tools to enhance these qualities to make the most of their young impressionable minds.   **$5 - $20**

CHILDREN'S PLAY / MUSICAL

Opening a little person's mind and exposing them to the arts can leave a powerful impression. I can still remember vividly the first live theatrical production I was taken to. Who knows, with this type of influence you might just be raising the next Lawrence Olivier or Audrey Hepburn. And even if a young child is not culturally enriched over night by a live show, they'll certainly be entertained. And you'll probably have just as much fun recalling the days when you saw the same play or musical as a youngster yourself. Check your local entertainment guide or call your community theatre for upcoming shows.   **$5 - $50 / ticket**

See also *MARIONETTE THEATRE*

DETECTIVE / SPY KIT

"Bond...James Bond." Prepare the recipient of this gift to be the next agent 007. A great learning and educational experience through make-believe adventure and excitement. The child will be fascinated with the technology of their new detective's tools. Just be forewarned that you will undoubtedly be their main subject. Something to keep in mind while shopping for this gift. You don't want their equipment to be too good. They'll see and hear everything...and I mean everything. If it is a rather hi-tech set-up, set some ground rules on how they can and can't use their equipment.

E.D.E.   **$20 - $100's +**
                                                                                       716-691-3476
   Surveillance equipment, bugs, tracking devises, scanners and more
HITEK - night vision glasses / binoculars   **$495 800-54- NIGHT**
INFORMATION UNLIMITED   **800-221-1705**
   electronic devices, laser window bounce listener
U.S. GENERAL TECH. - night vision products   **800-445-3300**
                                                                                       $249 and up
PALADIN PRESS - SOE secret operations manuals   **800-872-4993**
                                                                                       $8 - $35 / book
SONIC TECH.   **800-538-0787**
   lock picking kits, phone taps, stun gun, pepper spray and more
BRAINSTORMS - fun with fingerprints kit   **800-621-7500**
THE EDGE COMPANY   **800-732-9976**
   weapons, night vision, listening devises, voice changer, torch
U.S. ACADEMY OF PRIVATE INVESTIGATION   **213-879-1165**
SPY SUPPLY CATALOG   **800-544-4779**
JOHNSON SMITH CO.   **813-747-2356**
   things you never knew existed catalog, spy, undercover stuff, listening
   devises, night vision scope, hidden book camera, undercover manual
See also *DISGUISE KIT*   **$5 - $1300**

DIARY / JOURNAL / SCRAPBOOK

Many book and stationery stores as well as specialty shops carry a good selection of these bound volumes. Even if a person already has a book that they write in, one can always find another purpose to fill pages with thoughts, things to do and memories to keep. And when one is filled they'll always need another. A personal and rewarding gift that can be someone's best friend and stay with them the rest of their life. Have the front personalized with their name or initials. Don't forget to write your name and an inscription on the first page.

                                                                                       $2 - $45
PLAY FAIR TOYS - children's art portfolio **$20**   **800-824-7255**

PAPER JOURNEY   **800-827-2723**
   journals, scrapbooks, albums, notecards and more

ANTIOCH PUBLISHING   **513-767-7379**
   personalized book plates, albums, diaries, scrapbooks

SECRETS: AN INTIMATE JOURNAL FOR TWO, adults only (at bookstores)

CEDCO PUBLISHING CO. - datebooks, soft-cover books   **415-457-3893**

WRITEWELL CO.   **317-871-6710**
   postcard albums, leather-grained vinyl cover with personalization

THE DINOSAUR STORE

Through this unique source, you can get your hands on some real dinosaur skulls, skeletons, teeth, claws, eggs and more. Call for their catalog...you won't be disappointed.

THE DINOSAUR STORE   **310-589-5988**

DISGUISE KIT

Kids love to travel incognito. It's normal and natural for a kid's imagination to explore the world of different and interesting characters. A toy store or magic shop may have a complete kit all put together. If not, use your imagination and put one together yourself. You might want to include some safe but face altering make-up, a mustache or wig, creative wardrobe as well as other prosthetics and accessories. The young thespian or secret agent man (or woman) may become master of the theatre or stage of life even before they're paid to perform.   **$20 - $100 +**

EDUCATIONAL / GIFTS TO LEARN FROM

God bless the responsible companies and manufacturers who continue to create all that good stuff from where a child can develop their imagination, learning skills, curious nature and creativity. These gifts may not be as enjoyable as a video or arcade game to a child, but the lasting impact and developmental skills they unknowingly learn now, will be carried with them throughout their lives. It is the foundation and building blocks that are created so early in life that undoubtedly shape our destiny. Give a gift that prepares them for life...a good life.

PLAY FAIR TOYS   **800-824-7255**
   Dealing with Feelings Books   **$18 / set of 3**

 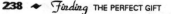

CD-ROM - MAC WAREHOUSE   800-255-6227
CD-ROM DRIVE: **$150 - $300 +**
GROLIER CD-ROM MULTI-MEDIA ENCYCLOPEDIA: **$180**
ANIMALS & ATLAS CD-ROM MULTI-MEDIA PACK

BRAINSTORMS CATALOG   800-621-7500
interesting & educational products for kids

TOYS FOR SPECIAL CHILDREN   800-832-8697
special communication devices, adapted activity toys, skill builder equipment, capability switches, computer training devices and other special devices for children with disabilities

THE SOFTWARE LABS   800-569-7900

A GENTLE WIND   518-436-0391
music & story cassettes for children ages 1 - 12

CHILDCRAFT   800-222-7725
educational toys & games for babies & young children

ALL BUT GROWN-UPS   800-448-1550
challenging toys for adults & children

ARISTOPLAY GAMES - educational games for all ages   800-634-7738

DISCOVERY TOYS   800-426-4777
toys for children encouraging physical, emotional & intellectual growth

THE GREAT KIDS CO   800-334-2014
developmental learning materials for early childhood education

HEARTH SONG   800-533-4397
toys & games that stimulate creativity, challenge, discovery & learning

KAPABLE KIDS - toys for the developing child   800-356-1564

TROLL LEARN & PLAY   800-247-6106
children's educational toys, books, puzzles, playhouse toys, videos and other recordings, costumes and more

RAISIN' COOKIE   800-866-6005
educational toys, books & videos for children 1 - 8

VIDEO REVOLUTION   800-342-3436
audio & video tapes for children

MAC'S PLACE   800-260-0009
fun, interesting, educational software for kids

See also ***CD-ROM / MULTI-MEDIA KIT, COMPUTER SOFTWARE, ELECTRONICS KITS, SCIENCE FAIR***

ELECTRONIC KEYBOARD / SYNTHESIZER

Casio, Yamaha and other electronic-music companies make a variety of synthesizers and electronic keyboards for the beginner to the concert or studio professional. Most of them have sound banks or samplers for an almost endless variety of different sounds and sound effects. Someone of the right age, mentality or curiosity will find it hard to put down. It may even lead to a promising career. A reasonably priced keyboard for the recreational beginner can be found at an electronics warehouse or music store.   **$80 - $100's +**

AKRON MUSIC - keyboards, amps, drums, guitars   **800-962-3152**

SAM ASH MUSIC - discounted music equipment   **800-472-6274**

CAVIN - guitars, amps, mixers, mics, other instruments   **800-854-2235**

KENNELLY KEYS MUSIC - discounted music instruments   **800-426-6409**

THOROUGHBRED MUSIC   **800-800-4654**
   keyboards, electronics, drum machines and accessories

TALKING OWNER'S MANUAL   **800-492-9999**
   electronic keyboard & "Rapping" accessories, videos, tapes by Casio

YAMAHA MUSIC CORP. - electronic keyboards   **800-541-6514**

SHOPPERS ADVANTAGE   **800-TEL-SHOP**
   best buys on name brand products,   electronic keyboards: **$79 - $249**

See also **MUSICAL INSTRUMENTS**

FIRST BANK ACCOUNT

There comes a time in everyone's young life to put their money in the bank bank. That means upgrading from Mr. Piggy to Mr. Biggy. After all, Mr. Piggy's interest rates are not very good. A wonderful learning experience for any kid or young adult to know first hand how to deposit and withdraw their money as well as earn interest...a fascinating and thought-provoking notion for young, innocent minds. Their good banking habits now could have a profound effect on their successful financial security and budgeting as an adult. As a gift idea, a nice contribution to initiate the account starts them off in the black.

Account Opening: FREE - contribution of $20 - $100's

FISH TANK...WITH FISH

A small fish tank with a couple of fish can be a child's introduction to being responsible for a living creature and its well being...along with hours of wonderment and fascination. Let the child know ahead of time a fish's life expectancy. You're doing pretty good if the fish lives longer than a few months. Check your local pet store or tropical

fish store. Some larger discount chains have inexpensive starter kits (not including fish). **$15 - over $100 (Including fish)**
JOHNSON SMITH CO. **813-747-2356, Fax: 813-746-7896**
    things you never knew existed catalog, live sea horses **$14**
    live sea monkeys **$11**
ACRYLIC CREATIONS - custom acrylic tanks and supplies **419-882-1287**
BUCKAROO MARINE - salt water fish and invertebrates **800-927-1050**
EXOTIC AQUARIA - tropical fish, algae, corals **800-622-5877**
MAIL ORDER PET SHOP - marine & other animal supplies **800-366-7387**
MARK'S AQUARIUM & PET WORLD - custom tanks & more **718-745-4001**
PET WAREHOUSE - tropical fish, bird, bog, cat supplies **800-252-7388**
REEF AQUARIUM DESIGNS - custom aquarium systems **904-760-0738**
WORLD CLASS AQUARIUM - aquariums, fish, accessories **718-258-0653**

FISHING POLE & EQUIPMENT

...Rod, reel, tackle, tackle box, fishing license, etc. A fishing pole and related equipment by itself is not all that creative or exciting, but to a kid, especially a boy, it means the great outdoors will soon be his. Wrap up the fishing pole and any accessories along with a card detailing a future fishing trip to the favorite hot spot. You'll find everything you need at a sporting goods store or one of your larger discount chains: Wal-Mart, K-Mart, etc. **$25 - $150**
L.L. BEAN - fly-fishing supplies and much more **800-221-4221**
BERKELEY - fishing equipment **800-237-5539**
HOOK & TACKLE CO. - fly-fishing tackle and accessories **800-552-8342**
FINGERHUT **4404 Eight St N, St Cloud Minnesota 56395**
    fishing package with 2 rods, reels, tackle, tackle box and more **$80**
BASS PRO SHOPS - fishing and outdoor equipment **800-BASS-PRO**
DIAWA CORP. - salt / fresh water fishing equipment **714-895-6645**
See also *FISHING TRIP, FISHING CHARTER, FLY-FISHING*

FISHING TRIP

This is really a gift disguised by dad, for himself...Or is it actually a gift for mom, a ploy to get them all out of the house for a little peace and quiet. Lake and stream fishing in the United States is thought to be the best in the world, especially for Trout, Bass, Steelhead, Catfish, Salmon, and Sturgeon among others. There are always a number of lakes and streams within driving distance...and the further

you drive the better the fishing. That's just how it works, don't ask why. If you're within reach of one of our coastlines, the odds are usually better to catch at least something, from a charter, public fishing boat, barge or local pier. If the little fishies are seen near the shoreline there are sure to be bigger ones lurking just beyond. Wherever you go, make sure there's plenty of other things to do for the kids during that down time between catches. The average kid gets board in about 30 seconds if nothing's biting. Fishing licenses and regulations are available at most sporting goods, fishing & tackle and bait stores. There to, you'll get all the latest details, info and supplies for your trip. Check also the local paper for the fish report and local hot spots. **COST: Gas, food, bait & fishing equip.**
Fishing Licenses $12 - $25 / person
Tackle, bait, expenses / person FREE - $25 / person
See also FISHING CHARTER, TROUT POND FISHING, OCEAN FISHING TRIP, FISHING ROD, REEL & EQUIPMENT, FLY FISHING

FOOTBALL'S DREAM WEEK

If there's a boy in the family between the ages of 8 and 18 and you want to give them a gift that will last them a lifetime, this is it; a 6-day football camp taught by the NFL stars, players and coaches. What else is there? **$300 - $500**
OFFENCE-DEFENSE, PRO CAMPS **800-554-1273**
instructional football schools operating in California & New York

FORT / TREE HOUSE KIT

No child should ever grow up without an awesome fort, tree house, or club house. Select a good location for development, then supply the plans and the raw materials. Oversee the operation so that everything is done safely, but allow the kids much creative freedom. They won't learn much if you do it for them. Include in the package general plans and all necessary materials...wood, nails, carpet, paint, tools, and other accessories and decorative items. And it's got to have character. Throw in a couple unique things...an old piece of furniture a port hole, a metal sign, a flag, a chest, a tire and other "cool" things to put into it or onto it. You won't find this gift idea neatly wrapped up in a box, ready to buy. You'll have to do it all on your own. Wrap up all the materials in a large wooden or cardboard box or a heavy canvas sheet.   **$35 - $150**

PRESTON'S   **67-T, Main St. Wharf, Greenport, NY 11944**
  ships and the sea, nautical ideas for the home
NAUTICAL FLAGS - nautical / U.S. / custom flags   **800-536-4002**
HAND CARVED - yacht and estate nameboards and more   **203-642-6008**
See also *TIPI*

FRAMED MOVIE POSTER

A nicely framed poster of someone's favorite movie, or movie star, can make for a uniquely exceptional gift. From one of the older classics to a film you just saw yesterday, there are several different sources that specialize in posters of movies and their stars. If you can't find a source that specializes in movie memorabilia try a theatrical or cinema bookstore. Mail order is also a possibility. Prices range dramatically depending on what you are looking for. Some rare original posters from films that were extremely popular could cost up to several hundreds or even thousands of dollars, whereas a poster from a fairly modern or unpopular film could cost as little as four bucks.   **$4 - $1,000's (without frame)**

RICK'S MOVIE GRAPHICS - movie Posters   **800-252-0425**
CINEMA CITY - all kinds of movie posters   **616-722-7760**
CINEMA COLLECTORS - movie posters / star photos   **213-461-6516**
JERRY OHLINGER'S - movie posters / star photos   **212-989-0869**
THE MOVIE POSTER SHOP   **403-250-7588**
AMERICAN ARTS & GRAPHICS   **800-524-3900**
  movie, giant, fun, all-star, pin-up, sports, art and photo posters
See also *FRAMED CELEBRITY PHOTO, MOVIE MEMORABILIA, WALL POSTER*

GIRLS / BOYS MAGAZINE SUBSCRIPTION

I couldn't recommend anything higher than a gift of interest...and education. As little reading as I did growing up, I still remember and apply some of those things I did read about. The only trouble was finding something interesting. As most parents know, it can be the hardest thing in the world to get a child to do something he or she doesn't want to do. If you find something readable for kids and interesting at the same time...you've struck gold and given a potentially powerful gift. A young impressionable mind is like a sponge or a mirror of all the influences around them and in their lives. A magazine subscription with a positive influence can help lead a child or teen in the right direction and even act as their surrogate parents for practical tools, knowledge and learning.

GIRLS

SEVENTEEN   800-388-1749
TEEN MAGAZINE   800-999-3269
AMERICAN GIRL - ages 7 and up   800-845-0005
   positive influence & education for girls: fashion, essays, trends, editorials
   and more   **$20 / year (6 issues)**
SASSY - for teen girls with an attitude   800-274-2622

BOYS

BOY'S LIFE   214-580-2366
JOHNSON SMITH CO.   813-747-2356
   things you never knew existed catalog, encyclopedia of card tricks **$8,**
   palm reading handbook **$13,** how to hypnotize book **$8,** understanding
   your dreams book **$13,** undercover manual **$12,** army survival manual
   $10, special forces handbook **$12**
VENTURE   312-665-0630
   wholesome entertaining reading for Christian boys ages 10 - 15

KIDS & TODDLERS

WEEKLY READER   800-446-3355
NATIONAL WILDLIFE FEDERATION   800-432-6564
                     Ranger Rick Magazine (12 issues): **$15 / year**
             Your Big Backyard, for ages 3-5 (12 issues): **$12 / year**
CHILD LIFE   800-342-0223
SESAME STREET - ages 2-6   303-447-9330
   education through entertainment for the little ones
CHILDREN'S DIGEST - for preteens   317-636-8881
CLUB KIDSOFT'S MULTIMEDIA KID'S STORE   800-354-6150
   computer software / CD-ROM magazine & catalog for kids & parents -
   responsible, educationally based
CREATIVE KIDS   800-354-6150
   ages 8-14, periodical for kids created by kids, accepts your own kid's
   written works for publishing consideration
SKIPPING STONES   503-342-4956
   children's magazine accepting art, photos and writings from children for
   publication   **$18 / year**

KID CITY - ages 6-10   303-447-9330
   the more mature version of "sesame Street" for kids a little older
STONE SOUP - ages 4-12   800-447-4569
   publishes children's stories and poems   **$23 / year (5 issues)**
MERLIN'S PEN - 6-12 graders   800-247-2027
   accepts stories, artwork, poetry, essays, reviews & more from 6th - 12th-
   graders for publishing   **$19 / year (4 issues)**
CREATIVE KIDS - ages 8-14   800-998-2208
   accepts photographs, plays, cartoons, interviews, book reviews, creative
   writing & artwork from children for publishing   **$20 / year (4 issues)**
See also *the PUBLISHED CHILD*

GO-CART / FORMULA RACING

For boys especially, this can wind up being their first addiction as they power their vehicles around a road racing course testing their driving skill, trying to beat the course record...set by dad. At many Go-Cart race courses you will also find an arcade along with many other fun-filled things to do. See also **Auto Racing** for a more serious level of cart racing for both father and son.   **$10 - $14 / run**

HARBOR CRUISE / EXCURSION

Any trip taken down to the sea or lake shore for a kid is difficult to top...put them on the water, even better. A harbor excursion while listening to all the historical background may rival the "Pirates of the Caribbean." Check your local directory under *"Cruises"* or *"Boat"* or call your designated shoreline recreation area. Make a day out of it, pack a picnic lunch and keep in mind that it also makes for a great day with grandparents, other family members or even a romantic date.   **$8 - $25**
See also BOAT RENTAL

HIGH PERFORMANCE KITES

Where were all these great hi-tech kites when I was growing up? Well, I got news for you. It's never too late to go fly a kite. The most serious kite hobbyists or collectors seem to be adults with investments often running into the hundreds or even thousands of dollars. If you haven't seen these kites in action take a jaunt down to a local park or shoreline on a windy day and you'll see why this gift idea for kids and many adults is hard to beat. Some find it relaxing and therapeutic to fly their kites for sometimes hours at a time, while others fly them with the competitiveness of a fighter pilot while indirectly achieving the same result.

KLIG'S KITES, BANNERS AND WINDSOCKS   **800-333-5944**

INTO THE WIND - Stunt Kites, boomerangs, how to books   **800-541-0314**
    the best kite catalog in the world, kites, accessories, and lots more

JOHNSON SMITH CO.   **813-747-2356**
    things you never knew existed catalog, world's easiest kite   **$27**
    world record paper airplane kit   **$13**

DR. KITES - kites and kite building supplies   **800-622-5483**

THE KITE LOFT - kites & accessories   **800-345-KITE**

SKYMASTER - acrobatic sport kites   **800-525-0980**

THE HOBBY SHOP

For boys especially, this gift source out-ranks just about any toy store for fun, interest and education. If you're ever at a loss to find something satisfactory for that hard to please kid, a good hobby store will more often than not solve that problem. I've never seen a hobby store that wasn't jam packed to the ceiling with great stuff from slot car sets, remote control and model cars, planes, helicopters, boats, ships and trains to kites, rockets and much much more. We can't all read minds, so trust your instinct. Go ahead and get them what you think they'd like, even if you're not sure.

AMERICA'S HOBBY CENTER   **212-675-8922**
    model airplanes, radio control stuff and more

HOBBY SHACK - radio control equipment & accessories   **800-854-8471**

WALT'S HOBBY - radio control kits for cars   **315-453-2291**

NORTH COAST ROCKETRY - rocket model kits   **800-877-6032**

TIFFANY HOBBIES of YPSILANTI - rocket model kits   **800-232-3626**

ROBBE MODEL SPORT   **908-359-2115**
    radio control model airplane kits, gliders, helicopters and more

See also *R.C. STUFF, REMOTE CONTROL GLIDER*

Homemade Playdough

You can't beat the price for fun. For kids, make your own with the right mixture of water, flour and a little salt. Add food coloring for a variety of different colors. A little thinner consistency and you can make your own sculptures, although if you bake it or let it sun dry it may change shape or crack...dramatically. Oh well, it was fun while it lasted. For an interesting more adult playdough for kids you might want to introduce them to safe molding clays and plasters.
See also *POTTERY MAKING KIT, SCULPTURE MAKING KIT*   **FREE**

Imaginarium

A great source of kid's stuff geared to expand the educational growth and creative imagination for babies on up to 15-year-olds. 69 stores throughout the country that pride themselves on carrying products of a non-violent nature. All Imaginarium stores carry a kid's library with their popular and current top-10 best-selling books, cassettes & videos. They even offer a book-club membership. Among the many educational products they carry, you will also find a whole bunch of fun stuff from face paints, kid's software, erector sets, animal puppets and lots lots more. You're sure to find something of interest for the little ones, and more than likely, they'll have to drag you out of there. Call Imaginarium for the store closest to your neighborhood. Imaginarium thinks so highly of their kids clientele, there is a "kids size" entrance built into every store. This unforgettable gift source gets our highest award for assisting in the responsible, positive growth of our next generation.
IMAGINARIUM   **800-765-TOYS**

Jewelry for Kids

Kids love jewelry, especially girls. It's as simple as that. For guys a simple ring, watch, masculine-looking necklace or bracelet is about all they'll wear when it comes to jewelry. For girls, they can never get enough and the options and styles are virtually endless. Know their tastes and try to figure out what they would like and appreciate the most. Below we've listed a few ideas for you to keep in mind and to stimulate your own ideas...and stick to the ears if piercing.

EAR PIERCING WITH DIAMOND STUD   TOE RING
PEARL NECKLACE / BRACELET   TURQUOISE
SIGNET / ENGRAVED RING   WATCHES of all kinds
COSTUME JEWELRY OF ALL KINDS   A COOL PENDANT
FRIENDSHIP BRACELET (leather, cotton, horse hair, beaded)
GOLD or SILVER RING, CHAIN, NECKLACE, BRACELET, ANKLET, EARRINGS

JOHNSON SMITH CO.   813-747-2356

things you never knew existed catalog, friends forever, sweetheart & best friends pendants **$8,** 10 million year old shark tooth pendant **$9,** Indian bead set **$10,** secret compartment ring **$10,** other pendants **$7 - $15**

JEWELRY MAKING KIT

For a little girl especially, this gift idea can fill their days with hours and hours of creative fun. She'll be able to outfit the whole family and neighborhood with her stunning creations. A gift that stimulates a young mind's curiosity, creativity and imagination is a gift second to none.

JEWELRY MAKER'S SOURCE BOOK   800-366-2218

jewelry making supplies

INDIAN JEWELRY SUPPLY CO.   505-722-4451

precious metals, semi-precious stones, shells, coral & equipment

KIDS STUFF : THE BIG 4

How would you like to never fight the toy store crowds again around Christmas time while shopping for that youngster? It's becoming more difficult to find something unique they won't lose interest in within the first 30 seconds. Let me introduce you to "The Big Four." Our selection of the greatest four kids catalogs in the world. The following is a short list of some of the more creative things they offer:

JOHNSON SMITH CO.   **813-747-2356, Fax: 813-746-7896**

MOTORIZED COIN-SEPARATING BANK $30   MILLIONAIRE'S CLUB MEMBERSHIP & CERTIFICATE $20

SLOT MACHINE / ONE-ARM BANDIT $20 - $130   3 to 4 BARREL COIN CHANGERS $22 - $27

CUSTOM STREET SIGN	$40
LIFE-LIKE HAND / LEG	$10 / $13
WORLD RECORD PAPER	
AIRPLANE KIT	$13
WORLD'S EASIEST KITE	$27
SPECIALTY PLAYING CARDS	$8
CARD SHUFFLER	$13
MAGICIAN'S COLLAPSIBLE	
TOP HAT	$25
PALM READING HANDBOOK	$13
UNDERSTANDING YOUR	
DREAMS BOOK	$13
INDIAN BEAD SET	$10
BONSAI TREE KIT	$12
CACTUS SEEDS	$2
REPLICA SHIP WRECK COINS	
(pieces-of-eight)	$28 (silver)
	$40 (gold)
10 MILLION YR OLD SHARK	
TOOTH PENDANT	$9
FLESH-EATING VENUS FLY TRAP	$5
BEER MAKING KIT (adults)	$30
LIVE SEA HORSES	$15
LIVE ANT FARM	$11
MILITARY POCKET WATCHES	$40
FLAGS: BRITISH, U.S., REBEL,	
MARINE, RUSSIAN	$15
ACTUAL FIRING CARBIDE CANONS	
(9 - 25in.)	$40 - $90
SECRET COMPARTMENT RING	$26
DETECTIVE'S BOOK CAMERA	$10
BIONIC EAR LSTNING DVISE	$115
REPLICA BADGES	$5
PERSONALIZED LOVE SONG	$14
SPORTS CARDS, COLLECTIBLES	
& MEMORABILIA	$7 - $130
NGHT VSION SCOPE	$300 - $1300
JELLY BELLY 40-FLAVOR BOX	$13

COUNTERFEIT MONEY	$3
GAG GIFTS	$1.50 on up
PHARAOH PENDANT	$50 - $300
FORTUNE TELLING CARDS	$9
MAGIC TRICKS AND KITS	$5 - $40
TRICK / MARKED CARDS	$8
CHINESE MAGIC BOX	$4
LUCKY POCKET COIN	$2
ENCYCLOPED. OF CARD TRCKS	$8
HOW TO HYPNOTIZE BOOK	$8
GIGANTIC VEGETABLE SEEDS	$10
FAMOUS VENTRILOQUIST	
FIGURES	$40 - $90
ACTUAL METEORITE / MOON	
ROCK	$8
COINS OF A DIFFERENT SHIP	
WRECK	$15
COIN SETS	$15 - $20
2000 YR OLD ANCIENT ROMAN	
COIN	$30
WINE MAKING KIT (adults)	$25
FLUORESCENT BLACK LIGHT	$28
LIVE SEA MONKEYS	$11
UNDERCOVER MANUAL	$12
ARMY SURVIVAL MANUAL	$10
SPECIAL FORCES HANDBOOK	$12
HANDCUFFS	$7 - $35
SWEETHEART PENDANTS	$15
FRIENDS FOREVER PENDANT	$8
WHERE THERE'S A WILL THERE'S	
A WAY VIDEO	$90
30 - POWER TELESCOPE	$20
CAMBRIDGE I.Q. TEST	$10
DOCTOR'S STETHOSCOPE	$13
SECRET BOOK SAFE	$3
HOW TO CONSTRUCT SECRET	
HIDING PLACES GUIDE	$10

SHOPPERS ADVANTAGE   800-TEL-SHOP
best buys on name brand products

TRAIN SET:	$29	RADIO FLYER WAGONS:	$15 - $49
COMIC BOOK SETS:	$15	BASEBALL CARD PACKAGES:	$29
WALKIE TALKIE SET:	$12	THE SINGING MACHINE:	$69
KIDS SIZE PING-PONG:	$69	ROLLER HOCKEY TABLE:	$69
KIDS SIZE POOL TABLE:	$69	KIDS SIZE FURNITURE:	$29 - $100
DOLL HOUSE:	$59	ROCKING HORSES:	$27 - $49
KTCHEN CENTER FOR KIDS:	$57	KIDS SIZE ACTION WORKSHOP	$39

SPORTING GOODS
CD-ROM & MULTI-MEDIA KITS
MUSICAL INSTRUMENTS
LARGE & SMALL TOYS

CAMERAS & PHOTO EQUIPMENT
ELECTRONIC GAMES - SEGA, GAME
BOY, NINTENDO, GENESIS
GAME CARTRIDGES & ACCESSORIES

BRAINSTORMS   800-621-7500
all kinds of great kids stuff from educational toys, books, games & crafts, gag gifts, fun & funny fashions, do-it-yourself kits and lots more

PICTURE FRAME WITH SOUND		LAVA LAMPS	$40
RECORDER	$20	"MINDTRAP" PARTY IN A BOX	$30
ALBERT: THE TALKING ROBOT		FACE PAINTING KIT	$17
TEACHES MATH & READING	$30	SOAP MAKING KIT	$11
BUBBLE MAKING KIT: MAKES		CANDLE MAKING KIT	$14
6 FOOT BUBBLES	$10	BUILD A TELEPHONE KIT	$25
NIGHT SKY STAR STENCIL		ROCK TUMBLER	$37
FOR THE ROOM	$20	ELECTRONICS KITS	$15 - $50
BRAIN QUEST GAME SERIES		ROBOT KITS	$15 - $50
FOR GRADES 1 - 7	$10	CRYSTAL GROWING KITS	
HOME REMEDIES / FAMILY			$17 - $30
HEALTH BOOKS	$20 - $70	HARD BOUND BOOK KIT - WRITE &
CAST-A-HAND MOLDING KIT		ILLUSTRATE YOURSELF	$25
	$17 - $28	CARTOONING KIT	$15
DRAWING KIT WITH		PAPER MAKING KIT	$23
INSTRUCTIONAL VIDEO	$15	VENUS FLY TRAP	$6
ENVIRONMENTAL KITS	$19 - $30	SCIENCE KITS	$16 - $60
WORM ACRES: WORM FARM	$37	PASTA MAKER	$30
FREEZE-DRIED SPACE SNACKS	$3	SCIENCE & CHEMISTRY	
LIVE FROG HATCHING KIT	$16	KITS	$13 - $120
THE COMPLETE HANDBOOK OF			
SCIENCE FAIR PROJECTS	$13		

PLAY FAIR TOYS   800-824-7255

PLAY TEPEES	$50 - $190	CHILDREN'S ART PORTFOLIOS $20
ELECTRONIC ROCK TUMBLER	$40	CHEMISTRY SET $30
COIN COLLECTOR'S STARTER		ROAMING ROBOT KIT $18
SET	$16	DEALING WITH FEELINGS BOOKS
WOODEN WORKBENCH WITH		SET OF 3 $18
TOOLS	$70	GERMAN MADE KETTCAR GO-CART
CAPSELA MOTORIZED SCIENCE		$200
KIT (BUILDS 30 MODELS)	$60	WOODWORKING KIT $30
POGO STICK	$28	VIDEO SWIM LESSONS $25
TOY BOXES	$25 - $80	SAND BOX $60
TOTS TRAMPOLINE	$250	

PERSONAL CREATIONS   800-326-6626
lots of great personalized stuff, toys & accessories for kids & babies

ANIMAL TOWN   800-445-8642
toys, novelties, games, puzzles, books & recordings for all ages

BACK TO BASIC TOYS   800-356-5360
raggedy ann dolls, lincoln logs, lionel trains, tinker toys, radio flyer
wagons, Disney classics, science sets, telescopes, play-in doll houses and
other great classic toys

CONSTRUCTIVE PLAYTHINGS   800-448-7830
toys novelties, games, puzzles, books, sports & fitness equip. & more

JUST FOR KIDS   800-443-5827
dolls, games, books, stuffed animals, science kits, building blocks, party
items and traveling games

WORLD WIDE GAMES   800-243-9342
casino games, outdoor games, kites & games from worldwide sources

R.E.A.L.IZMS   614-898-5464
skateboards, bicycles, skates, unicycles, mini-cars, pogo sticks, high-tech
games, dinosaurs, dolls, educational toys & lots more

F.A.O. SCHWARZ   800-426-TOYS
the world famous toy department store found in most major cities
Known for the "animals & toys" window display each year around
Christmas

See also *IMAGINARIUM*

Magic Kit

Timeless entertainment and curious fun for any youngster. I think it
was mandatory that everyone got a magic kit growing up...and
weren't we good at it? Half the pieces disappeared within a week.

Lost, I think is the correct word. I still remember a couple of great card tricks though. It may not influence your little one to become the next Hudini or David Copperfield, but it's fun. What more needs to be said?

$18 - $100 +

ABRACADABRA   **908-805-0200**
trick cards, vanishing cane, floating tricks, rings, ropes, magic hat a n d much more

JOHNSON SMITH CO.   **813-747-2356**
things you never knew existed catalog, magic kits, tricks, gag gifts and much more

MAGIC BY BRUCE CHADWICK   **817-927-0581**
custom illusions & transporting cases

MECCA MAGIC   **201-429-7597**
magic trick, ventriloquism, juggling, make-up, clown, puppet supplies

WHEELER-TANNER ESCAPES - accessories for escape artsts **406-453-4961**

KEN'S ILLUSIONARIUM   **604-875-9712**
magic, clown, juggler, puppeteer, ventriloquist stuff

MASTERCRAFT PUPPETS - hand-crafted puppets   **800-762-4514**

MECCA MAGIC   **201-429-7597**
puppet, juggling, clown supplies, magic tricks, theatrical make-up

MARIONETTE THEATRE

The most action-packed Schwartzeneggar film or hi-tech special FX will still not diminish the enjoyment of this timeless entertainment. Usually for kids under about 10 and over 35. May be hard to find in your area. Check local entertainment guide for kids or ask around.

FREE - $5 / person

METAL DETECTOR

A gift often overlooked, but something one should have at least once in their lifetime. Kids and old men seem to be fascinated with its discoveries and stick with it the longest. The rest of us seem to get board in about a half hour if we haven't found a rare coin or a diamond ring or something.

$45 - $100's

TESORO - metal detector catalog   **800-528-3352**

WHITE'S ELECTRONICS - metal detector catalog   **800-547-6911**

HEARTLAND AMERICA - metal detector **$100**   **800-229-2901**

KELLY COMPANY - metal detector distributer   **800-327-9697**

METAL DETECTORS OF MINNEAPOLIS   **800-876-8377**

D & K PROSPECTING HEADQUARTERS **800-542-4653**
metal detectors, prospecting equipment and supplies
HOUSE OF TREASURE HUNTERS **619-286-2600**
metal detectors and gold prospecting equipment
C & C DETECTORS - metal detectors **800-356-6636**

MINIATURE GOLF

...Is always a sure fire hit. A couple hours of guaranteed fun for the whole family, group of friends, co-workers, or kids. Many miniature golf courses also have a video arcade and other fun stuff available. Leave your #4 wood at home. Bring your putter if you wish. Check your area directory for local listings. **$6 - $12 / round**

MOVIE THEATRE GIFT CERTIFICATE

For kids or anyone, a series of tickets to their favorite movie theatre chain is easy, inexpensive and always appreciated. Many theatres sell gift certificates in the form of "movie money." A booklet of bills that can be used to buy their movie tickets, popcorn, Junior Mints or whatever. Check out your local theatre or theatre chain near you.

$15 / set of tickets
MOVIE MONEY: $20 on up

MUSICAL INSTRUMENT / EQUIPMENT

This gift should be left alone or be left up to the parents unless the child is impassioned with music or a particular instrument, or at least has an interest there. All in all, it's a terrific gift with the potential of shaping a young mind as well as their future. I often wish my parents had involved me in the musical arts at a young impressionable age and encouraged me to stick with it. With this list of instruments, keep in mind what the child's wants, needs, and desires are...and also what the parents can tolerate, especially the DRUMS. Keep costs down if for the beginner. One can always upgrade if they stick to it long enough. Look for a good used instrument in the local papers, music store or even a pawn shop.

DRUMS **$50 - $100's**
BONGO DRUMS

GUITAR	**$35 (used) - $100's (new)**
HARMONICA	**$5 and up**
KEYBOARD / PIANO / SYNTHESIZER	**$100 up to 1,000's**
TRUMPET	**$35 - $250**
SAXOPHONE	**$35 - $560**

THE MUSIC STAND - performing arts gifts — **802-295-7044**

ANYONE CAN WHISTLE — **800-435-8863**
unique musical instruments

SIGNAL'S - falling rain nature chimes — **800-669-9696**

AKRON MUSIC - keyboards, amps, drums, guitars — **800-962-3152**

SHOPPERS ADVANTAGE — **800-TEL-SHOP**
best buys on name brand products, electronic keyboards: **$79 - $249,** guitar: **$169,** trumpet & wind instruments: **$160 - $180,** electronic drums **$55,** singing machine: **$55**

SAM ASH MUSIC - discounted music equipment — **800-472-6274**

CAVIN - guitars, amps, mixers, mics, other instruments — **800-854-2235**

GIARDINELLI BAND INSTRUMENT CO. - brass, winds, more **800-288-2334**

KENNELLY KEYS MUSIC - discounted music instruments — **800-426-6409**

ST. CROIX KITS — **800-439-9120**
kits for harps, guitars, banjos, bag-pipes and more

THOROUGHBRED MUSIC — **800-800-4654**
keyboards, electronics, drum machines and accessories

YAMAHA MUSIC CORP. - electronic keyboards — **800-541-6514**

ZETA SYSTEMS - electronic guitars, violins and more — **800-622-6434**

TALKING OWNER'S MANUAL — **800-492-9999**
electronic keyboard & "Rapping" accessories, videos, tapes by Casio

See also *ELECTRONIC KEYBOARD / SYNTHESIZER*

NAVAL MUSEUM

No, this is not a museum of famous people's navals. This is our creative gift suggestion for those people living close to or visiting a naval port-of-call. There, you can usually find a battle ship, aircraft carrier and their aircraft, a submarine, or smaller vessels to explore and learn about. Make a day out of it with the whole family. You'll find it just as fascinating as your kids, really. **Free - $12**

PAINT GUN

A Paint Gun is a hand gun or rifle that shoots CO_2-propelled balls of paint that splatter upon impact. Definitely not for every kid as particular care and/or supervision must be taken. They can be very messy and can cause pain or injury. Check the warning and recommended age limit. They can be purchased at most major sporting goods stores. In some areas "war games" have become very popular and have been organized throughout the community for kids as well as adults. Some businessmen take this as a very serious weekend activity complete with fatigues and camouflage paint. When struck in simulated combat, there's no denying whether you've been hit or not by the paint splatter somewhere on your body. **$45 - $186**

PHOTOGRAPHY BAG

Wrap up together in a nice gift box or camera bag a person's first, or at least a new camera, a couple rolls of film, a photo album and any other accessories you can think of. The photographs they take at an early age will be fond memories to look back on as they pleasantly thumb through their first photo album later in life. They may not remember who gave them the gift that gave them all of these wonderful memories...but then again, maybe they will. For the hobby or photography enthusiast, giving a gift such as this allows them to express and develop their creativity. Hobbies often turn into careers...very successful careers. You just might be responsible for creating the next Helmut Newton or Avedon. As the say, "Do what you love and money will follow."   **$40 - $100's**

ABNER'S BY MAIL - camera equipment & accessories   **800-446-4148**
CAMERA WORLD   **800-634-0556**
    photo equipment for still, movie, video & underwater photography
47TH STREET PHOTO - photography / video equipment   **800-221-7774**
HELIX - camera, video, underwater video equipment   **800-621-6471**
PORTER'S CAMERA STORE - photo equipment, novelties   **800-553-2001**
ZONE VI STUDIOS - photo equipment & accessories   **800-457-1114**
SHOPPERS ADVANTAGE   **800-TEL-SHOP**
    best buys on name brand products, including photo equipment & accessories   cameras: **$39 - $359**
See also *POLAROID CAMERA & FILM*

POLAROID CAMERA & FILM

Getting a child started in the world of photography can be almost as enjoyable for you as it is for them. Watch their curiosity and excitement grow with the new power they now hold in their hot little hands. Exposing them to life's possibilities at an early age allows their artistic as well as their practical skills and desires develop. By the time they are of age to enter the working world, they may already know where their passions and desires lie, or at the very least they'll be better prepared. You can find a competitively priced polaroid camera at electronic, appliance, and camera stores. Be sure to throw in a couple of batteries and packets of film. Also, don't forget this idea as part of a gift package. A great accessory for any travel package, entertainment package, party, etc.   **$28 - $150**

See also *PHOTOGRAPHY GIFT PACKAGE*

THE PUBLISHED CHILD

What could be a better confidence builder or more motivating for a child than to be published in a magazine. Give to them this wonderfully powerful gift of education, creative expression and positive personality development. There are several kid's magazines for kids created by kids that accept stories, poems, artwork, photography, other written works and more for publication. Great for a child's self-esteem, creativity and knowledge. Keep in mind that the submissions to these publications can be many and highly competitive, but don't let this discourage you or your youngster. Most submitted pieces will receive positive feedback whether or not it is accepted for publication.

SKIPPING STONES   **503-342-4956**
   children's magazine accepting art, photos and writings from children for publication   **$18 / year**

STONE SOUP - ages 4-12   **800-447-4569**
   publishes children's stories and poems   **$23 / year (5 issues)**

MERLIN'S PEN - 6-12 graders   **800-247-2027**
   accepts stories, artwork, poetry, essays, reviews & more from 6th - 12th-graders for publishing   **$19 / year (4 issues)**

CREATIVE KIDS - ages 8-14   **800-998-2208**
   accepts photographs, plays, cartoons, interviews, book reviews, creative writing & artwork from children for publishing   **$20 / year (4 issues)**

THE RANGER RICK MAGAZINE AND NATURE CLUB MEMBERSHIP

Give to the special child on your list a gift of educational nature, through The National Wildlife Federation. The Ranger Rick Magazine is a wonder-filled nature magazine for kids 6-12. With a subscription the youngster will automatically become an official member of the Ranger Rick Nature Club. For youngsters 3-5 they have the always fun and entertaining magazine, Your Big Backyard.

THE NATIONAL WILDLIFE FEDERATION - membership   **800-432-6564**
Ranger Rick Magazine (12 issues): **$15 / year**
Your Big Backyard, for ages 3-5 (12 issues): **$12 / year**

RARE COIN / COIN COLLECTION

A child may not know the materialistic value of such investments, but, for them, to possess and to hold something in their hands that came from the 1800's or earlier is a fascinating notion. Teach them to hold on to it and to protect it, so that it may increase in value for as long as they wish to keep it. Create a story around it. Let them know that the coin was passed on from bank robber to bank robber in the old west, until it found its way into your Great Grandfather's pocket after one of these lowly robbers tried to stand up to him...or perhaps a golden doubloon from a sunken pirate ship...or something like that. You get the idea. A child's imagination will run wild with the thought of where this coin has been as they actually hold it in their hands. Take a trip into your local coin shop for something just right.   **$10 - $100's**

U.S. Franklin Mint   **800-523-7622**
THE WASHINGTON MINT - rare limited collectable coins   **800-926-MINT**
INTERNATIONAL COINS AND CURRENCY   **800-451-4463**
BLANCHARD - America's rare coin firm   **800-877-7633**
U.S. MINT BUREAU   **301-436-7400 415-556-6704**
    mint and proof sets, commemorative coins   **$8 - $12.50 / set**
    1/2 dollar - $5 commemorative coins in silver and gold   **$9.50 - $485**
BUREAU OF PRINTING AND ENGRAVING   Order processing center
P.O. Box 371594, Pittsburgh, PA 15250-7594
U.S. paper currency, in uncut sheets right from the printing press (frames available)   4 to 32 notes / sheet: **$10.25 to $46 (1-dollar bills)**
$14.75 - $78 (2-dollar bills)

JOHNSON SMITH CO. 813-747-2356
things you never knew existed catalog, old coins, mint sets, sunken treasure coins and much more
GOLDEN EAGLE COIN AND JEWELRY - rare gold coins 800-735-1311
SEVEN SEAS TRADING CO - Mike Dunigan 800-433-3715
pieces-of-eight, spanish treasure cobbs in jewelry and other rare coins from ship wrecks around the world
SOUTH PARK COINS - U.S. accumulation program 214-226-4277
you'll receive rare, high-quality, hand-picked U.S. coins **$25 / month**
COINAGE MAGAZINE - coins, knowledge, sources, etc. 805-643-3664
See also *U.S. MINT / PRINTING & ENGRAVING BUREAUS, SUNKEN TREASURE*

RC - REMOTE CONTROL STUFF

...Cars, planes, boats, and helicopters are always enjoyable gifts for kids, or grown-ups alike. There are some very serious clubs and organizations relating to these hobbies comprised primarily of adults. For some individuals, thousands and thousands of dollars have been invested into the hobby. These remote control miniatures of modern transportation have become quite sophisticated and are guaranteed to bring hours and hours of enjoyment...until it makes a crash landing, or finds a brick wall. You won't find the better quality ones in a toy store. Check out the local hobby shop. Other fun stuff include rockets, kites, model trains, and slot cars among a store full of other good ideas. **$166 - $1000**
MODEL EXPO INC.
AMERICA'S HOBBY CENTER 212-675-8922
model airplanes, radio control stuff and more
HOBBY SHACK - radio control equipment & accessories 800-854-8471
WALT'S HOBBY - radio control kits for cars 315-453-2291
ROBBE MODEL SPORT 908-359-2115
radio-control model airplane kits, gliders, helicopters and more
LESLIE'S SWIMMING POOL SUPPLIES 800-537-5437
radio-control sub, yacht, hydrofoil, jet boats **$40 - $150**
See also *HIGH PERFORMANCE KITES*

REMOTE CONTROL GLIDER

Not exactly a new idea, although the glider industry has enjoyed increasing success for over a decade now. Perhaps the most popular item in your local hobby store, they can range dramatically in price, performance ability and skill level, not to mention size. If they're a novice, start them off with an easy learning, inexpensive model. By the next gift-giving occasion, they'll be hinting around for that more expensive upgrade. Most remote control pilots get hooked and soon they'll have a whole room of gliders and planes hanging from the ceiling. You're local hobby store can be a great source of creative gifts from workable rockets, remote control helicopters, kites, do-it-yourself-models of all kinds and much more.   **$56 - $600**

AMERICA'S HOBBY CENTER   **212-675-8922**
          model airplanes, radio control stuff and more
HOBBY SHACK - radio control equipment & accessories   **800-854-8471**
ROBBE MODEL SPORT   **908-359-2115**
          radio control model airplane kits, gliders, helicopters and more

Rock / Stone Polishing Kit

Rock collecting sounds like a pretty dumb hobby...something a nerdy kid down the street did when you were growing up, but what you see on the surface is not always what you get. Rock hounding / collecting is taken very seriously by older enthusiasts as well as young. After a particular rock has gone through the polishing process, it emerges a beautiful swan, so to speak. Malachite, jade, opal, ruby and even diamond as well as other less precious stones sometimes look just like an ordinary rock or stone...until its mechanically polished. Even rocks in your own backyard will amaze you after they've gone through this polishing process. Mother of pearl (abalone, clams, scallops and other sea shells) too are a highly prized possession after the polishing process, often being turned into semi-expensive jewelry. Many of the nature, rock and shell stores that have these semi-precious stones and shells of brilliant colors and smooth surfaces are a result of this polishing process. A great gift to start any kid with curiosity, or adult for that matter, in this fascinating hobby.

BOURGET BROTHERS   **800-828-3024**
          rock-polishing equipment and jewelry-making supplies
EDMUND SCIENTIFIC CO.   **609-547-8880**
          rock polishers and much much more   **$80 - $225**
CONTEMPO LAPIDARY - beads, bead-stringing supplies   **800-356-2441**

CHARBONNEAU'S LAPIDARY SERVICE   **4020 Bow Trail, SW, Calgary**
rock polishing supplies   **Alberta, Canada**
ALPHA SUPPLY   **206-377-5629**
jewelry-making, prospecting and rockhounding equipment and supplies
GRAVES CO. - rockhounding / polishing equipment   **800-327-9103**

SCIENCE FAIR

For the logical youngster fascinated with science, astronomy, engineering or electronics there is a mountain of gadgets and other interesting, neat stuff out there. From lasers, robotics and put-it-together-yourself electronics to telescopes, microscopes and rock polishers. Given the equipment and supplies, a curious youngster might make for themselves an early career...or at least a brighter, more intelligent future. Be sure the child is of the right age and whatever is given to them is safe and/or used under supervision.

EDMUND SCIENTIFIC CO.   **609-547-8880**

MICROSCOPES	TELESCOPES	WEATHER BALLOONS
ROBOTS	LASERS	ELECTRIC MOTORS
LAB EQUIPMENT	MAGNETS	SOLAR ELECTRONICS
VOLCANOS	OPTICS	GEOLOGISTS MATERIALS
ROCK POLISHERS	AND MUCH MORE	

BRAINSTORMS   **800-621-7500**
brainstorms, science, anatomy and electronics products & kits

Lifescience lab kit: experiments in 12 sciences	**$37**
"10 science labs in one" kit	**$35**
educational solar energy kit	**$16**
Smithsonian world of nature set	**$30**
Earthlab: environmental kit	**$19**
world's safest chemistry set	**$60**
The complete handbook of science fair projects	**$13**
set of 12 science activity kits	**$13 / each, $120 / set**

HUBBARD SCIENTIFIC CO.   **800-323-8368**
science equipment & supplies for life, earth, physical science, energy experiments, health & physiology projects

INFORMATION UNLIMITED   **800-221-1705**
amazing, fascinating devices, plans, kits and products for hobby, science & education, including books, lasers, listening devises, solar energy, night vision, security, neon & neon car kits and more

RADIO SHACK   **817-390-3700**
science kits, electronics accessories, computers and more

HEATH CO.   **800-44-HEATH**
   practical kits for kids of all ages including computers, robots, TV sets,
   home convenience gadgets, security & educational projects

THE SINGING MACHINE

As with the computer revolution, music equipment is constantly
being updated, decreasing in price and size, while increasing in
quality and versatility. Following on the tail of the Karoke craze are
affordable at home participation entertainment systems that combine
your favorite tunes, karaoke videos with lyrics, and of course a
microphone. There are several different variations being put out on
the market by different companies at a reasonable prices. Do a little
research, fire your band, fire your singing coach and take your
singing machine on the road.   **$70 - $100's**
TALKING OWNER'S MANUAL   **800-492-9999**
   the "Rapping" machine & kit by Casio
SHOPPERS ADVANTAGE   **800-TEL-SHOP**
   best buys on name brand products,   the singing machine: **$70**

SKI SEASON PASS

If you know of a friend, relative or youngster who is an avid skier
(30 days or more a year) and are lucky enough to live within driving
distance of a ski resort, this can be a costly, but unparalleled gift.
There's nothing more important to the ski addict than getting those
runs in. If you're a parent, you'll be giving yourself plenty of free
time around the holidays and weekends as your kids enjoy your gift
day after day.   **$250 - $1200**
See also SKI LIFT TICKETS

SOCK PUPPETS

A simple homemade gift for kids of the right age. Use your creativity
and imagination to make some faces on some new or used socks.
Attach or draw distinctive eyes, mouth, and nose. Sew on a hat or
hair. Make a few distinct different characters and give them names.
Your natural acting ability will make the gift a complete success.
                                                 FREE - $5

SPORT CASSETTE-RADIO & HEADPHONES

...or Walkman, as they're more commonly referred to, is a great gift for any person, especially a child who is just starting to explore the world of popular music. Throw in a couple of tapes they might like...but try to avoid classical music for now. They might not appreciate it. One that's competitively priced can be found at an electronic or appliance warehouse or even swapmeets. You might not want to invest a large amount of money the first time around as even the best ones have a tendency to break under less than extreme conditions. If you're a parent buying for a child you might want to establish some ground rules such as when and where they are allowed to use it and even what type of music they can listen to. Can make a terrific part of many gift packages. **$19 - $180**

SHOPPERS ADVANTAGE **800-TEL-SHOP**
　　　best buys on name brand products　　personal stereos: **$20 - $119**
See also SPORT BAG, HEALTH CLUB GIFT PACKAGE

TELESCOPE

Give to someone the magic of the universe. The moon, planets, distant galaxies, colorful nebula, the solar system and thousands of other fascinating objects can now be within their eye sight.

$70 - $440 and up
EDMUND SCIENTIFIC CO. **609-547-8880**
　　　science products, microscopes to telescopes
JOHNSON SMITH CO. **813-747-2356, Fax: 813-746-7896**
　　　things you never knew existed catalog, 30 power telescope **$20**
ORION TELESCOPE CENTER - telescopes and accessories **800-447-1001**
HEARTLAND AMERICA - telescope: **$100** **800-229-2901**
COSMIC CONNECTIONS - telescopes and accessories **800-634-7702**
UNIVERSITY OPTICS - telescopes and accessories **800-521-2828**

A TENT

...and **camping equipment**. You don't need to have plans to go camping in the near future to give a little girl or boy a tent with all the amenities. As far as they're concerned, you've given them a home away from home...a portable fort. They'll set it up right there in the backyard and live there permanently if they didn't have to come in to eat once in a while. On summer nights it can bring kids of the right age many evenings of thought-filled, star-gazing, story-telling, safe adventures...right in their own backyard. A good tent can be found at any camping, sporting goods store, or larger discount chain. **$35 - $250**

CAMPMOR - camping and clothing catalog   **201-445-5000**
KELLY'S - camping / backpacking catalog   **800-69-KELLY**
ALL OUTDOORS MOUNTAIN EQUIPMENT   **800-624-1466**
L.L. BEAN - tents, backpacks, boats and much more   **800-221-4221**
CAMPING WORLD   **800-626-5944**
FLAGHOUSE CAMPING EQUIPMENT   **800-221-5185**
DAK INDUSTRIES - tents and much more   **800-325-0800**
     two, three and six-men tents   **$100 - $200**
SIERRA TRADING POST   **307-775-8000**
     name brand, discount outdoor clothing & equip.   **tents: $153 - $280**
FINGERHUT   **4404 Eight St N, St Cloud Minnesota 56395**
     Santa Fe 9' X 12' cabin tent, $129
See also ***CAMPING SURVIVAL PACK, GREAT EXPLORER GIFT PACKAGE***

TEPEE MAKING KIT

Don't waste your time trying to find this gift idea at your local toy or hardware store. It won't be there. Take the time and use your imagination to put this gift together yourself. Include all the appropriate materials - wooden poles or posts, a large canvas sheet or other material, twine, rope or some other strong fastening cord. Remember, the Indians didn't use nails. Create your own design instructions for the youngsters to follow and let them put it together themselves. Be sure to supervise and test the structure for strength and safety. We wouldn't want anybody to get hurt.   **$25 - $100**

WESTERN TEPEE - children's play tepee **$160 - $240**   **307-587-6707**
PLAY FAIR TOYS   **800-824-7255**
     all kinds of toys: big, little, outdoor, indoor, educational and more
     huge 12' tepee, sleeps 4 adults: **$190**
     5' indoor / outdoor tepee: **$50 (add $10 for name personalizing)**
See also ***FORT***

THEME PARKS, ATTRACTIONS & ADVENTURES

...Are a great gift for kids of any age...and most adults for that matter. Most any theme park across the country is a sure fire hit. Bring along their best friend, brother, or sister and be prepared for an exhausting, fun-filled...exhausting day. Most of the parks also offer season passes. You might not see the kids all summer...how awful.

$15 - $35 / person
$75 - $300 Season Pass

DISNEYLAND - Aneheim, CA	714-999-4565
Walt Disney Travel Co.	714-520-5050
BUSCH GARDENS - Tampa Bay, FL	813-987-5171
KNOTTS BERRY FARM - Buena Park, CA	714-220-5200
SIX FLAGS MAGIC MOUNTAIN - Valencia, CA	818-367-5965
SIX FLAGS OVER GEORGIA - Atlanta	404-948-9290
SEA WORLD OF TEXAS - San Antonio	512-523-3630
SEA WORLD - San Diego, CA	619-939-6212
SESAME PLACE - Longhorne, Pennsylvania	215-752-7070
UNIVERSAL STUDIOS - Universal City, CA	818-777-3750
- Orlando, FL	407-363-8000
MARINE WORLD AFRICA USA - Vallejo, CA	707-643-ORCA
WALT DISNEY WORLD FLORIDA - Orlando	407-W-DISNEY
OPRYLAND USA - Nashville, TN	615-889-6611
HERSHEYPARK - Hershey, Pennsylvania	800-HERSHEY
MGM GRAND ADVENTURES - Las Vegas	800-929-1111
PARAMOUNT'S KINGS DOMINION - Doswell, VA	804-876-5000
VIRTUAL WORLD - virtual reality theme park	San Diego: 619-294-9200

Chicago: 312-836-5977, Walnut Creek: 510-988-0700

See also *WILDLIFE EXPERIENCE, ZOO, MOVIE STUDIO TOUR, WATERPARK*

TOY STORE / HOBBY SHOP GIFT CERTIFICATE

When all else fails...A gift certificate to a child's favorite toy store or hobby shop is unsurpassed for getting them exactly what they want. It's an adventure for them roaming up and down the aisles looking for that perfect gift with their name on it. Give them the dollar amount set on the certificate and believe me they'll be within pennies of that limit (not including tax - they don't believe in tax at their age). With a child's limited appreciation of the gift-giving process, I think it's a gift far more appreciated than a random shot in the dark.

$10 - $100 +

TRAIN RIDE

Like a plane trip, a train ride will fascinate the youngster. From the engineers and engine, the caboose, to the ever changing countryside, they'll be in awe of their miniature train set come-to-life. For an adult, a train ride traveling the coastline, through the countryside, across the Americas, through the Rockies, or in some exotic land can be romantic, exhilarating, and inspiring, rekindling that childlike wonderment from within. Amtrak, America's only national train service, offers short day trips to first-class long distance runs at prices that run cheaper than air fares. Check out some of these nostalgic, majestic trains across the country and around the world.

RAILWAYS - travel publication   **818-500-0542**

AMTRAK - 800-872-7245   **$35 - $100's**

VIA RAIL   **416-366-8411 800-561-9181**
> Canadian rail, restored, stainless steel train cars from the 50's, travels between Vancouver and Toronto   **$230 - $1600 (3 nights)**

SILVERTON TRAIN - an 1882 adventure   **303-247-2733**
> travel through the Rockys from Durango to Silverton, Colorado (May thru October) Durango to Cascade Canyon, WY   **$37-$63**

RAIL EUROPE   **800-659-5028**

ALASKA RAILROAD CORP.   **800-544-0552**

THE ORIENT EXPRESS   **800-524-2420**
> leaves 2 times / week from London to Paris, Zurich, Insbruck & Venice
>   **$1300 - $1500 +**

THE EASTERN EXPRESS   **800-524-2420**
> Asia: Singapore to Bangkok   **$550 - $1,130 and up**

SIERRA MADRE RAIL EXCURSIONS - Copper Canyon, UT   **800-843-1060**

NORTHWEST RAIL   **P.O. Box 19342 Portland, OR 97280**
> 40's steam locomotive, travels infrequently from Portland to Klamath Falls, Oregon through the Cascade Mountains   **$180 - $240 (2 days)**

CASS SCENIC RAILROAD   **800-CALL-WVA**
> early 1900's locomotives in W. Virginia   **$5 - $25**

GETTYSBURG RAILROAD   **717-334-6932**
> 1920 & 1948 locomotives travel trough civil war country, Gettysburg, PA. Lincoln impersonator, October fall-foliage, civil war train raids
>   **$3.50 - $7**

GEORGETOWN RAILROAD   **303-670-1686 303-569-2403**
> 1920's locomotives, Georgetown, Colorado   **$1.50 - $10.50**

ST. LOUIS RAILROAD   **314-752-3148**
> 50's electric and diesel trains, runs along Mississippi   **$3 / private car**

ROARING CAMP & BIG TREES RAILROAD   **408-335-4484**

early 1900's steam locomotives, Roaring Camp to Felton, CA see a sawmill, general store, covered bridge, saloon. Other activities include chuckwagon barbecue, civil war reenactment, mountain-man rendezvous and handcar races   **$8.50 - $11.50**

VALLEY RAILROAD CO.   **800-561-9181**

1920's trains, travels up Connecticut River, Essex to Chester, can combine with steamboat ride, murder-mystery specials   **$4 - $8.50**

RAIL TRAVEL CENTER   **800-458-5394**

TROUT POND FISHING

If you've had poor luck in the past fishing in the great outdoors with son or daughter, you might want to make a quick trip to your local "private" trout pond. Here, you'll find an over abundance of trout herded into a small area that you can literally catch with an empty hook. It's a guaranteed catch on just about every cast...but you'll pay for it, usually by the pound or inch. It's worth the experience at least once to see the kids react with excitement. Check your local listings under fishing, trout, or ask around at your local bait or fishing store.   **$4 - $5 / pound**

U.S. MINT / PRINTING & ENGRAVING BUREAUS

It's not often that we mention one particular company, or agency in this case, as a gift idea source. The U.S. Mint Bureau and the Bureau of Printing & Engraving are Governmental Agencies that actually make our money. The U.S. Mint produce our coins and offer highly polished "uncirculated" and "proof" sets of coins, handsomely displayed in a case. And like an old rare coin, one of these sets of coins could start a youngster on a valuable coin collection. The bureau of Printing & Engraving also offers a few gift ideas equally as creative and interesting. This agency makes our paper money. They offer framed or unframed uncut sheets of bills right off the press in one-dollar or the more uncommon two-dollar denominations. Sorry, this is not the company that makes toilet paper rolls of hundred dollar bills. Not a useful gift, but one of those interesting fun gifts to give...and receive. The sheet of bills might also be appropriate for the graduate, the person starting a new job or someone starting a business.

U.S. MINT BUREAU 301-436-7400 415-556-6704
mint and proof sets, commemorative coins   **$8 - $12.50 / set**
1/2 dollar - 5 dollar commemorative coins in silver and gold
$9.50 - $485

BUREAU OF PRINTING AND ENGRAVING Order processing center
P.O. Box 371594, Pittsburgh, PA 15250-7594
U.S. paper currency, in uncut sheets right from the printing press (frames available) **4 to 32 notes / sheet: $10.25 to $46 (1-dollar bills)**
$14.75 - $78 (2-dollar bills)

See also *RARE COIN / COIN COLLECTION, SUNKEN TREASURE*

VIRTUAL WORLD

The future is here! Imagine yourself at the controls of a hovercraft...on the surface of a red planet or any number of other unique intergalactic delights. Be the first to introduce someone to the first digital theme park. Experience with them action and adventure in a variety of "Virtual Reality" environments.

VIRTUAL WORLD San Diego: 619-294-9200
Chicago: 312-836-5977
Walnut Creek: 510-988-0700

WALKIE-TALKIES, TWO-WAY RADIOS & CB's

A little out of date for us adults, but oh what fun the kids could have. Look into the walkie-talkies. You'll see that they've been upgraded since you were a kid. A good used CB / Ham Radio can be picked for a fair price. Just make sure the kid is old enough and responsible enough to operate this communication devise. Prices can range dramatically from a lower quality set purchased at a toy or hobby store to your professional electronics source. Check the classifieds in your local paper to find good-used electronics equipment that's more affordable.   **Walkie-Talkies & Two-Way Radios: $12 - $500 +**
CB'S: $50 and up (good used) - $300 + (new)

SHOPPERS ADVANTAGE **800-TEL-SHOP**
best buys on name brand products **walkie talkie sets: $12**
B&C COMMUNICATIONS - two-way radios **800-343-3004**
INFORMATION UNLIMITED - electronic devices **800-221-1705**
DAK INDUSTRIES - UHF radios and much more **800-325-0800**

ELECTRONIC EQUIPMENT BANK   800-368-3270
 shortwave radios and more
GATEWAY ELECTRONICS - electronics equipment 800-669-5810
HAM RADIO OUTLET   800-854-6046
 amateur ham radios, mobile units and more
HAM STATION - new / used amateur radio equipment 800-729-4373
MEMPHIS AMATEUR ELECTRONICS...and radio equipment 800-238-6168
MISSOURI RADIO EQUIPMENT   800-821-7323
 amateur radio equipment, hand-helds, remotes and more

WALL POSTER / PRINT

Kids of a certain age love to decorate their walls with their favorite person, star, hunk, babe, movie, singer, rock group, athlete...or, whatever they happen to be into that week. But, for God's sake, don't for one second think you can pick something out with your own taste. They'll reject it and find a deep dark hiding place for it as soon as the door closes behind you. Find out what they're into. Ask them or their parents...and they'll be forever greatful if you strike gold...you'll be the coolest. Good posters can be found through a good specialty, music, poster, or fine art print retailer and even some galleries, among other places. **$3 - $25 and up (without frame)**

MUSEUM OF FINE ARTS BOSTON 800-225-5592
 prints, objects de art and other gifts
APPLEJACK LIMITED EDITIONS - collectable art and prints 800-969-1171
POP POSTERS   800-666-7654
 one of the best selections for all kinds of mail-order posters
DAVIS & CO. - jewelry, prints, books and other gifts 800-876-9871
RICK'S MOVIE GRAPHICS - movie posters 800-252-0425
CINEMA CITY - all kinds of movie posters 616-722-7760
CINEMA COLLECTORS - movie posters / star photos 213-461-6516
JERRY OHLINGER'S - movie posters / star photos 212-989-0869
THE MOVIE POSTER SHOP 403-250-7588
AMERICAN ARTS & GRAPHICS 800-524-3900
 movie, giant, fun, all-star, pin-up, sports, art and photo posters
WILDLIFE ART NEWS - intl. magazine for wildlife art 800-626-0934
FINGERHUT - catalog **4404 Eight St N, St Cloud Minnesota 56395**
 MOVING PICTURE WALL LIGHT - a 17" X 14" oak framed scenic with waterfalls that appear to be actually flowing through a motorized filter mechanism **$90**

NATURE'S GALLERY 800-400-0090
  collectable fine art prints of wildlife / nature / Americana **$60 - $450**

WATERPARK

Set aside part of a day to take the little ones to a water wonderland... or, purchase a gift certificate for the person who needs a wet n' wild ride. As waterparks increase in popularity, they all try to out do each other with bigger slides, wave machines, and an endless array of other water rides and water related activities. Many of the water parks also stay open during those warm summer nights. Check your local listings for a water park close to you. **$12 - $25**

WILDLIFE EXPERIENCE

There are many wild animal parks, habitats and animal rescue centers around the country, aside from your local zoo. They have created as close to a natural environment as possible for these wild animals to be protected, studied, bread and enjoyed by the public. The animals at such a place might range from your native North American wildlife such as wolves, mountain lions and bears to the more exotic animals from around the world. A fascinating learning experience for anyone, especially kids. A nature walk in the right direction. Contact your local zoo or animal shelter and ask where you might find such a place and if they are open to the public. **FREE - $20**
See also *THE ZOO*

THE ZOO

What could be better, more wholesome, and more of a learning experience than the zoo? I don't think I've ever seen a child or an adult for that matter, that wasn't utterly fascinated with curiosity at the sight and behavior of zoo creatures. With so many of our wild animals in danger of extinction, be sure to allow your kids the opportunity to learn and respect this side of nature...and life. A positive influence such as this, has the power to shape their young lives in so many good ways. Children are our future. A great gift for anyone. **$6 - $25 / ticket**
See also *THEME PARKS, WILD ANIMAL EXPERIENCE, NATURE GIFTS*

Clients, Co-Workers...
THE BIG BOSS!

Work just so happens to be a large part of most people's lives, and in this, friendships and relationships can't help but develop in this environment. Whether you're trying to win an account, woo a secretary, bribe a boss, or enthuse your employees, we hope to provide you with more creative ideas then you'll know what to do with.

> *"We love those people who give with humility, or who accept with ease."*
>
> **FREYA STARK**

Clients, Co-Workers... THE BIG BOSS

QUICK REFERENCE LIST

BOOKS ON TAPE

...can be a wonderfully enlightening gift, for just about everyone from children to grandparents. How about the co-worker who flies, or commutes long distances...or short distances if they're stuck in traffic. An average book on tape may take anywhere between two and four hours of listening time. Imagine what could be accomplished if two hours of idle driving time were utilized, five days a week. In a year's time you could be fluent in three different languages. Also, as an ideal gift for kids, you'll find available pure enjoyment and entertainment to interest and learning. In the very near future you may find your local bookstore going through a similar transition as did music stores from LP's and tapes to CD's. Bookstores may very well become equally divided between books in print and books on tape. As of now there is limited availability on a wide variety of subjects from self-help/motivational, spy-thrillers and romance novels, to historical compilations, nostalgia and more. Mail order is a very viable source for this gift, where you'll find often times a better, more extensive collection than found at your local bookstore.

$8 - $20 + / book on tape

BOOKCASSETTE - all types of books on cassette   **800-222-3225**
BOOKS ON TAPE   **800-626-3333**
RECORDED BOOK INC.   **800-638-1304**
AUDIO EDITIONS   **800-231-4261**
      books on cassette: from mysteries to self-improvement
AUDIO DIVERSIONS - best selling books on tape   **800-628-6145**
DOVE BOOKS ON TAPE   **800-762-6662**
RECORDED BOOKS   **800-638-1304**
ADVENTURES IN CASSETTES   **800-328-0108**
      music, self-help and kids CD's & tapes
BLACKSTONE AUDIO BOOKS - catalog P.O. Box 969, Ashland, OR 97520

BUSINESS / FINANCE MAGAZINE SUBSCRIPTION

A great gift for the young businessman or businesswoman who is on their way to the top. They'll probably find more practical information from these periodicals then they did their entire college career. Don't feel limited to just business magazines. Keep in mind the person's interest or career aspirations, do a little research, find out the best trade publications and periodicals in their field of interest, then surprise them with an intelligent gift to be appreciated again and again. Start here, then look through this and other sections of this guide to complete a great start to a gift package. A great gift for graduates, entrepreneurs, workaholics and whiz kids.

MONEY	$59 / year (26 issues)	800-633-9970
FORTUNE	$57 / year (26 issues)	800-621-8000
FORBES	$57 / year (26 issues)	800-888-9896
SUCCESS	$20 / year (10 issues)	800-234-7324
INC.	$15 / year (monthly)	800-234-0999
BUSINESSWEEK	$47 / year (weekly)	800-635-1200

See also *NEWSPAPER SUBSCRIPTION*

CELLULAR / CAR PHONE

To rent or purchase...A little bit extravagant, but keep in mind that it could be a write-off under the right circumstances. For a woman, especially in a big crime-ridden city such as Los Angeles or New York, it has almost become a necessity, for fear of breaking down, or being stuck in some other compromising situation. Vital also for the man or woman on the move. This luxury item is becoming more and more affordable as prices continually drop...as seen by even a Ford Pinto sporting the familiar antenna. One helpful hint for the recipient to avoid looks of envy and disgust by all of us who hate people on their car phones, is to have the phone receiver installed in your visor. This way you can speak freely while driving safe, without anyone ever knowing you're on the phone. Again, know the person's particular needs as there are several different options both in hardware and monthly programs. Decide on either a simple car phone or a removable cellular phone. Check advertisements for deals, ask your cellular friends for their input & advice, or check your local listings under *phone companies, cellular, electronic* or *appliance dealers*.

$90 - $800 (to purchase phone)
$40 - $60 / month service (not including call charges)
monthly service: approx. $70 / month (light use, 80 minutes free)
approx. $100 / month (moderate use, 170 minutes free)
approx. $240 / month (heavy usage, 600 minutes free)

THE COMPANY STORE

Below are a few ideas for the company. If you happen to be the owner, office manager or loyal employee, the following gift ideas will bring unity, add morale and strengthen friendships. Plan well in advance for that office party, Christmas or company picnic. You'll be the star giving out these winning gifts. You'll receive more than enough reward watching everyone leave with a smile on their face with their new prized possession...either that or they're drunk. Go it alone if you feel daring enough...and have the finances, or consult a couple or few other co-workers and chip in together. You may come up with an even better idea together, while making it more affordable at the same time.

1) COMPANY FLAGS OR BANNERS - have the company name, logo, and colors beautifully designed and incorporated into a flag or banner. Make one or several. Try to capture the company's spirit and reputation. The sources listed below offer catalogs with examples and will assist you with the process.

> **NAUTICAL FLAGS - nautical / U.S. / custom flags   800-536-4002**

2) COMPANY HATS - have the company name and logo embroidered into the front of several baseball hats in a sharp design and appropriate colors.

3) COMPANY T-SHIRTS - capture the spirit of the company with a name and logo design on the front of some good quality beefy-t's in white or black. Inscribe a message on the back. Perhaps the company motto or the event taking place would be appropriate, or maybe something a little humorous. If you budget's a little bigger, have some company sweatshirts embroidered with your "team" logo.

4) COMPANY CALENDARS - remember all those great pictures from last years Christmas party or company picnic. Why not turn it into a company calendar. It'll be something everyone will treasure forever. No matter how much someone may hate their job at that time, they'll always look back at that calendar...and smile. One of life's better tricks played on us are the good memories remembered and bad memories forgotten...all through time.

See *PERSONAL CALENDAR* for more details

See *PERSONAL CALENDAR* for more details

5) COMPANY RESERVE - How about a couple of cases of company reserve. Fine wine or champagne with the company's custom label. The only bad thing about this gift idea is it's too good to drink. You're compelled to save it for posterity or something. Maybe when you get fired you won't feel so bad about drinking it...then smashing the bottle...through the company window.

See the selection of *WINERIES & FINE WINE* for more details

6) COMPANY AWARDS - employees tend to stay with companies longer if they're rewarded for their good services...even in jest. Whether you have a serious awards presentation or "fun" awards i t always turns into a smashing success allowing everyone to let their hair down (or up if it's an upscale dinner event). Company parties and events are always a welcome, needed break for everyone. It provides that second wind needed to get through another six months.

See *HONORING PLAQUE, AWARD, TROPHY* for more details

7) COMPANY PHOTO ALBUM - a great gift from the company, to the company. Organize all those company photos from past events and place them into a nice album with the company name monogrammed on the front. Leave it in the lobby for all your co-workers and clients to see. It also gives prospective clients and potential new employees an idea of the company's comradery and morale.

CUSTOM IMPRINTED BASEBALL CAPS　　　　　**800-535-5030**
For a company, group of friends, or family members: custom imprinted caps, t-shirts, aprons, jackets, tote bags, coffee mugs, pens, key chains, athletic wear, calendars, and more.　　**starting at $2 each**

PERSONAL CREATIONS　　　　　　　　**800-326-6626**
personalized and monogrammed gifts for home or office and more from desk clocks, frames, acrylic keepsakes, notebooks, stationery, travel accessories, bottles of wine and more

INITIALS - personalized / monogrammed gifts　　**800-444-8758**

THINGS REMEMBERED - engraved gifts　　　　**800-274-7367**

NAUTICAL FLAGS - nautical / U.S. / custom flags　　**800-536-4002**

HAND CARVED - yacht and estate nameboards and more　**203-642-6008**

ADVERTISING IDEAS CO.　　　　　　**800-323-6359**
luggage, desk accessories, caps, t-shirts and other promo novelties

SUPERGRAM - giant banners　　　　　**800-3-BANNERS**

GIFT SERVICES - custom corporate candies and chocolates　**800-562-4448**

AMSTERDAM PRINTING   800-543-6882
advertising novelties with custom printing
LUCKY DUCK FORTUNE COOKIES - custom fortune cookies   617-389-3583
B & F MAXAM   214-333-2111
promotional merchandise: luggage, knives, cameras, briefcases, more
BEST IMPRESSIONS CO.   815-223-6263
advertising promotions, incentives, gifts
CRESTLINE CO.   800-221-7797
badges, ribbons, buttons, portfolios, pens, gifts and other novelties
HUDSON INCENTIVES & IMPRINTS   800-942-5372
advertising novelties with custom printing
NAMARK CAP & EMBLEM CO.   800-634-6271
custom screen-printed emblems, caps, t-shirts, jackets
NOVELTIES UNLIMITED   800-647-1652
advertising novelties with custom logos
PRESTIGE PROMOTIONS   800-328-9351
pens, mugs, buttons, calendars and other novelties
SALES GUIDES   800-654-6666
promotional merchandise: pens, desk top items, foods, executive gifts, time pieces and more
N.G. SLATER CORP.   212-924-3133
advertising novelties: t-shirts, bags, pens, coins & medallions, buttons, jewelry and more
CARTOUCHE   800-AT-EGYPT
handmade pendants with your name in ancient Egyptian hieroglyphics
JOHNSON SMITH CO.   813-747-2356
things you never knew existed catalog, custom street signs   **$40**
PHOTO LOGO   800-887-3087
have any photograph printed on fun and useful products from hats, keychains and mugs to buttons and special frames   **$4 - $13 / Item**
See also **AWARDS, PLAQUES, TROPHIES, MONOGRAMMED / PERSONALIZED GIFTS**

COMPUTER SOFTWARE

...For the computer nut relative, co-worker, spouse, friend or kid, this idea is second to none. Be sure you know what their needs are as well as their system. You might want to consider a gift certificate to a software store for that person who spends an exorbitant amount of time on a computer, so that they may better pick out something for their needs. Include it in a computer gift package.   **$20 - $300**

SOME CREATIVE GIFT SOFTWARE SUGGESTIONS

ENCYCLOPEDIA	FAMILY TREE MAKER / GENEALOGY	WILL MAKER
COOKBOOK	GAMES FOREIGN LANGUAGES	EROTIC
EDUCATION	GRAPHICS VIRTUAL REALITY	BUSINESS
WINDOWS	MUSIC HOBBY	ASTROLOGY
ASTRONOMY	GAMBLING ATLAS	SPORTS
GRAMMAR	START-UP KITS...AN LOTS MORE	

TIGER SOFTWARE - 80 page catalog   **800-888-4437**

EGGHEAD SOFTWARE - computer software   **800-EGGHEAD**

COMP USA   **800-451-7638**
   DOS, windows, CD-ROM, PC's, cards, books, games, hardware, more

EDUCATIONAL RESOURCES - software and accessories   **800-624-2926**

MAC WAREHOUSE - Mackintosh software   **800-255-6227**

MAC'S PLACE - Mac computer software & accessories   **800-260-0009**

Q LABS   **800-443-6697**
   Apple business, entertainment, games, graphics, education, language

CLUB KIDSOFT'S MULTIMEDIA KID'S STORE   **800-354-6150**
   computer software / CD-ROM magazine & catalog for kids & parents -
   responsible, educationally based

SILICON EXPRESS - software, hardware accessories   **800-927-9555**
See also *CD-ROM*

EARTHQUAKE / DISASTER SURVIVAL KIT

Particularly appropriate for the California area, it's something most
people would never buy for themselves...and let's hope they never
have to thank you for it. There are different packages made for the
house, car, and business, ranging in price. If you want to get ultra-
creative, take a look at a few kits then model a homemade, less
expensive one after it. Also an appropriate, creative idea for flood,
tornado and hurricane prone areas.   **$45 - $150**

QUAKE KARE   **800-2-PREPARE**

EARTHQUAKE LADY - earthquake kits in L.A.   **310-275-8191**

EARTHQUAKE MANAGEMENT   **800-925-9744**
   kits and supplies   **$10 - $179**

THE SAFETY ZONE   **800-999-3030**
   helpful products for safety & security, for children, home, car and self
   SURVIVAL KITS: $40 - $90, HAND-HELD EMERGENCY CB (2-way radio):
   $70, FIRST AID KITS: $37, CAR EMERGENCY KIT: $60

CHC - earthquake & disaster preparedness kits   **310-477-7780**

FLOWERS, LUNCH AND THE REST OF THE DAY OFF

...with pay, for your secretary or other deserving employee. Generous perks such as these can only add to the working spirit of the individual and is guaranteed to promote a positive working atmosphere for all parties.   **$50 on up**

See *FLOWERS* for delivery services

FULLY STOCKED BRIEFCASE / ATTACHE

for the wife, husband, co-Worker, college or high school graduate ready to venture off into the working world, fill a monogrammed leather briefcase with all the appropriate accessories. If you really want to go overboard...and you're loaded...slip the briefcase into the trunk of their new car.   **$50 on up (including briefcase)**

A WALLET FILLED WITH CASH	BOOKS ON TAPE
A BEAUTIFUL ORGANIZER / DAY-PLANNER	A NICE PEN SET
A CELLULAR PHONE (OPTIONAL)	A LEATHER NOTEBOOK
NEWSPAPER / NEWSPAPER SUBSCRIPTION	BUSINESS CARDS
MAGAZINE / MAGAZINE SUBSCRIPTION	COMPUTER SOFTWARE
A WATCH / POCKET WATCH	BUSINESS SUPPLIES
INVESTMENT PORTFOLIO	STOCKS / BONDS

See *LEATHER BRIEFCASE* below for sources

HONORING PLAQUE, AWARD, TROPHY

Don't overlook this gift for adding a meaningful or humorous touch to any gift package or even by itself. Appropriate anytime for a co-worker, employee, achieving child, friend, parent or other family member. A gift that has no practical use but its purpose is great. It can give confidence, create a feeling of accomplishment, stimulate growth or simply produce a smile and a laugh. Perhaps more importantly, it will represent a lasting memory of a relationship and a place in time otherwise forgotten. Check your local directory for a trophy dealer. They'll be able to help tremendously with appropriate words, phrases and complementary style to better customize any idea you may have...That's what they do. It's their business.

CORNETTE RIBBON, TROPHY & AWARD CO.	**800-237-8930**
THINGS REMEMBERED - engraved gifts	**800-274-7367**

EMBLEM & BADGE   800-556-7466
  trophies, trophy cases, plaques, medals, pins, ribbons
JO SO CO TROPHY CO.   800-243-3428
  gavels, cups & trophies, plaques, medals, pins, ribbons
TAILOR GRAPHICS   800-777-1836
  award & recognition plaques, desk & doorplates, paperweights, brass I.D.
  plates, photo charm products, nameplates, business card cases
TROPHY SUPPLY   800-227-1557
  trophies, plaques, medals, club awards, neck medals, ribbons, pins
PERSONAL CREATIONS   800-326-6626
  personalized and monogrammed gifts
INITIALS - personalized / monogrammed gifts   800-444-8758
JOHNSON SMITH CO.   813-747-2356
  things you never knew existed catalog, horse's ass trophy   **$9**
**See *GIFT CERTIFICATES for helpful ideas and more details, COMPANY
STORE, MONOGRAMMED / PERSONALIZED GIFT***

LEATHER BRIEFCASE / ATTACHE

A nice leather briefcase falls into the same category as an organizer/
day-planner or leather notebook. Always a helpful tool for the first-
timer or as a beautiful, necessary upgrade for the briefcase veteran.
Know who you're buying for and their particular needs and tastes.
Filled with money would be a nice accessory. Have it monogrammed.
A good quality briefcase can be found through many sources
including luggage, leather and hand bag dealers. Try to avoid
department stores and other major chains for this item as the prices
have become very competitive through good wholesale outlets,
starting as low as $20.   **$20 - $250 +**
BALLY OF SWITZERLAND for MEN   212-751-9082
  men's shoe, luggage, small leather goods and accessories
CREATIVE HOUSE - attache / briefcases, luggage, wallets   800-527-5940
CROUCH & FITZGERALD - leather goods monogrammed   800-6-CROUCH
DOONEY & BOURKE - leather goods & accessories   800-243-5598
RETTINGER IMPORTING CO. - carry-alls, bags   800-526-3142
SHOPPERS ADVANTAGE   800-TEL-SHOP
  best buys on name brand products,   **4-piece leather attache set: $59**
SPORTS DYNAMICS CORP. - carry-alls, bags   800-322-DYNA
TIC-LA-DEX - attache / briefcases, pilot cases   800-827-9467
INITIALS - personalized / monogrammed gifts   800-444-8758

PERSONAL CREATIONS   **800-326-6626**
personalized and monogrammed gifts
GUCCI   **800-221-2590**
the most expensive...and perhaps the best leather goods
See also *STOCKED BRIEFCASE, LEATHER NOTEBOOK, ORGANIZER/DAY-PLANNER, MONOGRAMMED GIFTS*

LEATHER NOTEBOOK

A close relative of the organizer and the briefcase, falling somewhere in between, and can be found through many of the same sources and outlets. These beautiful notebooks are increasing in popularity and are very handy as a working file for scripts, large photographs, legal pads, etc. Most importantly it reads professionalism, class, and organization...three very important tools in the working world. Also a very nice gift to have monogrammed. The best quality notebooks can be found at art supply stores. Check also office supply, stationery, and some luggage stores.   **$45 - $195**

PERSONAL CREATIONS   **800-326-6626**
personalized and monogrammed gifts
INITIALS - personalized / monogrammed gifts   **800-444-8758**
HEARTLAND AMERICA   **800-229-2901**
soft leather portfolios, briefcases   **$80 - $90**
LEVENGER - tools for serious readers   **800-545-0242**
leather folio with monogramming   **$100**
soft leather or canvas travel briefcase   **$170 - $300**
SHOPPERS ADVANTAGE   **800-TEL-SHOP**
best buys on name brand products
4-piece leather attache set with leather notebook   **$59**
FLAX   **800-640-5641**
leather notebooks, portfolios, art supplies and much more
See also *ORGANIZER/DAY-PLANNER, MONOGRAMMED & LEATHER BRIEFCASE*

LOTTERY TICKETS

A little dry and impersonal by themselves. Can make a nice accessories or feature to any appropriate gift package. Be sure to claim your percentage before the winning ticket is announced...you just might be giving a gift worth...Ohhh...about 20 million or so.
See *GIFT PACKAGES*   **$1 and up**

MEMORY CARD

For a sick or departing co-worker, friend or family member, have everyone write a profound or touching word in a card. To get a little more creative, purchase a diary or book with blank pages. Title it, "THIS IS YOUR LIFE," and start a story either completely from imagination or exaggerate the past in good humor and let everyone add a page or paragraph. Make sure to keep the recipient the main character. Whether it's a story book, small card, or huge poster-board filled with love, kindness, and well-wishes, the recipient is likely to treasure it for years to come. **$1 - $10**

See also *CREATIVE CARDS*

MOTIVATIONAL BOOKS & TAPES

A potentially powerful gift capable of dramatically changing one's life...for the better. Not everybody's mind is so open as to receiving something of this nature. Others swear and live by it. Highly recommended...on our top ten gift idea list. Give to someone the technique of how to set goals, self-motivate, and to succeed. All you can do is provide them with the tools...It is up to them to use them. Combine a selection of motivational tapes with a good book of motivational quotes. Throw in any other accessories that may be appropriate and create a gift package geared toward the professional and their success or the individual in need of self-help.

THINK AND GROW RICH - books and tapes by Napolean Hill **Book $19**
Tapes $19 - $95

NIGHTINGALE CONANT **800-525-9000**
the greatest personal development & motivational products catalog for businessperson or anyone looking to better themselves goals / motivational / self-improvement / brain-power books, tapes, videos and more by such greats as Zig Ziglar, Anthony Robbins, Earl Nightingale, Napoleon Hill...and many others

PERSONAL POWER - Anthony Robbins **800-445-8183**
Book $19
Tapes $185
Weekend Seminars $600

SUCCESSORIES **800-535-2773**
The most attractive and powerful motivational products and visuals
GOAL QUOTES, BEST OF SUCCESS - of motivational quote books: **$6**

BOOKCASSETTE - all types of books on cassette   800-222-3225
AUDIO EDITIONS   800-231-4261
    books on cassette: from mysteries to self-improvement
ADVENTURES IN CASSETTES   800-328-0108
    music, self-help and kids CD's & tapes
RED ROSE COLLECTION   800-692-5145
    gifts to nurture the mind body & soul
GREAT QUOTES FROM GREAT WOMEN - book

NEWSPAPER SUBSCRIPTION

...will make a good part of many gift packages. For the co-worker, an industry related magazine or newspaper subscription is a vital part to anyone's career. Check your local news stands for a good selection or ask your peers for their recommendations. A fairly inexpensive gift that will stimulate interest, excitement, joy, and knowledge...day after day, month after month.

WALL STREET JOURNAL   800-568-7625
    $44 / 13 weeks, $78 / 6 months
LOS ANGELES TIMES   800-528-4637
    $42 / month (daily), $16 / month (Sundays)
WASHINGTON POST   800-627-1150
    $142 / 12 weeks (daily), $47 / 4 weeks (Sundays)
NEW YORK TIMES   800-631-2580
    $84 (daily), $49 (Sundays) / 3 months
    $154 (daily), $90 (Sundays) / 6 months
USA TODAY   800-872-0001
    $35 / 13 weeks, $65 / 6 months, $107 / year
See also *MAGAZINE SUBSCRIPTION*

ORGANIZER/DAY-PLANNER

An organizer / day-planner typically is a 3-ring, 5 1/2 x 8 1/2 leather binder filled with removable pages used for organizing your life, from daily appointments, "to do" lists, your personal phone book, goals, financial records and much more. Organizers come in a variety of different shapes, sizes & styles. This gift can be a helpful tool in not only a co-worker's life but for anybody in need of day-to-day organization. Know what the person needs. Get them their first, or a beautiful upgrade. Prices range dramatically from your cheap vinyl or hard cover planner found at a stationery store, to a specialty ordered, monogrammed, top quality leather book with custom features...or, go with a computerized pocket planner. Check also office supply stores for a better quality binder-organizer, or an electronic, computer, or specialty store for an electronic / computerized version. Pocket, purse, or notebook size for all professional or personal purposes can also be found.

COMPUTERIZED ORGANIZER

GLOBAL PRODUCTS - personal digital assistant   800-633-0633
    Casio's hand held computer organizer, converts and stores handwritten text   **$635**
SHARP WIZARD - electronic organizer   800-321-8877
    $100 - $720
SHOPPERS ADVANTAGE   800-TEL-SHOP
    best buys on name brand products, hand-held computer organizers
    $19 - $100
VOICE POWERED TECHNOLOGIES   800-743-2000
    beeper size, hand held voice organizer, recorder, reminder (uses computer chip)   **$200**
HEWLETT PACKARD PALMTOP   800-443-1254
    hand held computer/organizer   **$550**
NEWTON MESSAGEPAD 110 by Macintosh - **Mac Warehouse** 800-255-6227
    hand held organizer: notes, sketches, receive faxes and more   **$600**

DAY-PLANNER / NOTEBOOK ORGANIZER

DAY PLANNER - HARPER HOUSE, L.A.   **$40 - $120**
DAY RUNNER   **$40 - $120**
FILOFAX   **$12 - $85**
SHOPPERS ADVANTAGE   800-TEL-SHOP
    best buys on name brand products   **day planner: $29**
DAY-TIMER   **$20 - $120**   610-266-9000

PERSONALIZING ORGANIZERS

PERSONAL CREATIONS   800-326-6626
    personalized / monogrammed gifts
INITIALS - personalized / monogrammed gifts   800-444-8758
See also *MONOGRAMMED GIFTS, LEATHER NOTEBOOK, PORTFOLIO, CARRY-ALL and BRIEFCASE*

POCKET WATCH

...and other classic time pieces from the past are coming back into style with a flare. A wide selection can even be found for women. Not a gift for everyone, although these have to be seen to be appreciated. Some of the vintage replicas and nouveau pocket watches are irresistible in their beauty and their price. They can be found at a surprising number of places from your finer antique, collectors, and jewelry shops to your wholesale wristwatch and time piece dealers. They can range dramatically in price. A mint condition vintage original can run into the hundreds or thousands. Do try to stay away from your department stores, malls and other major chains when shopping for this gift...or even as a rule, as their mark-up is tremendous.

JOHNSON SMITH CO.   **813-747-2356**
      things you never knew existed catalog   **military pocket watches: $40**
FINGERHUT   **4404 Eight St N, St Cloud Minnesota 56395**
      catalog, two-tone eagle pocket watch   **$70**
See also ***WRISTWATCH, TIME PIECES***

WINE CONNOISSEUR'S CLUB

A favorite bottle of wine, fine champaign, sparkling wine or favorite spirit is always a hit with the "Yuppy" boss or Co-Worker who prides themselves on being a fine wine connoisseur. Keep this gift idea in mind if you happen to be traveling through the wine country, a few extra bottles picked up directly at the winery not only saves you money, but may stock your gift shelf for many occasions to come. Getting it from the source, you can also dress it up a bit with a prize winning, or reserve label and a nice oak box for one, three bottles, or a whole case. For a significant extra cost, many wineries can create a personalized label for one or more bottles, for virtually any occasion. Just provide them with the names, dates and any special inscription you would like to add. Perfect for weddings, anniversaries, birthdays, family or company reserve, etc.

                                      $10 - $100's

QUALITY, REPUTABLE NAPA VALLEY WINERIES
    CHARLES KRUG WINERY   **707-963-2761**
    VICHON WINERY   **707-944-2811**

NAPA VALLEY WINERIES CONTINUED

V. SATTUI WINERY	707-963-7774
ROBERT MONDAVI WINERY	707-963-9611
RUTHERFORD HILL WINERY	707-963-9694
STERLING VINEYARDS	707-942-5151
MONT ST. JOHN CELLARS	707-255-8864
BEAULIEU VINEYARDS	707-967-5200
CAKEBREAD CELLARS	707-963-5221
GRGICH HILLS CELLARS	707-963-2784
NIEBAUM - COPPOLA ESTATE	707-963-9435
STONEGATE WINERY	707-942-6500
SUTTER HOME WINERY	707-963-3104
PEJU WINERY	707-963-3600

QUALITY, REPUTABLE SONOMA VALLEY WINERIES

BUENA VISTA WINERY	707-938-1266
CHATEAU ST. JEAN	707-833-4134
GLEN ELLEN WINERY	707-996-1066
HACIENDA WINE CELLARS	707-938-3220
KENWOOD VINEYARDS	707-833-5891
ST. FRANCIS WINERY	707-833-4666
SEBASTIANI VINEYARDS	707-938-5532

NAPA / SONOMA VALLEY SPARKLING WINES (CHAMPAGNE)

DOMAINE CHANDON - sparkling wines	707-944-2280
KORBEL CHAMPAGNE CELLARS	707-887-2294

RECOMMENDED CAMPAGNE FROM FRANCE

MOET ET CHANDON	DOM PERIGNON
MUMM	TATTINGER

NAPA VALLEY TOURIST BUREAU	707-258-1957
THE WINE ENTHUSIAST	800-356-8466

wine accessories, cellars, racks, globe bars and much more

CHAMPAGNE, Wine, Liquors, Cordials, Gourmet Foods	800-BE-THERE
WINE FINDERS	800-845-8896

subscription club for wines delivered to your home or office

averages only $13 / month

THE BEST WINERIES OF NORTH AMERICA	800-LE-BEST

encyclopedia guidebook profiling over 400 wineries $18

See also *PRIVATE, COMPANY & FAMILY RESERVES*

THE PERFECT GIFT
HOTLINES

1-800-GIFT: THE PERFECT GIFTS DELIVERED

THE PERFECT TASTY GIFTS...
EXPRESSED !

*T*he modern age!...Boy is this world shrinking. With a simple phone call, one can have just about anything they want in the world...overnight, provided they know where to get it and can cover the cost. Think of us as your gift food connection, The Tasty Middleman, or your long distance refrigerator. We've provided you with the sources and access to the best gift foods in the country...and the world. Order your favorite chocolates from Belgium, a cajun dinner from the Bayou, fresh pineapples from Hawaii, Live Maine lobsters, or the best steak you've ever had, direct from Omaha. How can you go wrong with such a tasty surprise? You simply can't!...unless of course...oh, but it can't be...Is it?...It is...fruitcake!

SWEET TOOTH
DESSERTS, CHOCOLATES, CANDIES...AND ALL THAT GOOD STUFF

DESSERT OF THE MONTH CLUB   800-423-3091
DESSERT OF THE MONTH CLUB   800-800-CAKE
SEND-A-CAKE - to anyone, anywhere in 48 hours   800-338-7840
ARNOLD REUBEN JR's CHEESE CAKES   800-648-2253
SANTA FE COOKIE CO.   800-243-0353
JOHNSON SMITH CO.   813-747-2356
   things you never knew existed catalog, JELLY BELLY 40-flavor assortment box   **$13**
SWEET & almost sinful CHEESECAKE - homemade, 20 diff. **800-84-CAKES**
MRS. BARRY'S KONA COOKIES   800-862-KONA
   personally sampled by ourselves for quality and safety...and they are delicious. Choose between Mac nut chocolate chip, shortbread, white chip, peanut butter, oatmeal, coconut shortbread and more
   $3.50 / bag, gift boxes: $18 - $35
LUCKY DUCK FORTUNE COOKIES - custom fortune cookies   617-389-3583
OUT OF A FLOWER   800-743-0696
   sorbets & ice-creams from edible flowers, herbs, spices & wines
PEPPERIDGE FARM   800-243-9314
   the best commercial soups cookies and other pastries, cheese & sausage, breakfast mixes
GRAFTON VILLAGE APPLE CO. - Vermont maple syrups   800-843-4822
RENT MOTHER NATURE   617-354-5430
   lease a maple tree or sap bucket and receive 25 - 50 ozs. or 100% real maple syrup   **$30 - $40**
IMPROV GOURMET FOOD BASKETS & GIFTS   800-322-4438
   gift assortments: beverages, cakes, cookies, breads, pates, tea and other international gourmet favorites
COASTAL EXPRESS FOOD & SPIRITS   800-243-7466
   fruit, chocolates, cakes, spirits, wines and other favorites
OLD FASHIONED SNACK TIN OF GOODIES   800-GOODIES
See also CHOCOLATE CLUB

FLYING SEAFOOD

ABBOTT'S LOBSTER - Atlantic lobster overnight expressed   **800-325-3346**
CHESAPEAKE EXPRESS   **800-282-2722**
   Maryland's crab cakes, oysters and soft shell crabs delivered
LIVE from MAINE LOBSTER CO.   **800-766-6246**
   overnight expressed live lobsters, steamer clams and all the tools
OLDE MAINE LOBSTER CO. - lobsters overnight expressed   **800-562-7909**
OUTER BANKS SEAFOOD   **800-852-3028**
   seafood entrees that serve 4 with seasonings and instructions
NEW YORK'S CAVIARTERIA   **800-422-8427**
   The best Beluga Caviar   **$70, 1 1/2 ounces**
PACIFIC NORTHWEST TRADING COMPANY   **800-445-0737**
   giftboxes of smoked Salmon, seafoods, jellies, honey, jams, etc.
CAVIAR HOUSE - smoked Salmon, caviar, truffles   **800-522-8427**
DUCKTRAP RIVER FISH FARM   **800-828-3825**
   naturally bread Salmon, trout, mussels and scallops
CLAMBAKE CELEBRATIONS   **800-423-4038**
                          From 1 to 10 servings: $80 - $464
LOBSTERLINE - Live Main Lobsters gift package   **800-47-FRESH**

THE HEARTLAND'S PRIME CUTS
BEEF AND OTHER FRESH MEATS

AMERICA'S BLUE RIBBON BEEF   **800-US-FILET**
   half dozen prizewinning filet mignons, 6 ozs. each   **$30**
THE FORST MOUNTAIN SMOKEHOUSE   **800-453-4010**
   caviar, smoked meats, steaks, cheeses
HEARTLAND / MINNESOTA   **800-544-8661**
   swedish baked goods, cider syrup, sausage & smoked meats, preserves,
   and wild turkey
HONEY BAKED HAMS   **800-854-5995**
   hams, smoked turkey, barbecued ribs & gift baskets   **from $24 - $89**
PREFERRED STOCK - Fresh beef gift packages   **800-47-FRESH**
OMAHA STEAKS - Filet Mignon and other cuts   **800-228-9055**

THE SPICE OF LIFE
EXOTIC SPICES, SEASONINGS AND ETHNIC FOODS

COMMUNITY KITCHENS 800-535-9901
cajun spices, creole seasonings, Louisiana corn bread, jambalaya & more
WATKINS 800-373-2630
the finest spices, condiments and food accessories / gift boxes
PENDERY'S TASTE MERCHANTS 800-533-1870
quality exotic spices and other cooking accessories
LUZIANNE BLUE PLATE FOODS 800-692-7895
coffee, tea, jambalaya, gumbo, creole Louisiana / New Orleans style
MELISSA'S BY MAIL 800-468-7111
gourmet & exotic produce, herbs, catalog of cookbooks
EL PASO CHILI CO. 915-544-3434
cactus salsas, chili & spice blends, beer & tequila BBQ sauces
TAKE MAUI HOME 800-545-MAUI
Hawaiian foods gift baskets: $53 - $89
pineapples, maui onions, papayas, macadamia nuts, Maui chips, mac nut
brittle, Kona coffees, syrups, dressings, jams & more
GOURMAIL - foods & spices from India 215-296-4620
GOURMET JERKY - homemade beef jerky, $9 1/2 lb. 818-288-8682
TEXAS PRIDE BEEF JERKY - 2 1/4 lbs. $40 800-472-6661
THE JERKY HUT 800-2BF-JRKY
33 kinds of homemade beef jerky and smoked meats $8 - $25 / lb.
HELEN'S TROPICAL EXOTICS 800-544-JERK
dips, sauces, tropical spices and more
HAWAIIAN PLANTATIONS 800-767-4650
candies, jams, syrups, dressings & condiments from Hawaii
ROSSI PASTA - homemade pastas 800-227-6774
G.B. RATTO & CO. - imported ethnic & specialty foods 800-228-3515
TSANG & MA WOKERY 415-595-2270
oriental herbs, spices, sauces & veggies, woks & steamers, and more
HERB & SPICE COLLECTION 800-365-4372
natural herbal care products, spices, teas
COMTESSE DU BARRY 33-62-67-9813
fine cuisine direct from France
SAN FRANCISCO HERB CO. - cooking herbs & spices 800-227-4530

CREATIVE GIFT BASKETS, PACKAGES

*B*oring, useless, impersonal gift baskets have been traditionally given to the friendly co-worker, distant relative, client, and acquaintance...usually out of guilt, necessity, and/or laziness. If they're not your best friend and you don't care about them a great deal...let's not lie about it.

If you're thinking about someone you care about, don't just hand over one of those shrink-wrapped sausage, cheese and jam combo-thingys. Create something exciting, useful, and practical. Put it together yourself and save some money, or for that matter put together a few of them at the same time.

We've listed some good ideas to start with. Feel free to mix & match and create your own with the recipient's needs, wants, and desires in mind. Stick to a theme and accessorize. If you take a little time and put a little thought into it, you'll be quite surprised how imaginative you can be. The result will most certainly be a really fabulous gift. You'll most likely find yourself keeping them or wanting to go into business making them. There aren't many things more fulfilling then creating something with your own two hands that you're proud of...then giving it to someone else to enjoy.

Don't limit yourself to using just gift baskets. Men aren't too fond of them. You can come up with an endless number of ideas to package a gift for just about anything, for just about anyone. Also, many establishments will help construct a gift basket or package if it means a sale. All you have to do is ask. If any of the following ideas peak your interest, look them up individually in this guide for details on creating your own Perfect Gift.

. . . AND SURVIVAL KITS

GIFT BASKETS

WINE & CHEESES
FACE, HAIR, BODY PRODUCTS
BATHROOM IN A BASKET
EXOTIC FOODS
COFFEES & TEAS
TOYS
CHAMPAGNE & CAVIAR
TEXAS BARBECUE
PASTAS
CHOCOLATES
SWEETS
STOCKED PICNIC BASKET
THE WEDDING GIFT BASKET

SURVIVAL KITS

VACATION SURVIVAL BAG
CAMPING SURVIVAL PACK
EARTHQUAKE SURVIVAL KIT
GREAT EXPLORER TRAVEL PACK
ROAD TRIP SURVIVAL KIT
TOOL BOX
FIRST AID KIT
CHILD SAFETY KIT
ANTI-CRIME KIT
EMERGENCY CAR KIT
CARE PACKAGE
TRAVEL KIT / BAG

GIFT PACKAGES

FULLY STOCKED BRIEFCASE
PET LOVERS GIFT PACKAGE
HEALTH CLUB GIFT BAG
BEACH BAG
ADULT TOY BOX
SKI BAG
CD ROM / MULTI-MEDIA KIT
VIDEO GIFT PACKAGE
PHOTOGRAPHY BAG
THE 'BON VOYAGE' WRITING KIT
ENTERTAINMENT GIFT PACKAGE
GARDEN KIT
EROTIC GIFT PACKAGE
SPORT BAG
FANTASY GIFT PACKAGE
TACKLE BOX
ROMANTIC GIFT PACKAGE
SKI VACATION PACKAGE

GIFT BASKET DELECTIBLES

MAIL ORDER GOURMET DIRECTORY   800-989-5996
$12 / year (12 Issues)
MAYTAG DAIRY FARMS - Iowa cheeses   800-247-2458
NEW ENGLAND COUNTRY FARE - New England gift assorts   800-274-FARE
WHET YOUR APPETITE   800-228-9438
food gift assortments from around the world
FIGIS GIFTS IN GOOD TASTE - gift foods & accessories   715-387-6311
ALASKA WILD BERRY PRODUCTS   907-235-8858
berry jams and sauces
THE BLUE HERON COMPANY   800-237-3920
Winter fruit from Florida   **$22 1/4 bushel, $40 full bushel**
HARRY & DAVID   800-345-5655
fresh fruits, veggies, flowering plants, baked goods, gourmet gift baskets
and the fruit-of-the-month club   **$10 - $300**
800-BASKETS - Favorite munchies and sweet treats   **800-BASKETS**
BASKETS BY DAWN - custom gift baskets   **800-THINK-OF-U**
See also **CHOCOLATE CLUB, COFFEE / TEA LOVER'S DELIGHT, THE SPICE OF LIFE**

THE PERFECT GIFT CATALOG COLLECTION

OVER 200 of the MOST UNIQUE, CREATIVE GIFT CATALOGS...EVER LISTED

ADVENTURES IN CASSETTES   800-328-0108
    music, self-help, kids CD's & tapes
AMERICAN ACCOMPANIMENT TRACK TAPES   800-525-7155
    karaoke sing-a-long cassettes
AMERICAN FORESTS   800-320-TREE
    famous and historical tree saplings
AMERICAN NATIONAL PARKS   800-821-2903
    gifts that commemorate American History
AMERICA'S GREATEST RESORTS   212-807-7100
ANITA BECK CARDS - greeting cards   800-328-3844
ANYONE CAN WHISTLE - unique musical instruments   800-435-8863
APPLEJACK LIMITED EDITIONS - Collectible prints and art   800-969-1171
AUDIO EDITIONS   800-231-4261
    books on cassette from mysteries to self-improvement
B&C COMMUNICATIONS - two-way radios   800-343-3004
BART'S WATERSPORTS - water toys and accessories   800-552-2336
THE BEST OF EVERYTHING   800-722-7226
BIKE NASHBAR - serious mountain bikes & accessories   800-NASHBAR
BITS & PIECES - great puzzles, unique objects and more   800-884-2637
BOOKCASSETTE - all types of books on cassette   800-222-3225
BOOKS ON TAPE   800-626-3333
BOSE EXPRESS MUSIC - the CD and tape music source   800-444-2673
BROOKSTONE - innovative, new, hi-tech gifts   800-846-3000
CAMPMOR - camping and clothing catalog   201-445-5000
THE CELEBRATION FANTASTIC - some unique gifts   800-527-6566
CHEERS - Bar and TV show memorabilia   800-852-9692
CHEYENNE OUTFITTERS   800-234-0432
    various southwestern inspired fashions and gifts
CINEMA COLLECTORS - movie posters / star photos   213-461-6516
THE COFFEE CONNECTION   800-284-JAVA
CO-OP ARTIST'S MATERIALS   800-284-3388
    paints, brushes, canvases and more
COLLECTOR'S ARMORY - replicas of past weaponry   800-336-4572
COWBOY CHUCK CO.   800-378-6400
    unique, charming cartoon pictures personalized with the names of your choice, 200 picture choices for all occasions

HOTLINES

CRATE AND BARREL   800-323-5461
country-style indoor and outdoor housewares & furniture
CREATIVE CALLIGRAPHY - personalized lithographs   800-942-7471
CRITIC'S CHOICE VIDEO - over 2,200 videos under $15   800-544-9852
CRUISES, INC. - a cruise directory   800-762-7447
CRUTCHFIELD - home electronics   800-336-5566
DAK INDUSTRIES   800-325-0800
electronic technologies devices and other neuvoux products
DAMARK INTL.   800-729-4744
audio, video, computers, spting goods fitness equip, tools & more
DAVIS & CO. - unique jewelry, prints, books and more   800-876-9871
DESIGN TOSCANO - deco objects and sculptured pieces   800-525-1733
DESSERT OF THE MONTH CLUB   800-800-CAKE
DESSERT OF THE MONTH CLUB   800-423-3091
DICK BLICK ARTIST MATERIALS   800-522-5786
DIRECT BOOK SERVICE DOG & CAT CATALOG   800-776-2665
over 2,000 books & videos
EARTH CARE PAPER   800-347-0070
environmental cards, stationery, gift wrap, books and other gifts
EDIBLE LANDSCAPING - fruitful and other edible plants   800-524-4156
EDMUND SCIENTIFIC CO. - science resource catalog   609-547-8880
microscopes to telescopes
EGGHEAD SOFTWARE - computer software   800-EGGHEAD
ELECTRONIC EQUIPMENT BANK   800-368-3270
shortwave radios and more
EXIMIOUS OF LONDON - various gifts   800-221-9464
EXPOSURES - photo accessories, frames, albums, etc   800-222-4947
FIGI'S - valentine gifts   715-384-6101
FIGI'S: GIFTS IN GOOD TASTE - gift foods & accessories   715-387-6311
FORTUNE'S ALMANAC   800-331-2300
FREDERICK'S OF HOLLYWOOD - hot lingerie   800-323-9525
FUSION VIDEO COLLECTION - hard to find TV & film videos   800-959-0061
GAMES MAGAZINE - fun games   800-886-6556
GLOBAL CRAFTS - Christian children's fund   800-366-5896
GREENPEACE - environmental / nature gifts   800-456-4029
HAMMACHER SCHLEMMER - various gifts   800-543-3366
HEARTLAND AMERICA   800-229-2901
best prices on name brands from leather backpacks, slot machines, low
electronics, office equipment, personal accessories and more
INFORMATION UNLIMITED   800-221-1705
products, kits, electronic devices for hobby, science, education

INITIALS - personalized / monogrammed gifts · 800-444-8758
INTERNATIONAL MALE - men's hottest, sexiest fashions · 800-854-2795
INTO THE WIND KITES · 800-541-0314
IT'S A SECRET LINGERIE - lingerie, lotions, games, etc. · 800-390-3528
J. CREW - classic, high quality fashions · 800-562-0258
JACKSON & PERKINS - roses & gardens · 800-872-7673 · 800-292-GROW
JERRY OHLINGER'S - movie posters / star photos · 212-989-0869
THE JERRY'S CATALOG! - art supplies · 800-U-ARTIST
JOHNSON SMITH CO. · 813-747-2356
   things you never knew existed catalog: one of the greatest catalogs o n
   earth for kids and adult kids, from magic tricks, gag gifts, sea horses and
   venus fly traps to moon rocks, Roman coins, slot machines and sunken
   treasure...and lots lots more
JUST FOR KIX / DANCE ETC. - dance apparel, gifts, etc. · 800-345-0307
KATHERINE MARCH, LTD. · 800-876-2724
   European soaps and luxuries for the bath
KELLY'S - camping, backpacking catalog · 800-69-KELLY
KLIG'S KITES, BANNERS AND WINDSOCKS · 800-333-5944
KOALA - men's hottest swimwear from around the world · 800-238-2941
KRISTI'S BY OVERTON - hot swimwear and other fashions · 800-334-6541
L.L. BEAN · 800-543-9089
LESLIE'S SWIMMING POOL SUPPLIES - water toys & prods · 800-537-5437
LEVENGER - tools & accessories for the serious reader · 800-545-0242
LIGHT IMPRESSIONS - photo albums and storage systems · 800-642-0994
LILLIAN VERNON - personalized items and various gifts · 800-285-5555
MAITRESSE - lingerie from small to plus sizes · 800-456-8464
MANNY'S BASEBALL LAND - sports apparel · 800-776-8326
MARLAR PUBLISHING CO. · Box 17038, Minneapolis, MN 55417
   New age, science, religious, arts & crafts, hobbies
MASTER OF LIFE WINNERS - new age / psychic gifts · 800-421-6603
MCA / UNIVERSAL PROPERTIES - TV Show and Movie stuff
METROPOLITAN MUSEUM OF ART · 800-468-7386
   art, jewelry & other unique collectibles
MINKUS - american stamps · 800-476-6284
THE MOVIE POSTER SHOP · 403-250-7588
MOVIES UNLIMITED - huge movie catalog, 30,000 titles · 800-523-0823
MUSEUM OF FINE ARTS BOSTON · 800-225-5592
   prints, objects de art and other gifts
THE MUSIC BOX COMPANY · 800-227-2190
THE MUSIC STAND - performing arts gifts · 802-295-7044
MYSTIC STAMP CO. - collector's stamp catalog · 800-433-7811

HOTLINES

NATIONAL PARKS AND CONSERVATION ASSOC.   800-NAT-PARK
  nature products to help preserve national parks
THE NATURE COMPANY   800-227-1114
NATURE'S GALLERY   800-400-0090
  collectable fine art prints of wildlife, nature, Americana   **$60 - $450**
NATURE'S JEWELRY   800-333-3235
  jewelry & gifts depicting nature's animals & scenics. Some items made
  from nature's naturally beautiful semi-precious stones, minerals & shells
NIGHTINGALE CONANT   800-525-9000
  one of the greatest personal development products catalog
NOAH'S ANIMALS - animal art & collectibles   800-368-6624
THE NOBLE COLLECTION   800-8-NOBLE-8
  replicas of the arms and armor from the medieval times and the Samurai
  to antique guns and cannons
NORTHERN   800-533-5545
  home & outdoor accessories, equipment, tools and recreational products
  at great prices
NORTHSTYLE - nature gift catalog   800-336-5666
OLD TOWN - canoe catalog   800-848-3673
ONE STEP AHEAD - helpful gifts for baby   800-274-8440
OVERTON'S - discount boating accessories   800-334-6541
PACIFIC ARTS PUBLISHING - public home video   800-538-5856
  the best of public TV and other fine quality programs
PAPER JOURNEY   800-827-2723
  journals, scrapbooks, albums, notecards and more
THE PARAGON - various gifts   800-343-3095
PEARL - art and graphic supplies (discount centers)   800-451-PEARL
PEERLESS COFFEE COMPANY - coffees, teas, spices, etc.   800-372-3267
PERFECTLY SAFE   800-837-KIDS
  safe stuff; toys and such for kids and toddlers
PERSONAL CREATIONS   800-326-6626
  personalized and monogrammed gifts
PET OWNERS RESOURCE BOOK   800-562-7169
  for the health and happiness of your pet
PLANE STUFF - the aeronautical gift catalog   800-637-9057
  airplane, helicopter and hot air balloon stuff
PLAYBOY - videos, magazine, lingerie and other gifts   800-423-9494
THE PLEASURE CHEST - adult toys   800-75-DILDO
THE POTTERY BARN   800-922-5507
  indoor & outdoor, country-style furniture, housewares, accessories
POURETTE - candle and soap making supplies   800-888-9425

PYRAMID BOOKS AND THE NEW AGE COLLECTION   800-247-1889
   new age & mystical stuff
REAL GOODS   800-762-7325
   solar power goods, electric cars, environmentally friendly goods, unique
   tools, safety products & more
RED ROSE COLLECTION   800-692-5145
   gifts to nurture the mind body & soul
RICK'S MOVIE GRAPHICS - movie posters   800-252-0425
THE SAMPLER - free and hard to find stuff   800-950-0852
SEASONS - various gifts   800-776-9677
SEATTLE FILMWORKS - photography school   800-445-3348
SELF CARE - tools for healthy living   800-345-3371
SERRV - African handcrafts   800-423-0071
SERVICE MERCHANDISE CATALOG SHOWROOM   615-251-6666
   quality discount department store merchandise
THE SHARPER IMAGE   800-344-4444
   unique, high-tech gadgets and the best of things
SHEPLER'S - western wear and accessories   800-833-7667
SHIP'S HATCH   703-691-1670
   nautical decorative items and pieces
SHOPPERS ADVANTAGE   800-TEL-SHOP
   best buys on all kinds of name brand products
SIERRA TRADING POST   307-775-8000
   discount, name brand outdoor clothing & equipment
SIGNAL'S - falling rain nature chimes   800-669-9696
SIMPLY SOUTHWEST - southwest fashions, jewelry & decor 800-447-6177
SKY MALL - various gifts   800-424-6255
SOUND CHOICE - karaoke sing-a-long tapes & CD's 800-788-4487
SPIEGEL - fashions & furnishings   800-345-4500
STAMP GIFT CATALOG   800-228-8035
STASH TEAS BY MAIL- teas and accessories   800-826-4218
STRATTON & COMPANY - romantic gifts   408-464-1780
SUCCESSORIES   800-535-2773
   The most attractive, powerful supply of motivational products &
   visuals
SUNDANCE   800-882-8827
   Founded by Robert Redford: unique southwestern gifts
TARTAN BOOKS - 3,500 titles at serious discounts 800-233-8467
THANKSGIVING COFFEE COMPANY   800-445-6427
   award winning coffee's and accessories
THINGS REMEMBERED - personalized / engraved gifts 800-274-7367

THINK BIG! - big stuff   800-487-4244
TIFFANY & COMPANY   800-421-4468
TIME CAPSULES   800-225-5800
TIME WARNER'S SOUND EXCHANGE - music, and more   800-854-1681
TIME WARNER'S VIEWER'S EDGE - videos for under $10   800-847-6753
TOYS TO GROW ON - educational toys for kids & toddlers   800-542-8338
TRUMBLE GREETINGS - fine art cards and gifts   800-525-0656
U.S. GAMES - tarot & fortune telling cards   800-448-4263
U.S. SALES   818-891-5588
    wholesale prices on hundreds of items from fashions, home and office items, to personal accessories and more
U.S. STAMPS   800-823-9355
UNDERGEAR - sexy men's underwear catalog   800-854-2795
UPPER DECK AUTHENTICATED   800-873-7332
    autographed sports memorabilia
VICTORIA'S SECRET - lingerie & swimwear catalogs   800-888-8200
THE VIDEO CATALOG   800-733-2232
VINOTEMP WINE CELLARS   800-777-8466
    38 handmade models, mostly wood, 24 - 3,400 bottles
THE WARM STORE   800-889-WARM
    non-profit, cruelty free nature and environmental products
WARNER CUSTOM MUSIC   415-592-1700
    you pick the songs they make the tape
THE WINE ENTHUSIAST - wine cellars & accessories   800-356-8466
WIRELESS - various gifts   800-669-9999
WHAT ON EARTH   216-963-6555
    fun stuff, fashions and collectibles from around the world
WHOLE EARTH ACCESS   800-829-6300
THE WOODLAND CATALOG - Smokey the Bear stuff   800-610-8800
WORLD OF PRODUCTS   800-289-2869
    over 3,500 decorator items and gifts
WORLD TIME WATCH CO. - name brands discounted   800-327-7682
WORLD'S GREATEST GAMING CATALOG   800-282-6666
    gambling products, equipment and games

THE PERFECT GIFTS'
INTERNATIONAL CATALOG COLLECTION

AMAZING GRACE ELEPHANT CO.   GPO Box 12206, Hong Kong
jewelry, decorative items, watches, silk, books and much more

BJORN WIINBLADS HUS   Ny Ostergade II, 1101 Copenhagen, Denmark
posters, jewelry, decorative items from Denmark

CASHS OF IRELAND   P.O. Box 47 St. Patrick St, Cork, Ireland
the most famous Irish catalog with merchandise from all over the world
and Europe. beautiful catalog, low prices

CHARBONNEAU'S LAPIDARY SERVICE   4020 Bow Trail, SW, Calgary
rock and precious metal tools and polishing equip.   Alberta, Canada

CHARMS INTL. Alpha House, 27 Nathan Rd, P.O. Box 6192, Kowloon, HK
mail order with many different lines of merchandise

CHINESE ARTS AND CRAFTS   233-37 Nathan Rd, Yaumati, Kowloon,
all kinds of gifts and crafts from China   **Hong Kong**

EDEN   212 Rue De Rivoli, 75001 Paris, France
name brand perfumes and scarves at Paris discounts

EMERALD, BALLIN GEARY   County Cork, Ireland
Christmas and religious items and lots of other great buys

EQUAL EXCHANGE   P.O. Box 2652 Cambridge, MA 02238
food importing from farmers around the world

FOYLES   113 Charing Cross Rd, London WC2, England
largest book store in the world

FRIENDS OF THIRD WORLD   611 W Wayne St, Fort Wayne, IN 46802
Food, coffee, books and gifts imported from around the world

GENERAL TRADING CO.   144 Sloane St., London SWIX 9BL, England
Christmas catalog, gifts of all kinds

HANDCRAFT HOUSE   110 W Esplanade, N Vancouver, BC, Canada
clays, kilns, potter's wheels and other ceramic supplies

HAWAIIAN HOUSE GIFTS BY MAIL   808-955-3575
Hawaiian calendars, clothes, foods and shell jewelry

HAYIM PINHAS MEERSCHAUM PIPES   P.O. Box 500 Istanbul, Turkey
exotic smoking pipes in all shapes and sizes

HEDONICS   302 Bridgeland Ave, Toronto, Ontario, Canada M6A 124
unusual electronics and health care items for home or office

HERITAGE ATLANTIC   Box 39, Lake Cjarptte, MS, Canada BOJ 1YO
gift items, clothing, foods and more from the Canadian Atlantic

HOUSE OF TYROL   800-443-1299
gifts & collectibles from around the world from beer steins to cuckoo
clocks

KUNG BROTHERS STORES   GPO Box 13324, Hong Kong
furniture, camera equip., jewelry and more

THE MYSTIC TRADER   800-637-9057
old world and new age gifts from exotic places around the world

ONE WORLD TRADING CO.   P.O. Box 310 Summertown, TN 38483
Guatamalan arts and crafts

OUT OF AFRICA   12 Lock St, Saint Catharines, Ontario, Canada L2N 5B5
very unusual hand crafted items from all over Africa

OXFAM AMERICA TRADING CATALOG   800-426-3282
a non-profit hunger relief agency offering hand crafted gifts from Asia, Africa and the Americas

PUEBLO TO PEOPLE   800-842-5220
hand-made gifts and collectibles from central and south America

R. CARENTON PORCELAINE   Porcelains Peintes A La Main
                Z.A. Des Alles, 45680 Dordives, Orleans, France
thousands of high quality decorative pieces at low prices

RAFFAELLO ROMANELLI   Lungarno Acciaioli 72-78 r., 50123 Firenze
                                              Florence, Italy
statues, fountains, tables, marble, bronzes, stone and art

ROYAL ONTARIO MUSUEM   100 Queens Park, Toronto, Ont.,
artifact repros, sculpture, jewelry and more   Canada M5S 2C8

SAVE THE CHILDREN CRAFT SHOP   54 Wilton Rd, West Port, CT 06880
crafts, decorative and gift items from around the world

SMALL COMBE CLOCKS Glee House, Globe Industrial Estate, Rectory Rd
                                Grays, Essex, RM 17 6ST, England
grandfather clocks, wooden marine barometers, mantle clocks

STEPTOE AND WIFE ANTIQUES   322 Geary Av, Toronto, Ont.,
spiral stairs and architectural pieces   Canada M6H 2C7

THAI INTL. DISPLAY   6030 90th Ave N, Pinellas Park, FL 33565
hand-made clothes, crafts, gifts from Asia

WALLACH   Residentzstrasse 3, 8 Munich 2 Germany
wood carvings, beer steins, crafts, costumes etc. from Germany

WITTAMER   Place Du Grand Sablon 12-13, 100 Brussels, Belgium
The best chocolates in the world

WORLDWIDE CURIO HOUSE   Box 17095, Minneapolis, MN 55417
unusual gifts, jewelry and more from around the world

YUE HWA CHINESE EMPORIUM   301 Nathan Rd, Kowloon, Hong Kong
jewelry, carvings, rugs, wall hangings, furniture and more

GIFT GIVING CALENDAR

GIFT GIVING HOLIDAYS AND SPECIAL OCCASIONS

NEW YEAR'S DAY . . . . January 1

VALENTINE'S DAY . . . . February 14

ST. PATRICK'S DAY . . . . March 17

EASTER / PASSOVER . . Sun., late March, early April

SECRETARY'S DAY . . . . April

CHILDREN'S DAY . . . . May 5

MOTHER'S DAY . . . . second Sunday in May

MEMORIAL DAY . . . . . May 30 (celeb. on Monday)

FATHER'S DAY . . . . 3rd Sunday in June

INDEPENDENCE DAY . . . . July 4

GRANDPARENT'S DAY . . . . . 1st Sunday in October

ROSH HASHANAH . . . . fluctuates, September

YOM KIPPUR . . . . . fluctuates, September / October

VETERANS DAY . . . . November 11

HANUKKAH . . . . fluctuates, December

CHRISTMAS . . . . December 25

NEW YEAR'S EVE . . . . December 31

PERSONAL BIRTHDAY LIST

FAMILY / RELATIVES

NAME	BIRTH DATE

PERSONAL BIRTHDAY LIST

FRIENDS / CO-WORKERS

NAME	BIRTH DATE

PERSONAL
BIRTHDAY / CHRISTMAS CARD LIST

NAME / ADDRESS	NAME / ADDRESS

PERSONAL
GIFT GIVING LIST

WHO	WHAT	WHEN

PERSONAL
BIRTHDAY / CHRISTMAS WISH LIST

WHAT **I** WANT

CHRISTMAS

BIRTHDAY

Gift Certificates

Awards

A gift doesn't necessarily have to be a materialistic possession traditionally wrapped in a box. A gift can take any form or shape and be given in as many different ways. And, as mentioned before, a good portion of our creative gift ideas have to do with events, things to do, and places to go, and you can't very well wrap up in a box something so intangible as a good time. Gift Certificates for our purpose happen to be a wonderfully versatile gift. There are virtually an endless number of ways you can create and present a gift in the form of a gift certificate, for as many different gift ideas.

A gift certificate to a hobby, sport, desire, hidden talent, or other interest thought about, but not acted upon, can suddenly open a new door to a different world, given the kindness and generosity of a good friend, loved one, or family member.

Gift certificates are, and will always be, the old stand by, which is by no means a bad thing. A young boy or girl reaching that early teen or pre-teen age would much rather do the shopping themselves...or take the cash. Believe me, they'll know exactly what to do with it. At this age, it's truly their favorite gift.

Whether you start out with a gift certificate from an establishment or make it yourself, it truly comes alive with the creativity you put into it...and the emotions shared between giver and receiver. Make a gift package or gift basket centered around your gift certificate. Add a theme, style and personal touch with written words or any accessories that may add a nice touch...a classy envelope and a rose...roll it up in a scroll and tie it off with nice ribbon...calligraphy or computer design...there are hundreds of simple little things you can do to give a gift that extra little something, that says so much.

THE PERFECT GIFT CERTIFICATES & AWARDS

QUICK REFERENCE LIST

HOMEMADE GIFT CERTIFICATES

LINGERIE OF THE MONTH CLUB....69
WEEKEND GETAWAY....71
EVENING ON THE TOWN....105
VACATION PACKAGE....125
STOCK CERTIFICATE....149
BEER-OF-THE-MONTH CLUB....193
TRAVELER'S CLUB
ONCE IN A LIFETIME SHOPPING SPREE
RESTAURANT OF THE MONTH CLUB
FINE WINE OF THE MONTH CLUB
GIFT CERTIFICATE FOR INSTRUCTION
GIFT SUBSCRIPTION

AWARDS

THE GREATEST LOVER IN THE WORLD....67
THE GREATEST FATHER IN THE WORLD....225
MOTHER OF THE YEAR....227
WIFE APPRECIATION DAY
SPORTSMAN OF THE YEAR
SALESPERSON OF THE YEAR

OLD STAND-BY'S

FAVORITE MUSIC STORE
FAVORITE SPORTING GOODS STORE
FAVORITE CLOTHING STORE
OTHER FAVORITE RETAIL STORE
FAVORITE DEPARTMENT STORE

See **ORDER FORM** in back of book to order these and other
custom **GIFT CERTIFICATES & GIFT COUPONS**

HOMEMADE
GIFT COUPONS
& COUPON BOOK

Gift coupons or a gift coupon book is an ideal, clever gift for the one you love, a friend, your parents, or kids. Set up a few pieces of paper and start putting your ideas down in equal sized rectangular boxes so that they may be cut out and stapled together as a booklet later. Think of any favors, services, or future plans you would like to share together or simply give as a gift. Make dollar bill coupons for kids, roommates, lovers. Include your picture on them. Make a hundred, put denominations on them and make a list of chores and things to do, what each is worth and what the redeeming value is. See ideas listed here and place "your" dollar value on each. Take your time with an attractive design. Use nice paper and put your personal touch into it. Use these coupons to stimulate your own imagination. Do whatever you want. I guarantee the more involved you get, the more you'll enjoy your very own imaginative, creative process.

Below we've given you several different gift coupons to start with. Of course the ideas are endless and vary from age to age and from male to female. Feel free to cut these coupons out to put together in a booklet. That's what they're there for. Keep in mind that many of these coupon ideas also double under other categories. Coupons also add wonderfully as an accessory to many gift ideas & packages. Use your own judgement and creativity in putting this gift together for the person you're thinking of. Make sure you also put in some general guidelines so your generosity is not taken advantage of. Also, make them aware that the fulfillment of some of these gift coupons need to be planned appropriately around everyone's schedule. For children, the most wonderful part of this gift is giving them the opportunity to make the decision of what, where, when and how...more importantly, it tells them you are willing to spend this quality time with them.

See **ORDER FORM** in back of book to order these and other custom made **GIFT COUPONS & GIFT CERTIFICATES**

THE PERFECT GIFT COUPONS

QUICK REFERENCE LIST

FOR KIDS

ONE SECRET
FAVORITE RESTAURANT
AN ICE CREAM CONE
TRIP TO THE ZOO
AN AMUSEMENT PARK
TRIP TO THE BEACH
A PANCAKE BREAKFAST OUT
A HOT FUDGE SUNDAE
A HORSEBACK RIDE
A MOVIE
ONE TOY OF THEIR CHOICE
AN ALL NIGHTER OF FUN
HOMEMADE COOKIES
OVERNIGHT CAMP OUT
ONE DAY OF FUN FUN FUN

FOR PARENTS

DINNER OUT
DAY'S WORTH OF YARD WORK
AUTO DETAIL / WASH & WAX
ONE NIGHT OF BABY-SITTING
ONE BREAKFAST IN BED
A HOME COOKED MEAL
ALL HOUSEWORK FOR 1 WEEK
A HUG

FOR FRIENDS

A NIGHT ON THE TOWN
ONE BIRTHDAY DINNER
A MOVIE
A PROFESSIONAL MASSAGE
A HOME COOKED MEAL
A SHOPPING SPREE

FOR LOVERS

A HOME COOKED MEAL
NIGHT ON THE TOWN
A SENSUAL MASSAGE
BREAKFAST IN BED
A HUG
A KISS
A FANTASY FULFILLED
A PICNIC LUNCH
ALL HOUSE WORK FOR 1 WEEK
DINNER & MOVIE
ONE SKINNY DIP
AFTERNOON DELIGHT
A NIGHT OF FOREPLAY
ONE LOVE MAKING SESSION
ALL-NIGHTER BEING TOGETHER
ONE EROTIC ADVENTURE
ONE TRUTH / SECRET
ONE DARE
KING / QUEEN FOR THE DAY

THE PERFECT GIFT COUPONS FOR KIDS

This gift coupon entitles you to

ONE TRIP TO THE ZOO

redeemable at your local zoo

This gift coupon entitles you to

ONE HOT FUDGE SUNDAE

redeemable at home or wherever ice cream sundaes are sold

This gift coupon entitles you to

ONE TOY OF YOUR CHOICE

(NOT TO EXCEED $_____)
redeemable at your favorite toy store

THE PERFECT GIFT COUPONS FOR KIDS

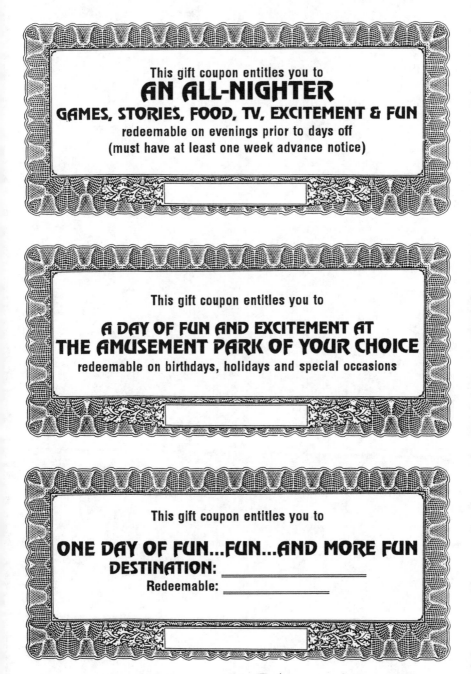

This gift coupon entitles you to
AN ALL-NIGHTER
GAMES, STORIES, FOOD, TV, EXCITEMENT & FUN
redeemable on evenings prior to days off
(must have at least one week advance notice)

This gift coupon entitles you to

A DAY OF FUN AND EXCITEMENT AT
THE AMUSEMENT PARK OF YOUR CHOICE
redeemable on birthdays, holidays and special occasions

This gift coupon entitles you to

ONE DAY OF FUN...FUN...AND MORE FUN
DESTINATION: _____
Redeemable: _____

THE PERFECT GIFT COUPONS FOR PARENTS

This gift coupon entitles you to

AN EVENING OF WINING AND DINING

redeemable at your favorite restaurant

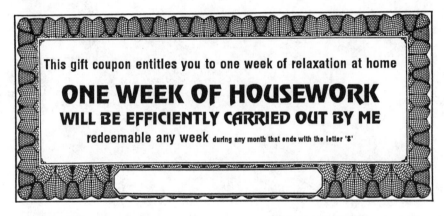

This gift coupon entitles you to one week of relaxation at home

ONE WEEK OF HOUSEWORK
WILL BE EFFICIENTLY CARRIED OUT BY ME

redeemable any week during any month that ends with the letter 'S'

This gift coupon entitles you to

BREAKFAST IN BED

redeemable any morning you wish
(desired menu items must be submitted in advance)

THE PERFECT GIFT COUPONS FOR FRIENDS

This gift coupon entitles you to

A HUG

redeemable at any time, anywhere

This gift coupon entitles you to

A BATCH OF HOMEMADE COOKIES
(favorite kind must be ordered in advance / milk included)
redeemable at any time

This gift coupon entitles you to

A $___ SHOPPING SPREE

AT YOUR FAVORITE RETAIL STORE

THE PERFECT GIFT COUPONS FOR LOVERS

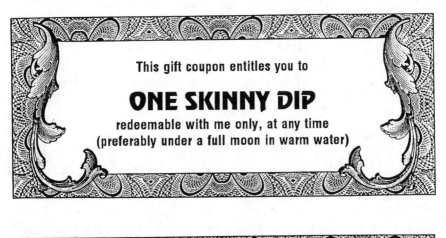

This gift coupon entitles you to

ONE SKINNY DIP

redeemable with me only, at any time
(preferably under a full moon in warm water)

This gift coupon entitles you to

A KISS

redeemable any time, anywhere

This gift coupon entitles you to

A FANTASY FULFILLED

EROTIC OR OTHERWISE
YOUR WISH IS MY DESIRE
redeemable at any time

THE PERFECT GIFT COUPONS FOR LOVERS

This gift coupon entitles you to

AN AFTERNOON DELIGHT

an afternoon rendezvous of making love
redeemable any day you wish

This gift coupon entitles you to

AN ALL-NIGHTER
OF MAKING LOVE AND BEING TOGETHER

redeemable with me only, any special night you wish

This gift coupon entitles you to

A PICNIC

redeemable:
on the day and at the destination of your choice

MAKE YOUR OWN PERFECT GIFT COUPONS

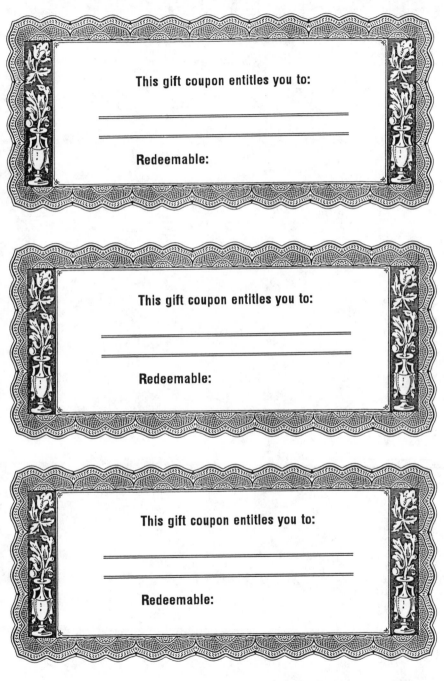

This gift coupon entitles you to:

Redeemable:

This gift coupon entitles you to:

Redeemable:

This gift coupon entitles you to:

Redeemable:

GIFTS CROSS-REFERENCED

GIFTS CROSS-REFERENCED

GIFTS CROSS-REFERENCED

GIFTS CROSS-REFERENCED

GIFTS CROSS-REFERENCED

THE B - LIST

FOR THOSE GIFT IDEAS THAT DIDN'T QUITE MAKE THE CUT

AUTH. LEATHER BOMBER JACK.	HOME GYM
SINGLES DATING SERVICE	WATER PURIFIER
CAMCORDER	RADAR DETECTOR
HOMEMADE BREAD MAKER	LAPTOP COMPUTER
ICE CREAM MAKER	MASSAGE CHAIR
ELECTRONIC MASSEUSE	JUKEBOX
MODEL TRAIN SET	SLOT CAR SET
HATS: WESTERN / SAFARI	WESTERN BOOTS
GOLFING EQUIP. & SUPPLIES	POOL TABLE
WOOD & BRASS WORLD GLOBE	BIRD FEEDER
EXERCISE EQUIPMENT	BOOMERANGS
NOTEBOOK COMPUTER	POOL TABLE
BICYCLES & ACCESSORIES	TEDDY BEAR
AIRBRUSHING KIT	PASTA MAKER
3-WHEEL EXERCISE STROLLER	BIRD FEEDER

INDEX

INDEX

INDEX

INDEX

INDEX

Gift Certificates & Awards Packages

PACKAGE #1 (12 Gift Certificates & Awards) $12.95

MOTHER OF THE YEAR	LINGERIE-OF-THE-MONTH CLUB
EVENING ON THE TOWN	VALENTINE'S DAY CERTIFICATE
STOCK CERTIFICATE	HUSBAND APPRECIATION DAY
VACATION PACKAGE	SALESPERSON OF THE YEAR
TRAVELER'S CLUB	RESTAURANT-OF-THE-MONTH CLUB
BIRTHDAY CERTIFICATE	GIFT CERTIFICATE FOR INSTRUCTION

PACKAGE #2 (12 Gift Certificates & Awards) $12.95

WEEKEND GETAWAY	THE GREATEST LOVER IN THE WORLD
GIFT SUBSCRIPTION	THE GREATEST FATHER IN THE WORLD
WIFE APPRECIATION DAY	ONCE-IN-A-LIFETIME SHOPPING SPREE
BEER-OF-THE-MONTH CLUB	FINE WINE-OF-THE-MONTH CLUB
SPORTSMAN OF THE YEAR	THE GREATEST FRIEND IN THE WORLD
ANNIVERSARY CERTIFICATE	BLANK CERTIFICATE

Gift Coupons Package
(See coupon details, page 312)

COUPONS FOR KIDS PACKAGE (15 Coupons) $4.95
COUPONS FOR PARENTS PACKAGE (15 Coupons) $4.95
COUPONS FOR FRIENDS PACKAGE (15 Coupons) $4.95
COUPONS FOR LOVERS PACKAGE (21 Coupons) $4.95

Combination Variety Package

A MIX OF 12 GIFT CERTIFICATES & AWARDS, 15 COUPONS $15.95

Order Form

If you like the **Gift Certificates, Awards** and **gift coupons** found throughout this guide...then you'll love our **custom packaged assortments.**

Each gift certificate, award and coupon has been beautifully laid out on quality paper stock in attractive, subtle shades of color. This, combined with our striking design and tasteful, heart-felt words makes for a perfect gift either by itself or as part of any gift package. An intangible gift appropriate for almost any occasion, or for no occasion at all.
See Previous Page for Package Details

NAME _____

COMPANY NAME _____

ADDRESS _____

CITY   STATE   ZIP

Package #1 & #2   ($12.95 each).....................$_____
Coupon Packages   ($4.95 each)........................_____
Combination Package   ($15.95)......................._____
    Shipping: $1.50 for each package................_____
    50 cents for each additional package..........._____
    Sales tax: California residents add 8.25% ._____

Total...$_____

Payment: Make **check** or **money order** payable to:

DOG GONE BOOKS
P. O. B o x 4 0 5 4 - 7, M a l i b u, C A 9 0 2 6 4
310 - 572 - 6450

Order Form

If you'd like to order additional copies of *FINDING THE PERFECT GIFT: THE ULTIMATE GUIDE*, for **yourself, friends, a function, an organization** or **your company,** please use this form.

Please send me ____ copy(ies) of *FINDING THE PERFECT GIFT: THE ULTIMATE GUIDE.*

_____

NAME

_____

COMPANY NAME

_____

ADDRESS

_____

CITY   STATE   ZIP

    $12.95 each book...$_____
    Shipping: $2.00 for the 1st book................._____
        75 cents for each additional book.........._____
        Air Mail: $3.50 per book ...._____
    Sales tax: California residents add 8.25% .._____

    Total...$_____

Payment: Make **check** or **money order** payable to:

DOG GONE BOOKS

P. O. B o x 4 0 5 4 - 7, M a l i b u, C A 9 0 2 6 4
310 - 572 - 6450